The Architect as Worker

Praise for
The Architect as Worker

The Architect as Worker is completely relevant to understanding the architect's current professional and political predicament. At once historical, theoretical, practical and clear-eyed, it should start urgent conversations across the design disciplines, not just architecture. **Simon Sadler, University of California, Davis, USA**

Architects, students, academics — workers of all kinds — concerned with the question of how the fragmented, homogenized, financialized, blind field that is architecture can simultaneously exploit and allow us to produce new forms of knowledge, need this book. It represents a point of departure for research and a call to act. **Nick Beech, Oxford Brookes University, UK**

The Architect as Worker

Immaterial Labor, the Creative Class, and the Politics of Design

Edited by
Peggy Deamer

Bloomsbury Academic
An imprint of Bloomsbury Publishing Plc

BLOOMSBURY
LONDON • NEW DELHI • NEW YORK • SYDNEY

Bloomsbury Academic
An imprint of Bloomsbury Publishing Plc

50 Bedford Square	1385 Broadway
London	New York
WC1B 3DP	NY 10018
UK	USA

www.bloomsbury.com

BLOOMSBURY and the Diana logo are trademarks of Bloomsbury Publishing Plc

First published 2015

© Selection and Editorial Material: Peggy Deamer, 2015
© Individual Chapters: their Authors, 2015

Peggy Deamer has asserted her right under the Copyright, Designs and Patents Act, 1988, to be identified as Editor of this work.

All rights reserved. No part of this publication may be reproduced or transmitted in any form or by any means, electronic or mechanical, including photocopying, recording, or any information storage or retrieval system, without prior permission in writing from the publishers.

No responsibility for loss caused to any individual or organization acting on or refraining from action as a result of the material in this publication can be accepted by Bloomsbury or the authors.

British Library Cataloguing-in-Publication Data
A catalogue record for this book is available from the British Library.

ISBN: HB: 978-1-4725-7050-5
PB: 978-1-4725-7049-9
ePDF: 978-1-4725-7052-9
ePub: 978-1-4725-7051-2

Library of Congress Cataloging-in-Publication Data
The architect as worker : immaterial labor, the creative class, and the politics of design / Edited by Peggy Deamer.
pages cm
Includes bibliographical references and index.
ISBN 978-1-4725-7050-5 (hardback) -- ISBN 978-1-4725-7049-9 (paperback) 1. Architectural practice--Social aspects. 2. Work--Social aspects. I. Deamer, Peggy, editor.
NA1995.A725 2015
720.1'03--dc23
2014048286

Typeset by Fakenham Prepress Solutions, Fakenham, Norfolk NR21 8NN
Printed and bound in India

I would like to dedicate this book to the members of the Architecture Lobby who have supported, enhanced, and focused the thinking that lies behind the assembly of this book. I owe you my ongoing thanks.

Contents

List of illustrations	xi
List of contributors	xiii
Acknowledgments	xx
Foreword *Joan Ockman*	xxi
Introduction *Peggy Deamer*	xxvii

Part I The commodification of design labor   1

1 Dynamic of the general intellect   3
Franco Berardi

2 White night before a manifesto   13
Metahaven

3 The capitalist origin of the concept of creative work   30
Richard Biernacki

4 The architect as entrepreneurial self: Hans Hollein's TV performance "Mobile Office" (1969)   44
Andreas Rumpfhuber

Part II The concept of architectural labor   59

5   Work   61
Peggy Deamer

6   More for less: Architectural labor and design productivity   82
Paolo Tombesi

7   Form and labor: Toward a history of abstraction in architecture   103
Pier Vittorio Aureli

Part III Design(ers)/Build(ers)   119

8   Writing work: Changing practices of architectural specification   121
Katie Lloyd Thomas and Tilo Amhoff

9   Working globally: The human networks of transnational architectural projects   144
Mabel O. Wilson, Jordan Carver, and Kadambari Baxi

Part IV The construction of the commons   159

10   Labor, architecture, and the new feudalism: Urban space as experience   161
Norman M. Klein

11   The hunger games: Architects in danger   171
Alicia Carrió

12   Foucault's "environmental" power: Architecture and neoliberal subjectivization   181
Manuel Shvartzberg

Part V The profession — 207

13 Three strategies for new value propositions of design practice — 209
Phillip G. Bernstein

14 Labor and talent in architecture — 219
Thomas Fisher

15 The (ac)credit(ation) card — 228
Neil Leach

Afterword — 241
Michael Sorkin

Index — 249

List of illustrations

3.1	Friedrich Jakob Tromlitz after Karl Moritz Berggold.	34
4.1	Mobile Office, 9'21".	45
4.2	Mobile Office, 9'40".	45
4.3	Mobile Office, 10'11".	45
4.4	Mobile Office, 10'20".	46
4.5	Mobile Office, 10'33".	46
4.6	Mobile Office, 10'55".	46
5.1	*Casual Fridays, Table Top,* 2002, Maureen Connor.	62
5.2	*Casual Fridays, Exhausted,* 2002, Maureen Connor.	71
6.1	Comparison between nominal fee scale structures and fees actually charged or due, all indexed at 2011 construction costs.	86
6.2	Example of the surface-based Tariff of Fees for Architectural Services recommended by the Architectural Institute of British Columbia (AICB).	87
6.3	The time-based logic of the contract agreement for professional services (1002/2003) of SIA, the Swiss Society of Engineers and Architects, where construction budget is translated into "average time required in hours" (Tm).	89
6.4	International comparison of percentage differences in building costs in PPP dollars per square meter of internal area in 2013.	92
8.1	"Articles of Agreement for a Town House for Sir William Heathcote at St James Square, London," (1734–6).	126
8.2	"The particulars and estimates of the several works," Tendring Hall, (1784).	128
8.3	Joiner title block, *Specification* (1898).	130
8.4	Contents page, *Specification* (1898).	131
8.5	Cover, *National Building Specification* (1973).	137

9.1	Aerial view, Doha, Qatar.	145
9.2	Education City Central Library, Doha, Qatar, designed by OMA.	146
9.3	Foreign national workers in Qatar from Amnesty International *Dark Side of Migration*.	150
9.4	Case study Ras Laffan Emergency and Safety College from Amnesty International *Dark Side of Migration*.	153
13.1	Basic practice business model.	210

List of contributors

Foreword

Joan Ockman is currently Distinguished Senior Fellow at the University of Pennsylvania School of Design and Visiting Professor at Cooper Union and Cornell. She directed the Temple Hoyne Buell Center for the Study of American Architecture at Columbia from 1994 to 2008. Among her book publications are *Architecture Culture 1943–1968* (1993), *The Pragmatist Imagination: Thinking about Things in the Making* (2000), and *Architecture School: Three Centuries of Educating Architects in North America* (2012). She began her career at the Institute for Architecture and Urban Studies in New York in the 1970s and was an editor of its journal *Oppositions* and of the Oppositions Books series.

Chapter 1

Franco Berardi, born in Bologna, Italy in 1949, is a writer, media-theorist, and media-activist. As a young militant he took part in the experience of Potere operaio in the years 1967–73, then founded the magazine *A/traverso* (1975–81) and was part of the staff of Radio Alice, the first free pirate radio station in Italy (1976–8). Involved in the political movement of Autonomia in Italy during the 1970s, he fled to Paris, where he worked with Félix Guattari in the field of schizo-analysis. He has been involved in many media-projects, including "Telestreet" and "Recombinant.org." Berardi has published the following books: *The Uprising* (2012), *After the Future* (2011), *The Soul at Work* (2010), *Felix* (2001), *Cibernauti* (1994), and *Mutazione e Cyberpunk* (1993). He has contributed to the magazines *Semiotext(e), Chimères, Metropoli*, and *Musica 80*, and is currently collaborating with *e-flux* journal. As Coordinator of the European School for Social Imagination (SCEPSI), he has taught at Ashkal Alwan in Beirouth, PEI-Macba in Barcelona, Accademia di belle Arti di Brera (in Milan), and has lectured in social centers and universities worldwide.

Chapter 2

Metahaven is a studio for design and research, founded by Vinca Kruk and Daniel van der Velden. Metahaven's work—both commissioned and self-directed—reflects political and social issues in provocative graphic design objects. Metahaven released *Uncorporate Identity*, a book on politics and visual identity, published by Lars Müller in 2010. Solo exhibitions include "Affiche Frontière" (CAPC musée d'art contemporain de Bordeaux, 2008) and "Stadtstaat" (Künstlerhaus Stuttgart/Casco, 2009). Group exhibitions include "Forms of Inquiry" (AA London, 2007), "Manifesta8" (Murcia, Spain, 2010), the "Gwangju Design Biennale 2011" (Gwangju, Korea) and "Graphic Design: Now In Production" (Walker Art Center, Minneapolis, 2011). In 2011, Metahaven was selected by *Rolling Stone Italia* as one of the world's twenty most promising design studios.

Chapter 3

Richard Biernacki teaches in the Department of Sociology at UC Berkeley. He received his Ph.D. from UC Berkeley in 1989. In *The Fabrication of Labor: Germany and Great Britain, 1640–1914* (1995), he compares the influence of culture on the execution of factory manufacture. His interests are classical and contemporary theory, comparative method, and culture. His research focuses on the historical invention of key forms of cultural practice in Europe, including the categories of labor as a commodity, ethnic identity, and property in ideas.

Chapter 4

Andreas Rumpfhuber is an architect. His research focuses on the intersection of architecture and economics. He is presently heading the research project "The Office of Society," funded by the Austrian Science Fund, and has recently completed the project "Scarcity and Creativity in the Built Environment," co-initiated by Rumpfhuber and supported by the European Research Council (ESF/HERA). His publications include *Architektur immaterieller Arbeit* (2013), *The Design of Scarcity* (with Jeremy Till et al., 2014), and *Modeling Vienna: Real Fictions in Social Housing* (2015). Rumpfhuber presently teaches at the Academy of Fine Arts Vienna and is the initiator of the non-institutional seminar series "Theoriesalon" (founded in 2011). More info at: www.expandeddesign.net.

List of contributors xv

Chapter 5

Peggy Deamer is Assistant Dean and Professor of Architecture at Yale University. She is a principal in the firm of Deamer Architects. She received a B.Arch. from the Cooper Union and a Ph.D. from Princeton University. She is the editor of *Architecture and Capitalism: 1845 to the Present* (2014), *The Millennium House* (2004), and co-editor of *Building in the Future: Recasting Architectural Labor* (2010) and *BIM in Academia* (2011) with Phil Bernstein. Recent articles include "Office Management" in Office*US*'s *Agenda*; "Work" in *Perspecta 47*; "The Changing Nature of Architectural Work" in *Design Practices Now, Vol II: The Harvard Design Magazine* no. 33; "Detail Deliberation" in *Building (in) the Future: Recasting Labor in Architecture* (2010); and "Practicing Practice" in *Perspecta 44*. Her research examines the nature of architectural work/labor. She is the organizing member of the advocacy group, The Architecture Lobby.

Chapter 6

Paolo Tombesi is the Chair in Construction at the University of Melbourne, where he teaches construction technology, construction policy, and building innovation subjects. A former Fulbright Fellow and a Ph.D. in architecture from the University of California, Los Angeles (UCLA), he has held several visiting positions in Europe and the United States. An international authority on the analysis of the building process and the organization of contemporary practice, he has contributed to many of the world's most prestigious architectural publications. In 2000, his essay "The Carriage in the Needle", on the industrial restructuring of the building and architectural sector, won the *Journal of Architectural Education* Award. In 2005, he received the Sisalation Prize, the research award of the Royal Australian Institute of Architects. To date he has given numerous public addresses and advanced seminars around the world, and lectured at several universities, including Harvard, Yale, and the École Polytechnique Fédérale de Lausanne (EPFL). The overarching concern of his work remains the relationship between the intellectual dimension of architecture and the socio-technical aspects of its physical construction.

Chapter 7

Pier Vittorio Aureli is an architect and educator. His projects, researches, writings, and teaching focus on the relationship between architectural form, political theory, and urban history. He is the author of publications including

The Possibility of an Absolute Architecture (2011) and *The Project of Autonomy: Politics and Architecture Within and Against Capitalism* (2000). Aureli studied at the Istituto di Architettura di Venezia (IUAV), before obtaining his Ph.D. from Delft University of Technology. He teaches at the Architectural Association and is Davenport Visiting Professor at the School of Architecture at Yale University. He has taught at Columbia University, the Barcelona Institute of Architecture, and Delft University of Technology. Together with Martino Tattara, Aureli is the co-founder of DOGMA, an office focused on the project of the city.

Chapter 8

Katie Lloyd Thomas is Lecturer in Architecture at Newcastle University where she co-directs ARC, the Architecture Research Collaborative, and is an editor of the international journal *arq*. Her research is concerned with materiality in architecture and with feminist practice and theory. She is co-founder of the feminist collective *taking place* (www.takingplace.org.uk), and edited *Material Matters* (2007). Her monograph *Preliminary Operations: Material Theory and the Architectural Specification* is in preparation.

Tilo Amhoff is Senior Lecturer at the University of Brighton as well as teaching fellow and Ph.D. candidate at the Bartlett School of Architecture (University College London). His research investigates plans for various entities such as the factory, the city, and the economy. He is a founder member of *Netzwerk Architekturwissenschaft* (www.architekturwissenschaft.net).

Chapter 9

Mabel O. Wilson's practice *Studio &* operates between the fields of architecture, art, and cultural history. As the Nancy and George E. Rupp Professor, she teaches architectural design and history/theory courses at Columbia University's Graduate School of Architecture Planning and Preservation (GSAPP) and was appointed as a senior fellow at the Institute for Research in African American Studies.

Jordan Carver is a writer, researcher, and educator whose work investigates the intersection of space, law, and political rhetoric. He is the 2014–15 Peter Reyner Banham Fellow at the University at Buffalo. Jordan is a core member of Who Builds Your Architecture? and a contributing editor to *The Avery Review*.

List of contributors   xvii

Kadambari Baxi is an architect and educator based in New York. Her current architecture and media projects focus on design, visual culture, and globalization. She is a professor of practice in architecture at Barnard College, Columbia University.

Chapter 10

Norman M. Klein is a critic, urban and media historian, and novelist. His books include: *The History of Forgetting* (1997): *Los Angeles and the Erasure of Memory* (1997); *Seven Minutes: The Life and Death of the American Animated Cartoon* (1993); *The Vatican to Vegas: The History of Special Effects* (2004); *Freud in Coney Island and Other Tales* (2006); the database novel *Bleeding Through: Layers of Los Angeles, 1920–86* with Marsha Kinder, Rosemary Comelia, and Andreas Kratky (2003), and in 2014 with Margo Bisits, the media science-fiction and archival novel, *The Imaginary 20th Century*, available online (an interactive archive of 2,200 images and a 231 page ebook). The paper edition will be available in 2015. Klein's next book is entitled *History of the Present: The Dismantling of the American Psyche* (2016). He is a professor at California Institute of the Arts, in Los Angeles.

Chapter 11

Alicia Carrió was born in Buenos Aires, Argentina, where she studied Architecture at the Universidad Nacional de Buenos Aires, Facultad de Arquitectura y Urbanismo. In 1976, she moved to Barcelona to study Graphic Design at the Eina School. In 1979, Carrió settled in Malaga, Andalucía, where she has developed her autonomous practice as an architect. She holds an M.A. in Urbanism with a focus on Gender, and an M.A. in Environmental Studies from the NOW (New Opportunities for Women) European program, and is in the process of finishing her Ph.D. She has an extended practice in drawing, painting, and etching. Carrió has made stage and costume designs for Community Theater, and she is an active member of *La Casa Invisible*, a cultural and social self-organized center in the city of Malaga.

Chapter 12

Manuel Shvartzberg is an architect and researcher. He has worked, among others, for OMA/Rem Koolhaas and David Chipperfield Architects in London. He is currently based in New York City where he is a Ph.D. candidate in Architecture

History and Theory and a researcher at the Temple Hoyne Buell Center for the Study of American Architecture, GSAPP, as well as a graduate fellow of the Institute for Comparative Literature and Society, all at Columbia University.

Chapter 13

Phillip G. Bernstein is a vice president at Autodesk, a leading provider of digital design, engineering, and entertainment software, where he leads Strategic Industry Relations and is responsible for setting the company's future vision and strategy for technology as well as cultivating and sustaining the firm's relationships with strategic industry leaders and associations. An experienced architect, Phil was formerly with Pelli Clarke Pelli Architects where he managed many of the firm's most complex commissions. Phil teaches Professional Practice at the Yale School of Architecture where he received his both his B.A. and his M.Arch. He is co-editor of *Building (In) The Future: Recasting Labor in Architecture* (2010) and *BIM In Academia* (2011). He is a senior fellow of the Design Futures Council and former Chair of the American Institute of Architects (AIA) National Contract Documents Committee.

Chapter 14

Thomas Fisher is a professor in the School of Architecture and Dean of the College of Design at the University of Minnesota, having previously served in various editorial positions at *Progressive Architecture* magazine. With degrees from Cornell and Case Western Reserve Universities, he was recognized in 2005 as the fifth-most published architecture writer in the United States, with eight books, over fifty book chapters or introductions, and over 325 articles.

Chapter 15

Neil Leach is an architect, curator, and writer. He is currently Professor at the University of Southern California, and a NASA Innovative Advanced Concepts Fellow. He has also taught at SCI-Arc, Architectural Association, Columbia GSAPP, Cornell University, Dessau Institute of Architecture, Institute for Advanced Architecture of Catalonia (IaaC), London Consortium, Royal Danish School of Fine Arts, Escuela Superior de Arquitectura (ESARQ), University of Nottingham, University of Bath, and University of Brighton. His research interests fall broadly into two fields, critical theory and digital design. In the field of critical theory, he has published a number of monographs and edited volumes, dealing largely with the impact of importing theoretical tools from critical theory into an architectural arena. In the field of digital design he has curated several exhibitions and published numerous edited volumes. He is currently working on a NASA-funded project to develop a robotic 3-D printing technology for the Moon and Mars.

Afterword

Michael Sorkin is Principal of the Michael Sorkin Studio, a global design practice working at all scales with a special interest in the city and green architecture; President and founder of Terreform, a non-profit institute dedicated to research into the forms and practices of just and sustainable urbanism; and Co-President of the Forum and Institute for Urban Design. He is Distinguished Professor of Architecture and Director of the Graduate Program in Urban Design at the City College of New York, author or editor of numerous books on architecture and urbanism, and architecture critic for *The Nation*. In 2013, he won the National Design Award as "Design Mind."

Acknowledgments

I am indebted to all of the contributors to this book. Many are writers admired from afar now brought close by the work on these chapters, I have learned from all of them. Others already close have moved beyond positions previously digested to produce surprising and ever-informative speculations. Phil Bernstein and Paolo Tombesi are past collaborators to whom I am particularly and consistently indebted, Phil for his insights into building information modeling (BIM) and new structures of practice and Paolo for demonstrating the advantage of calling all buildings agents "designers." In addition, Reinhold Martin, and Keller Easterling, not represented here, provide ongoing provocations to my own thinking on how architecture operates in the current global economy. The Vera List Center for Art provides an inspiring model of politically engaged aesthetics currently lacking in architecture. Students in my seminars and my studios at Yale School of Architecture have always made me see architectural design and what it takes to work at it in a new and often inspiring light. The members of the advocacy group The Architecture Lobby (to which I belong and which picks up where the AIA leaves off in advocating for architectural value) have drawn my attention to the full gambit of traumas faced by architecture workers and inspired me as both a thinker and an activist. The members of the women's group ArchiteXX ("We ask how, not Y,") and its leaders Lori Brown and Nina Freedman have been at the forefront of identifying the indignities architecture offers most harshly to women but that are experienced by all. And finally, I am beholden to my Assistant Editor, Dariel Cobb, who has made the work of editing this book shared, fun, and consistently provocative. She deserves a great deal more than my thanks.

Foreword

Joan Ockman

> A bee would put many a human architect to shame by the construction of its honeycomb cells. But what distinguishes the worst architect from the best of bees is that the architect builds the cell in his mind before he constructs it in wax.[1]
>
> *Karl Marx*

Marx wrote the above in 1867 in the first volume of *Das Kapital*. Today, according to the post-Marxist concept of "immaterial labor," the old divide between mental and manual labor has been transcended. Under the currently dominant economic regime known (among many other names) as "cognitive capitalism," new technologies of design and communication and new forms of work involving the creation of symbolic products and intangible services have short-circuited traditional relationships between conceptualization and realization. Architecture, for its part, understood as a production of not just physical objects but also social relations and images, is deeply implicated in these processes. With the advent of digital fabrication, BIM, and the (eventual) robotized building site, the hive and the idea of the hive are being integrated as never before. At the same time, the architect's performance can now be stretched geographically over thousands of miles, thanks to new affordances of computerization and sophisticated long-distance control.

So we are all worker bees now… Well, sort of. While some have hailed the most recent transformation of capitalism for its potential to engender new subjectivities, new socialities, and also new, emancipatory politics, others have seen the collapse of the distinction between older forms of labor and knowledge-based work as vastly expanding the realm of capitalist oppression, from the sweatshop to the office cubicle and beyond. As architects fly from job site to job site, as they restock their 3D printers with wax, they may resemble Marx's drones more than ever. As many commentators have pointed out, intellectual labor has become increasingly arduous and stressful today by virtue of the expansion of the workday to the 24/7 cycle, "flexible" hiring and firing policies, insecurity with respect to healthcare and other social benefits, and—in the particular case of young, highly educated architects—low compensation and unpaid internships.

In fact, in the same chapter where the passage about bees and architects appears, titled "The Labor Process and the Valorization Process," Marx himself writes in a note,

> The distinction between higher and simple labor, 'skilled labor' and 'unskilled labor,' rests in part on pure illusion or, to say the least, on distinctions that have long since ceased to be real, and survive only by virtue of a traditional convention; and in part on the helpless condition of some sections of the working class, a condition that prevents them from exacting equally with the rest the value of their labor-power.[2]

What Marx is suggesting here is that certain workers have historically been incapable of demanding the worth of their labor power from their bosses, whether because of their inferior position or because the value of their labor is difficult to measure or because it is subject to economic fluctuations and changes in the mode of production.[3] These problems are compounded today in the context of a disorganized global "precariat" that has to market its own skills as "entrepreneur of itself." Yet what all forms of labor share under conditions of capitalism—high- or low-skilled, blue-, white-, or pink-collar, at all stages of development and in every part of the world—is the condition of exploitation for the sake of profit. And although theorists across a wide political spectrum have celebrated the immaterialization of work—from neoliberal apologists, to techno-utopians and end-of-work prophets, to post-Workerist militants—the fact is that "real people with real bodies have contributed real time" to the development of the new "weightless" commodities on offer today; and that this labor, despite its cyborg prosthetics and fleetness, does not escape being subsumed by capitalist power.[4] As George Caffentzis has argued in "The End of Work or the Renaissance of Slavery?" capitalism thrives precisely on uneven development. "The very capital that owns 'the ethereal information machines which supplant industrial production,'" he writes, "is also involved in the enclosure of lands throughout the planet, provoking famine, disease, low-intensity war and collective misery in the process."[5]

As far as architecture is concerned, the focus by theorists like Antonio Negri and Michael Hardt on the most advanced sector of capitalism obfuscates a deeper understanding of the contradictions between—and interdependencies of—the different forms of labor that go (have always gone) into the physical realization of buildings. Today both the actual construction site and the factory where—hardly weightless—building materials are produced continue to be hazardous places, particularly when they have moved offshore and out of the range of enforceable safety codes. Just as the glass panels for Joseph Paxton's 1851 Crystal Palace in London emerged out of a smoke-belching factory near Manchester that employed child labor, so the metallic shingles that clad Frank Gehry's Guggenheim Museum in Bilbao originated not only from the aerospace-derived software subsequently patented by Gehry Partners in Los Angeles but also from the *terra incognita* of titanium mining in central Russia, where the raw material was extracted.

Today the issue of architectural sourcing and outsourcing is more than a banal matter to be relegated to the business of construction management. More than ever before, it is clear that not very many degrees of separation exist between "here" and "there." A recent book by Mark Schapiro connects the dots between the greening of the once polluted city of Pittsburgh and the blackening of Guangzhou, an industrial hub in China's Pearl River Delta of over 15 million people whose population has more than quadrupled since the 1960s. Whereas Pittsburgh's economy used to be based on greenhouse-gas-intensive manufacturing, the emissions that formerly spewed from its factories have now been replaced by "one of the highest concentrations of green buildings in the United States" and a "greenwalk" running alongside its once toxic rivers. Meanwhile, jobs in the steel industry have migrated to China, and American cities are purchasing that steel to construct their buildings. "The Chinese, in short, are producing greenhouse gases on our behalf," Schapiro writes.[6]

It is worth recalling that at certain moments in the last century architects sought—however quixotically—to involve themselves directly in questions of labor and production. In 1968, striking architecture students at the École des Beaux-Arts in Paris took as one of their rallying cries "three deaths a day on the construction site," demanding the amelioration of dangerous practices in the French building industry. Further back, after the Bolshevik Revolution, Productivist designers in the Soviet Union, including Alexander Rodchenko, Varvara Stepanova, and Liubov' Popova, strove to reform working conditions in the factory. They not only dressed in and designed factory uniforms to express their solidarity with the new proletariat, but in the case of the two women, went directly into textile plants to collaborate with female workers on the production of mass-consumer goods. A new category of "worker-inventor" was put forward at this time to stimulate Soviet workers' creativity and to help reduce alienation in the Taylorized workplace.[7]

In architecture today, despite the proclaimed integration of all phases of the building process through high-tech management techniques, the rhetoric of immaterial production contributes to absolving architects from accountability to material bodies and places, not to mention provides an alibi from legal liability. In the countries of the Persian Gulf, in the context of one of the largest construction booms in history, migrant workers, mostly from South Asia, are treated by government-sanctioned private construction companies as indentured servants, housed in miserable camps, and forced to labor under brutal conditions. Western architects, hired to design the spectacular monuments that are transforming this region into a twenty-first-century showplace, have for the most part washed their hands of responsibility. Apropos of his current commission to design another satellite for the Guggenheim in Abu Dhabi, scheduled to be completed in 2017, Gehry notoriously declared in an interview with *Foreign Policy* magazine that he preferred working for "benevolent dictators" who "have taste."[8] At the same time, amid a mounting storm of condemnation of building practices in this part of the world by groups like Human Rights Watch, he hired a human rights lawyer to vet the situation. Most recently—and in the wake of the hornet's nest stirred up by Zaha Hadid's even more unfortunate comments on the architect's responsibility to concern herself with such matters[9]—Gehry, who is also fond of flaunting his own working-class origins, has released a statement asserting that his firm has had "a substantial and on-going dialogue over many years now [concerning labor conditions on his building sites] that has involved government, the construction industry, architects, project sponsors and NGOs."[10]

With such high-profile attention being paid, as well as the appearance of books like the present one, perhaps a paradigm shift is at hand. Certainly serious reflection on labor in architecture today must entail a recognition that buildings begin in *both* embodied and disembodied—material and immaterial—production, not just in architects' designs but also in raw materials from the ground and bodies on the construction site; and they also end there, in physical objects located in actual places as well as in images or "effects" that enter into a cycle of future reproduction and commodification. Nor is the architect's labor just a finite moment in this chain of production; it is implicated in both immediate and deferred ways at every stage of the building's existence.

Ultimately what we are talking about with respect to present-day architecture is a division of labor that exists at a planetary scale, an expanded "construction site" that encompasses all the far-flung but environmentally interconnected actors and factors involved in bringing a building to fruition. If material and immaterial processes have always been intertwined in the production of architecture, what is unprecedented today is the degree of interconnection. As far as the architect-as-worker—that is, the architectural worker as a producer of culture[11]—is concerned, we would like to pose the following questions:

> How can the architect both *represent* and *embody* the historical conditions and contradictions of architecture's coming into being?

How can the architect think *all at once* material resources, manufacturing technologies, laboring bodies, the fetish of the commodity, and the production of real, habitable space?

How can the architect give creative and imaginative expression to ideas about how people might live—and the planet might thrive—in the future while also making manifest the collaborative, social nature of all architectural work? If individual signature is a reactionary mark of the marketplace, can the architect be a *de-signer* today as well as a *designer*?

Notes

1. Karl Marx, *Capital*, vol. 1, trans. Ben Fowkes (London: Penguin Books, 1990), 284.
2. Ibid., 305.
3. Marx goes on to say in the same note that the work of a bricklayer may, through market-related circumstances like labor shortages, come to be valued as highly as that of "men of letters, artists, schoolmasters" and other middle-class workers.
4. For a critique of the concept of immaterial labor, see, among others, Ursula Huws, "Material World: The Myth of the 'Weightless Economy,'" *The Socialist Register* 35 (1999); quoted phrase, p. 44; and Steve Wright, "Reality Check: Are We Living in an Immaterial World?" *Mute* 2, no. 1 (2005), online at http://www.metamute.org/editorial/articles/reality-check-are-we-living-immaterial-world. Notably, after initially embracing the concept of immaterial labor in their 2000 book *Empire*, Hardt and Negri shifted their vocabulary to "immaterial production," and also acknowledged that workers involved primarily in this sphere of activity represent only a small fraction of the global workforce. See Michael Hardt and Antonio Negri, *Multitude: War and Democracy in the Age of Empire* (New York: Penguin Press, 2004), 65. Yet in insisting on the inexorable hegemony of immaterial production and downplaying the continued existence of older forms of labor, their theory both serves to reinforce the traditional binary, privileging those in the more developed economies of the world, and converges with mainstream capitalist ideology.
5. George Caffentzis, "The End of Work or the Renaissance of Slavery? A Critique of Rifkin and Negri," *Common Sense* 24 (1999), 34; the quote within the quote comes from Antonio Negri and Félix Guattari, *Communists Like Us: New Spaces of Liberty* (New York: Semiotext(e), 1985), 21.
6. *Carbon Shock: A Tale of Risk and Calculus from the Front Lines of the Disrupted Global Economy* (White River Junction, VT: Chelsea Green, 2014). See excerpt in *The Nation*, "A Tale of Three Cities: How Pittsburgh's Pollution Became Guangzhou's Problem—and Manchester Found a Solution," 27 October 2014, 22–25.
7. See Maria Gough, *The Artist as Producer: Russian Constructivism in Revolution* (Berkeley: University of California Press, 2005), esp. 167–78.
8. Benjamin Pauker, "Epiphanies from Frank Gehry: The Starchitect on His First Project in the Arab World—and Why It's Hard These Days to Find a Benevolent Dictator

with Taste," *Foreign Policy*, 24 June 2013, online at http://www.foreignpolicy.com/articles/2013/06/24/epiphanies_from_frank_gehry

9. See the contribution to this volume by Mabel O. Wilson, Jordan Carver, and Kadambari Baxi, "Working Globally: The Human Networks of Transnational Architectural Projects" (Chapter 9).

10. See Anna Fixsen, "What Is Gehry Doing About Labor Conditions in Abu Dhabi?" *Architectural Record*, September 25, 2014, online at http://archrecord.construction.com/news/2014/09/140922-Frank-Gehry-Works-to-Improve-Worker-Conditions-on-Abu-Dhabi-Site.asp

11. Despite the fact that it was written in the context of an industrial rather than postindustrial society and by a committed socialist, Walter Benjamin's classic essay "The Author as Producer" (1934) has not lost its relevance. While Benjamin does not mention architects specifically, what he demands of any artist or intellectual who does not wish to be branded a hack is a radical engagement with the processes of production. His concept of authorship is shorn of romantic notions of autonomy and suspicious of celebrity, but it does not deny the artistic producer a degree of agency.

Introduction
Peggy Deamer

In 1995, I watched a subcontractor plastering the rooms of a house my partner and I had designed. It was clear that he knew every corner of the house in a way we never would. Whose contribution mattered more, his material labor of construction or our immaterial labor of thinking, drawing and model-making? I also felt it clear that if the owners ever gave up the house, they would not be able to sell it to just anyone; they'd be forced to donate it to my partner and me, the only ones who loved it as they did. (Yes, they have since sold it, and no, we weren't its recipients.) Which of us—designer, builder, owner—could rightly say this house was "theirs," I wondered? What value—emotional, monetary, social—could be placed on our particular role as designers?

Writing about detail in an article for *Praxis* a few years later,[1] when computer-aided manufacturing and prefabrication became hot, the relationship between design, production and ownership was again weighing on me. Who determines the design of the prefabricated house, the fabricators or the architect? And without a patron, could the architecture of prefabrication be commission-free? In factory-based production, design not only could not be distinguished from construction, but the definition of "detail" expanded from the joining of materials in an object to the joining of steps in the production process. Theoretically, I felt it was important to rescue the appreciation of detail from the hands of the phenomenologists who too easily, it seemed to me, equated good design with the sentimental craft attached to the handiwork of beautiful drawings, the traditional product of architectural work.[2] Not only did their conservative position reject digital production and paperless outputs (which just weren't going to go away), but it also kept design in the realm of the elite, since the crafty, one-off buildings they so admired could never find an underprivileged, urban audience. Surely architectural work could move through these procedural changes and still keep alive the flame of detail, craft, and quality design.

My article for *Praxis* in turn led to two "a-ha" moments. One was reading, in Edward Ford's *Details of Modern Architecture*, this quote:

> Insofar as twentieth-century architects have concerned themselves with the social consequences of their work, they have focused on the way in which buildings affect the behavior of their occupants. Insofar as 19th century architects concerned themselves with the social consequence of their work, they focused

on the way in which buildings (and particularly their ornaments) affect those who build them. There is perhaps no greater difference between the architects of the 19th century and those of the 20th than that each group was so indifferent to the social concerns of the other.[3]

Why did we architects give up on the worker? And didn't the present emphasis on the intricacies of environmental façades and material performativity invite a reconsideration of the fabricators' essential role in design? In addition to this, the outsourcing of drafting, rendering, and model-making to distant countries implied that even the craft of representation was not an intimate, office-based activity. Shouldn't the larger family of building-makers—fabricators, factory workers, engineers, HVAC consultants, energy specialists, drafters—be consulted about their creative, social, and monetary satisfaction?

The other such moment occurred during research initiated by the *Praxis* article that led to the symposium (2006) and eventual book entitled *Building in the Future: Recasting Architectural Labor* (Princeton, NJ: Princeton Architectural Press, 2010) that Phil Bernstein and I organized and edited. A grant from Yale University allowed me to interview engineers, metal and glass fabricators, steel and aluminum factory workers, architects, and software developers to determine their role in the current chain—or was it now a network?—of design command. Besides confirmation of the thought that building work was no longer linearly handed down from architectural auteur, to staff, to contractor, to subcontractor, the interviews indicated the importance of new software supporting building information modeling (BIM) and new contracts allowing Integrated Project Delivery (IPD), frameworks with the potential to change the old design/construction hierarchies for good.

Beyond these explorations into the material and social nature of architectural design, seminars I taught at Yale School of Architecture—"Architecture and Capitalism" and "Architecture and Utopia"—continued the exploration of architectural work and, as a not-too-subtle aside, responded to architectural theory's pathetic avoidance of issues raised by 9/11 or the 2008 financial crisis. "Architecture and Capitalism" examined an alternate historiography of architecture that looked beyond the standard focus on formal, stylistic progression, and attempted to link those changes to transformations in capitalism. Issues of labor are not always paramount in this history, but labor is certainly an important ingredient. The book that this seminar research yielded, *Architecture and Capitalism: 1845 to the Present*,[4] can be seen as the precursor to this more contemporary book. Likewise, "Architecture and Utopia" (a more optimistic alternative to "Architecture and Capitalism") examined societies with varying attitudes about work: societies like Robert Owen's New Lanark made the work day short so pleasure and leisure could follow. Other societies such as William Morris's in *News from Nowhere* and Charles Fourier's *Phalanstere* promoted work as inherently creative and pleasurable. Marx's utopian society freed the worker from the alienation imposed by capitalism—alienation from one's fellow workers via job competition, from one's products by the division of labor, and from oneself by the false needs of consumption. These latter utopias not only offered a glimmering view of work that many of us entering architecture thought we would experience (designing is fun!), but indicated how work was integral to society in general: how one felt about one's work and how it was assigned value formed the basis of social relationships.

While none of these utopian societies addressed architectural work per se, it became impossible to feel good about the architecture profession. It had become commonplace to see architecture graduates with $100,000 in debt begging for internships that paid little more than minimum wage, honored to be working 15 hour days, seven days a week as a sign of their being needed; principals of firms working almost exclusively for the rich, trying to prove that their meager fees weren't paying for hubristic self-serving experiments; young architects hoping to move beyond bathroom renovations to possible suburban additions.

Things came to a head on two separate occasions during the last three years. One was an architectural symposium where a young audience member asked the panel what to expect from a career in architecture, to which one prominent, intelligent speaker fervently answered, "Architecture isn't a career, it is a calling!" What? How had we fallen into the same ideology that Christianity used to make the poor feel blessed for their poverty? How could architecture have become so completely deaf to the labor discourse that it could so unself-consciously subscribe to the honor of labor exploitation?

A few months later I was part of a "Who Builds Your Architecture?" panel at the Vera List Center for Art and Politics at the New School in New York. Organized by Kadambari Baxi and Mabel Wilson in collaboration with Human Rights Watch monitoring the labor abuse of indentured workers building projects in the Emirates, South Asia, and China, they hoped to initiate pressure on architects designing these buildings to in turn put pressure on their clients to monitor construction protocols. Not a single architect working in these geographic areas would concede to participate in talks, sign a petition, or consider interfering in labor issues. This response was in contrast to the many artists who refused to have their work shown at the Guggenheim Museum in Abu Dhabi, possibly the most infamous of these questionable projects. How could artists, with less professional security, more easily identify with indentured workers than did architects? How ironic that if architects thought they were outside the work/labor discourse because what they did was art or design instead of "work" per se, that artists themselves didn't abdicate the social responsibility that accompanies the self-identification as a laborer.

In retrospect, I shouldn't have been surprised. Critical theory has embraced the field seemingly most distant from architecture's economic engines—art—to prove the extensive realm of capitalist ideology. Art history and theory has examined the tense, historical relationship between art and politics. Having taught courses in Architectural Critical Theory, I was very aware of the fact that teaching architects about these issues meant reading the essays of art theorists and hoping students could grasp the implications for architecture.

A few examples in architecture theory have proved the exception, most notably the work circling around the writings of Manfredo Tafuri, the Marxist architecture historian who argued that there could be no socially beneficial architecture as long as there was no socialism. This intricately considered argument leaves little hope for architecture to be more than capitalism's pawn, but it is singular in its reading of architecture as operating in a dialectical fashion with art as both struggle to adjust to the traps of industrial capitalism. The legacy of his writing resides in one of two types of response, both of which we learn from: architectural thinkers who defend their relevance within capitalism, either by leaving overt Marxism behind or by rereading architecture's opportunities; or non-architecture, neo-Marxist theorists who occasionally extend their thinking to architecture.

One portion of the architectural response has capitalized on Tafuri's belief in architecture's inability to be socially relevant in capitalist society—that it is savvy to limit aspirations to (mere) formal exploration. This has allowed many architects, Peter Eisenman primary among them, to be pure formalists while claiming to be Tafurian/Marxist readers. Another neo-formalist group has analyzed the proposition that the autonomy of architecture—its uniquely formal language—allows it to mirror the ethical void of capitalism. The nuanced work of this latter group, exemplified most clearly by K. Michael Hays, has been largely historical and focused on the effects and consumption of architecture. Another group of thinkers, less interested in the formal or autonomous side of Tafuri than his critical stance regarding capitalism, are defenders of criticality against those "post-critical theorists" who want to fully indulge the advantages offered by capitalism's new modes of production.[5] While sharing post-criticality's rejection of Tafuri's gloom and doom fatalism, the anti-post-criticality group—Keller Easterling, Reinhold Martin, and Felicity Scott among them—redirect (if not reject) Tafurianism for a global, slippery, non-monolithic capitalism whose contradictions and mistakes offer opportunities for infiltration. And finally, Ken Frampton's work centering on critical regionalism moves the discourse away from Marxism proper toward Hannah Arendt's humanist, phenomenological social analysis. Frampton's *Labour, Work, and Architecture* (New York: Phaidon Press, 2002), an influential collection of polemical essays arguing for an "arrière-garde" resistant to technical optimization, is less an examination of labor and work per se than the types of spaces "good work" yields, but it still extends a critical look at how we architects have come to work.[6]

These exceptions aid architecture's social and cultural consciousness and bring the terms of labor to an architect's table. Tafuri's declaration that architecture would resist relevance until the user/public controls the means of production set in motion my own interest in digital fabrication, the source of much of this book's inquiry. Frampton's reference to Arendt's distinction between work and labor—one that I here resist because it's an unhelpful division when both are ignored by architects (but which is astutely explored by other authors, especially Paolo Tombesi)—directs our attention to the ethos of making, as does Richard Sennett in his *The Craftsman*.[7] Easterling, Martin, and Scott remind us that capitalism's historical particularity constructs the boundaries of production opportunities. K. Michael Hays reminds us that architecture resides not merely in the base but in the superstructure; or, more accurately, in his Althusserian outlook, dispenses with this distinction altogether. However, all of these exceptions spin around an empty center that still requires more focused attention, a center that examines architecture's peculiar status of material embodiment produced by its immaterial work, work that is at once very personal and yet entirely social.

The chapters assembled here are meant to fill that void. While it might be missing both the Robin Evans of digital production ("Architects don't make drawings, they make drawings of buildings") and the Andrew Ross of architecture labor,[8] and while it might also lack research on the specifics of contemporary architectural time-based work (typing in commands; talking on the phone; searching the internet; sketching on yellow trace; staring at a screen; attending meetings, etcetera), the totality of the texts herein cover the essentials embedded in the question of contemporary architectural labor. There are articles by non-architects that demonstrate the arena of issues in which architectural theory could and should operate. There are articles by architects who don't see their writing in terms of critical theory but whose grasp of the facts puts the urgency of the architectural labor condition before us. If this set of chapters is still circling around a more data-driven examination of architectural work, it hopefully invites that next set of investigations which will entail a professional study of considerable scale.

The book you are holding is divided into five parts, moving generally from the most aesthetically broad to the most architecturally specific, but negotiating as well the different territories that architectural design labor marches through—creativity, autonomy, value and compensation, the connection to or division of design (mental labor) from construction (material labor), labor's construction of subjectivity and its resultant public realm—there are many subjects that architectural labor touches on and the authors here find their individual point of entry.

Part I, "The commodification of design labor," includes articles by thinkers largely outside the field who look at how immaterial labor gets categorized, spatialized, and monetized. The first chapter by Franco "Bifo" Berardi—one of the original Italian theorists associated with automatism and its embrace of immaterial labor (and hence an honor to have in this collection)—titled "Dynamic of the general intellect" looks at the artist as a subcategory of "the Intellectual," itself part of the triumvirate, Intellectual, Warrior, Merchant that dominates modernism's self-characterization. In this framework, Berardi suggests that the intellectual's subordinate position to the other two is a result of its own internal ambiguity that misreads the artist's particular and proper role. Metahaven's "White night before a manifesto" is a meditation by this graphic design firm on the role of the enlightened creative professional *vis-à-vis* the corporate global clients who benefit from their skills. The claim that what is valued in this exchange is a "surface" of virtual assets independent of the corporate objects themselves leads Daniel van der Velden and Vinka Kruk to create a manifesto protesting this form of exchange. Richard Biernacki's "The capitalist origin of the concept of creative work" looks at the manner in which writers' work was commodified when this new "creative class" fell into the protocols of Taylorization. While "architectural" only in the sense that Taylorization implied specific work spaces, this chapter nevertheless is an essential story of the period when creative work was placed—in this case clumsily—into a system of capitalist value.[9] Andreas Rumpfhuber's "The architect as entrepreneurial self: Hans Hollein's TV performance 'Mobile Office' (1969)" is the sole chapter in this part addressing architecture proper, but it connects to the larger theme of aesthetic commodification in its analysis of a video by Hans Hollein that is as much performance art as it is architecture. Hollein's performance/critique of uncentered, apparatus- and client-driven work anticipates contemporary aspects of the architect's "daily grind," mirroring an organization that has made us all entrepreneurs. The "Mobile" Office presciently portrays and begs contemporary self-reflection on our entrepreneurial selves. This chapter then neatly forms a bridge to the next section dealing with architectural work.

Part II, "The concept of architectural labor," includes chapters that speculate on the nature of architectural work *vis-à-vis* other forms of labor, identifying both the specific and shared characteristics of architectural work. My chapter, "Work," addresses architects' blindness to the fact that they perform labor and examines two of the underlying suppositions contributing to this ignorance: that creative work, like architectural design, isn't labor; and that work in general is laborious and uncreative. Looking at various examples of how work is conceived in utopian literature, I speculate that architecture can and should now conceive of its work in a positive, utopian manner. Paolo Tombesi's "More for less—Architectural labor and design productivity" argues that architectural practice as it is now constructed—caught in the web of fiduciary professionals, technical analysts, transnational building systems, local normative frameworks, and idiosyncratic architectural ambitions—makes it almost impossible to design a building "well." Tombesi also predicts both the demise of the canonical architectural worker and the necessity to dis-aggregate geographic practices and technical conventions. Pier Vittorio Aureli's "Form and labor: Towards a history of abstraction in architecture" examines the role that abstraction plays in both the Marxist exposition of industrial labor in general and in architectural labor—design—in particular. By connecting aesthetic abstraction to industrial production, the article links architecture theory's infatuation with autonomy to its primary role in creating spaces of production.

Part III, "Design(ers)/Build(ers)" includes two chapters that address the fundamental cause of the conceptual ambiguity surrounding architectural work: the separation of architectural design and mental labor from construction and material labor even though architectural design "manages" that construction. "Writing work: Changing practices of architectural specification" by Katie Lloyd Thomas and Tilo Amhoff gives an historical account of the changing nature of architectural work in the UK from the eighteenth century to the present as indicated by specifications—that written work that instructs the builder on how, not just what, to build. The historical changes, from procedures based on personal relations, speech, and trust to ones based on professional relations, writing, and legal obligations, indicate a shift in spec writing from determining the building as an object to prescribing it as a process of work. These changes are today matched by a shift from process-based to performance-determined specifications written by specialists outside the design team; a change that, the authors argue, increasingly jeopardizes the architects' identification with the builders enacting their designs. Mabel Wilson, Jordan Carver, and Kadambari Baxi's "Working globally: The Human Networks of Transnational Architectural Projects" examines the expanded human labor networks—clients, technical consultants, contractors, labor contractors—that form around transnational building projects in the Middle East and Asia. It argues that the abuse of migrant laborers on construction sites is allowed by a system where fault is pervasive—and hence difficult to allocate—across a network of actors, at the same time that it insists that architects can no longer not account for the role they play within it. This chapter, in describing the camps that migrant laborers are forced to live in (a logical development of their disempowered status), links this one to the next, spatially focused, section.

Part IV, "The construction of the commons," includes chapters that analyze the subtle and not-so-subtle ways in which capitalism, in organizing work in a particular way, produces both impoverished subjects and spaces. Norman Klein's "Labor, architecture, and the new feudalism: Urban space as experience" examines how the new economy—disempowering unions and dismissing a labor theory of value—enacts a "feudalism" only mildly different from its original construct but different in its effects, now scripted spaces of entertainment and media. This chapter calls for a grammar for changing a social network definition of labor within the built environment. Alicia Carrió's "The hunger games: Architects in danger" looks at the development of professionalization as a new form of labor intended to offer—but radically failing to deliver—personalized and responsible attention to the public realm. Linked as the architectural profession is to speculation, it precludes addressing the basic needs of shelter and public assembly, as Carrió's case study of the Casa Invisible in Spain shows, by way of exception. Manuel Schwartzberg's "Foucault's 'environmental' power: Architecture and neoliberal subjectivization" examines Foucault's notion of governmentality—in which neoliberal society must "govern for the market, rather than because of the market"—to probe Foucault's underdeveloped idea of the "environment" which, Foucault indicates, is an essential construct of neoliberalism. Pointing out that Foucault did not intend this term metaphorically, he identifies architects as essential products and makers of this construct. The discipline of architecture must be rewired, Schwartzberg insists, to produce subjects resistant to neoliberalism's framework.

Part V, "The profession," includes chapters that look specifically at the potential for the profession of architecture to fully capture the value of architectural knowledge and creativity. Phil Bernstein's "Three strategies for new value propositions of design practice" examines the damage done to a profession when it characterizes itself as a "lowest cost commodity" in the construction supply chain. Given that architects are "extensively educated, carefully screened, and certified through licensure," why, Bernstein asks, is the value proposition of architecture so poorly converted? Tom Fisher's "Labor and talent in architecture" compares architectural talent to talent in other fields—that of football players, film and music stars—in which talent translates into high salaries, and speculates on why this does not happened for those with architectural talent. Pointing out that the global economy increasingly needs architects as the demand for innovative environments becomes more pressing, Fisher looks at how the design fields can move away from the position of oppressed labor towards that of high-demand talent. Finally, Neil Leach's "The (ac)credit(ation) card" connects the concerns laid out by Bernstein and Fisher to the architectural academy. The institutional blocks that prevent true creativity and innovation in schools of architecture in the US and Europe are outlined, and new models for accreditation encouraging multi-disciplinarity and "porous relations between industry" are put forward.

While this organization of texts is logical, it also misses affinities and disagreements that transcend the authors' specific subject matter. A clearly Marxist orientation runs through many of the texts (how could it not, given the origin of the "immaterial labor" discussion in Italian automatism, or given Tafuri's critique of a profession that doesn't own its means of production?) while others emphasize architecture's need to simply play capitalism better; others avoid an ideological position to describe the internal illogic of our current concept of architectural work. Some texts assume architecture's essential creative nature (that may be its escape from commodification or commodification's particular partner), while others assume architecture's essential social obligation. Some blame and want to transform the profession, others blame a system that vastly transcends the profession. But as a totality, they form an outline of the issues implicated in architectural work.

Notes

1. Peggy Deamer, "Detail: The Subject of the Object," *Praxis: Detail* 1.1 (2000): 108–15
2. Marco Frascari, Alberto Perez-Gomez, David Leatherbarrow, Peter Carl, and Juhani Pallasmaa, for example.
3. Edward R. Ford, *The Details of Modern Architecture, vol 1* (Cambridge, MA: MIT Press, 1990), 9.
4. Peggy Deamer, ed. *Architecture and Capitalism: 1845 to the Present* (New York: Routledge, 2013).
5. These include, amongst others, Silvia Lavin, Bob Somol, Michael Speaks, and Sarah Whiting.
6. Fredric Jameson, Hal Foster, and Richard Sennett are the non-architectural cultural theorists who have left the most substantial impression on architecture. Fredric

Jameson, in *Postmodernism, or the Cultural Logic of Late Capitalism* (Durham, NC: Duke University Press, 1990), and in "Architecture and the Critique of Ideology," in *Architecture, Criticism, and Ideology* (Princeton, NJ: Princeton Architectural Press, 1996), addresses the possibility that architecture can thwart ideological complicity by pushing its utopian aspirations. Holding a Marxist position that avoids the fatalism of Tafuri, Jameson expresses an architectural optimism lodged in postmodernism's fluidity of signification. Hal Foster—in his Dia publications such as *Vision and Visuality* (New York: The New Press, 1998) and his *October* articles like "What is Neo about the Neo-Avant-Garde?" and more recently in his *The Art-Architecture Complex* (London: Verso, 2013)—has consistently addressed art in Frankfurt School-inspired terms broad enough to encapsulate architecture, keeping alive the possibility of socially motivated, critical architectural production even as he outlines the complex tentacles of capitalist cooption and socially motivated theory. Richard Sennett has consistently addressed the particularities of craft and work in architecture, especially in *The Craftsman* (New Haven, CT: Yale University Press, 2009). Linking subjective work satisfaction to larger economic issues, his argument for the value of craft is exemplary if nostalgic.

7. Richard Sennett, *The Craftsman* (New Haven: Yale University Press, 2008).
8. Robin Evans (1944–93) analyzed architectural drawings for both evidence of social constructions of space and indication of the world-view of their authors. See Robin Evans, *Translations from Drawing to Building and Other Essays* (London: AA Publications, 1997), and Robin Evans, *The Projective Cast: Architecture and Its Three Geometries* (Cambridge, MA: The MIT Press, 2000). Andrew Ross has analyzed, critiqued and historicized the labor practices producing contemporary fashion. See *No Sweat: Fashion, Free Trade, and the Rights of Garment Workers* (London: Verso, 1997), and *Low Pay, High Profile: The Global Push for Fair Labor* (New York: The New Press, 2004).
9. Biernacki's *The Fabrication of Labor: Germany and Britain, 1640–1914* (Berkeley, CA: University of California Press, 1995) presents the model with regard to weavers of that period of the analysis and research needed for architecture. His research on the quantification of the movement of weavers' hands, the timing of their work, and the relation of these acts to their monetization, and later to the construction of the notion of authorship, is both concrete and theoretically expansive. See also: Richard Biernacki, "Contradictory Schemas of Action: Manufacturing Intellectual Property," lecture, Havens Center at the University of Wisconsin-Madison, Spring 2004, 82:04 minutes (23.48 MB), Mono 44kHz 40Kbps (CBR), http://www.havenscenter.org/audio/richard_biernacki_contradictory_schemas_action_manufacturing_intellectual_property

Part I

The commodification of design labor

Chapter 1

Dynamic of the general intellect
Franco Berardi

Sick at heart

Recently I read the words uttered by Mario Savio during a meeting in Berkeley, California on 2 December 1964. He was relating a conversation with the director of the Board of Regents of the University of California. I guess that many of you know these justifiably famous words by heart. However, please, let's read these words again:

> The answer we received, from a well-meaning liberal, was the following: He said, "Would you ever imagine the manager of a firm making a statement publicly in opposition to his board of directors?" That's the answer!
>
> Well, I ask you to consider: If this is a firm, and if the Board of Regents is the board of directors; and if President Kerr in fact is the manager; then I'll tell you something. The faculty are a bunch of employees, and we're the raw material! But we're a bunch of raw materials that don't mean to be—have any process upon us. Don't mean to be made into any product. Don't mean … Don't mean to end up being bought by some clients of the University, be they the government, be they industry, be they organized labor, be they anyone! We're human beings!
>
> There's a time when the operation of the machine becomes so odious, makes you so sick at heart, that you can't take part! You can't even passively take part! And you've got to put your bodies upon the gears and upon the wheels … upon the levers, upon all the apparatus, and you've got to make it stop! And you've got to indicate to the people who run it, to the people who own it, that unless you're free, the machine will be prevented from working at all![1]

Fifty years have passed since that day. The world has changed exactly in the direction that Mario Savio then sensed as a frightening possibility.

In his words I see an astounding anticipation of the relation between knowledge and the capitalist economy, the process of submission and privatization of the University and of research, and also a sort of premonition of the destiny of the movement that in 1964 was dawning: the student movement that spread to everywhere in the world in the legendary year of 1968.

The first point that I want to emphasize in Savio's speech is the understanding that the University is (becoming) a firm, an economic entity whose leading principle is profit. The relationship between the economy and knowledge was an important subject in the consciousness of the students, researchers, and intellectuals involved in the Free Speech Movement of the 1960s and 1970s. That relationship has become absolutely crucial in the thirty years since the digital revolution. In this period, which has also been marked by market globalization, the neoliberal ideology has gained the upper hand, and the subjugation of cognitive labor has become a main factor of capital valorization. Collaboration has been turned into competition, and social aggressiveness has prevailed over solidarity.

The second point of interest in this speech is the heart sickness that Savio is talking about. Knowledge, creativity, and language have become labor. The brain is the work force, and the concept of general intellect noted by Marx, *Grundrisse*, comes to life in the global network of the digital flow of signs.[2] Simultaneously, the activity of the brain is disconnected from the social existence of the body. The work of the brain is subjected to the heartless rule of finance, and this subjection makes people sick at heart in many ways.

Mario Savio and his colleagues were protesting against the submission of research to the demands of the Vietnam War. Today, war is proliferating at the margins of the cognitive sphere of production, and competition is fueling war in every niche of daily life.

The third point that impresses me in Savio's speech is the gesture he suggests: "you've got to put your bodies upon the gears and upon the wheels … upon the levers, upon all the apparatus, and you've got to make it stop."[3] Gears, wheels, levers. This is the metaphor that the Free Speech Movement of 1968 had for the machinery of power. The factory and the working class kindled our imagination of social conflict. But the Free Speech Movement did not understand that the most important thing to do was to take hold of the cognitive machine. This is why we missed the point.

In that crowd, five thousand young people were listening to Mario Savio speak in the main square of the premiere university in California; five thousand young people were participating, were breathing together. Many of them have become animators of the processes that led to the creation of today's global network. Steve Jobs and Steve Wozniak were possibly there.

Because of the industrialist imagination that prevailed in the political culture of the Movement, we missed the opportunity to start a long lasting process of the self-organization of the general intellect. As professionals, we built the high-technology network, but as activists, we were trapped in a nineteenth-century industrialist imagination.

The only possibility of avoiding the subjection of knowledge to profit, which equals the subjection of knowledge to war, was the conjunction of the general intellect with the needs of society. But we were trapped by the old Leninist concept of political revolution.

Knowledge and the automation of work

Since 1968, the relationship between cognition and automation has framed the crucial issue of social transformation involving knowledge and the economy, technology and war.

Haunting the culture of modern times, automation is sometimes viewed as an empowerment of human enterprise, but at other times it is viewed as its enslavement, sacrificing the human soul, personal freedom, and social autonomy.

In the 1960s, critical thought focused on the issue of the automation of work as a dilemma open to two different possibilities: liberation and control.

Herbert Marcuse, who embodies the intersection of European philosophy and American technology, published two books that approach the prospect of automation from two opposing although complementary points of view: *Eros and Civilization* and *One Dimensional Man*.[4] In *Eros and Civilization*, Marcuse expressed the idea that the technical automation of work may be the condition required for the process of emancipation of social life from its own alienation to take place.

> A progressive reduction of labor seems to be inevitable, and for this eventuality, the system has to provide for occupation without work; it has to develop needs which transcend the market economy and may even be incompatible with it.[5]

In the same book, the philosopher emphasizes the prominent role that cognitive work will have not only in the future of production, but also in the social movement against exploitation.

> To the degree to which organized labor operates in defense of the status quo, and to the degree to which the share of labor in the material process of production declines, intellectual skills and capabilities become social and political factors. Today, the organized refusal to cooperate of the scientists, mathematicians, technicians, industrial psychologists and public opinion pollsters may well

> accomplish what a strike, even a large-scale strike, can no longer accomplish but once accomplished, namely, the beginning of the reversal, the preparation of the ground for political action.[6]

Linking the emancipatory force of technology to the organized refusal of scientists and technicians to cooperate with the status quo, Marcuse outlines the possibility of overcoming the alienation or discontentment that Freud saw as a defining feature of civilization.

In *One Dimensional Man*, the book that canonized Marcuse's work as an expression of the anti-authoritarian movement, the prospect seems different. The focus is still on the crucial function of intellectual labor, but here such labor is not seen as an emancipatory force, rather as a tool for domination and control.

> The capabilities (intellectual and material) of contemporary society are immeasurably greater than ever before—which means that the scope of society's domination over the individual is immeasurably greater than ever before. Our society distinguishes itself by conquering the centrifugal social forces with Technology rather than Terror, on the dual basis of an overwhelming efficiency and an increasing standard of living.[7]

Technology is taking the place of terror in the organization of social control: this is why Marcuse's man is becoming one-dimensional.

> For "totalitarian" is not only a terroristic political coordination of society, but also a non-terroristic economic-technical coordination which operates through the manipulation of needs by vested interests. It thus precludes the emergence of an effective opposition against the whole. Not only a specific form of government or party rule makes for totalitarianism, but also a specific system of production and distribution which may well be compatible with a "pluralism" of parties, newspapers, countervailing powers.[8]

The mobilization, organization, and exploitation of the technical, scientific, and intellectual productivity are the conditions of the new high-tech totalitarianism.

In these two books, Marcuse signals the dilemma of automation in the architecture of knowledge and technology. The neoliberal triumph, the annihilation of the Workers' Movement (*movimento operaio*), the catastrophic turn that we have been living during the last thirty years led to the submission of the general intellect to the economy and its war machine.

Meritocracy versus solidarity in the age of cognitive labor

In the second part of the twentieth century, mass education opened the way to the emancipation of the working class: the worker's "refusal of work" joined the "general intellect," and the result was a dilemmatic situation whose outcome was not predictable. The student-led Free Speech Movement of 1968 can be seen as the first insurrection of the general intellect: the solidarity between students and workers was not only an ideological effect, but also the alliance of two social subjects sharing a common possibility. Industrial workers pushed toward the reduction of work time, and students acted as harbingers of the intellectual potency of cognitive work, announcing the technological possibility of emancipation from the slavery of physical labor. This alliance between refusal of work and technological innovation paved the way for the digital revolution and the replacement of industrial labor with the info-machine. However, this process of emancipation was disrupted in the last decades of the twentieth century, diverted toward the financial form of semio-capitalism as the neoliberal counter-revolution twisted the force of the general intellect against workers' autonomy.

The increase in productivity that could have potentially opened the way to a general reduction of work time was turned into a tool for increased exploitation. Limitations to work time were removed, and unemployment rose as a side effect of increased individual work time. The potential of the general intellect has thereby been turned against the wellbeing of the working population.

As cognitive labor became the main force of valorization, economic power tried to submit cognitarians to the ideology of merit—meritocracy—in order to destroy the social solidarity of the intellectual force. Reducing intellectual ability through economic reward, meritocracy acts as the Trojan Horse of neoliberal ideology. Meritocracy, the hotbed of precariousness, is fostering competition: when individuals are obliged to fight for survival, intellectual and technical ability are reduced to tools for economic confrontation. When solidarity is broken and competition rules, research and discovery are disassociated from pleasure and solidarity.

Submission of knowledge to the rule of economy

A crucial passage in the process of the submission of knowledge to economics is the current dismantlement of the public education system, the privatization of the university and the operational submission of research to the rule of finance. This implies the epistemic primacy of the economy. The defining feature of the modern university was knowledge autonomy, namely autonomy from theology. Today, the asserted primacy of the economy implies the cancellation of knowledge autonomy, and the establishment of a new sort of theology.

Since the end of the twentieth century, the university crisis has been embedded in the inability of modern humanism to cope with the networked infosphere. The institution of the university in the age of modernity was unfit to deal with networked intelligence. The humanist legacy was in need of a reformation. Yet what is happening is different from a reformation; public education has been simply emptied, dismantled, and replaced with a system of market-driven evaluation that kills autonomous research. Innovation is celebrated, but only through the framework of profit and growth, amounting to a new theological dogma.

The old industrial bourgeoisie was a strongly territorialized class; it was the class of the *bourg*, of the city, and in the age of bourgeois civilization the welfare of the community was essential to the process of industrial growth. Present financial accumulation, on the contrary, is based on a game of buying and selling financial products whose usefulness is nil. The architecture of financial knowledge is therefore intended to produce nothing.

In the industrial age, money was a tool for the production of goods, as the production of goods was a necessary step in the increase of exchange value and the accumulation of money (money, goods, money). Financialization has transformed this process: money accumulates without the production of useful things. Financial products are just simulations, triggering the accumulation of more simulation. The effect of this process of valorization through simulation is a sort of minus-value realized through the concrete annihilation of the product of social knowledge and activity. The dismantlement of the educational system and the current destruction of European social civilization are dramatic demonstrations of the financial architecture of annihilation.

Artist, engineer, economist

The Intellectual, the Merchant, and the Warrior have been the dominant characters of the fable we call Modernity. The Warrior and the Merchant have managed to subjugate the knowledge and skills of the Intellectual to the demands of war and accumulation. In order to do this, not only has knowledge been fragmented, but the social bearers to the access of knowledge have been fragmented as well. Intellectual cooperation is technically mediated, and the general intellect is functionally recombined by the networked information-machine.

During the twentieth century, intellectual life was a space of exchange between the so-called "two cultures," techno-scientific and historico-political, but the anti-capitalist movement did not invest enough energy in its own interdisciplinarity. The process of specialization was pushed to the extremes, and the common ground of intellectual exchange—which was the public sphere of the social movements—was erased. Everybody is busy working in conditions of isolation and competition; engineers and poets belong to two distant dimensions that today never meet.

Nevertheless the intellectual function is traversed by an internal conflict, whose dynamics I'll try to sketch. I'll call the Artist, the Engineer, and the Economist the main characters of the fable of the General Intellect. Their interaction forms the core of the social dynamics of intellectual life. The Artist (by this word I mean both the poet and the scientist who is not involved in functional technology but rather in conceptual research) creates an excess of knowledge and language, an excess that produces a breach in the established framework of language and knowledge. The Artist is the creator of new concepts and new percepts, disclosing new possible horizons of social experience. The Artist speaks the language of conjunction: in artistic creation the relationship between sign and meaning is not conventionally fixed, but pragmatically displaced and constantly renegotiated.

The Engineer is the master of technology, the Intellectual who transforms concepts into projects, and projects into algorithms. The Engineer speaks the language of connection. The relationship between sign and meaning is conventionally inscribed in engineering. The Engineer is a producer of machines, of technical combinations of algorithms, and of physical matter which performs in accordance with accepted concepts.

The third figure of the contemporary General Intellect is the Economist, a fake scientist and real technologist who is charged with the task of separating the Artist and the Engineer, keeping them isolated within their specialized tasks.

Economists are more priests than scientists. Their discourse aims to subjugate the activity of other Intellectuals to the rule of economic expansion. They denounce the bad behavior of society, urging people to repent for their debts, threatening inflation and misery for people's sins, worshipping the dogmas of growth and competition. Their scientific conventions are not based on experience, nor in purely conceptual abstractions, but on the particular interest of the social class at the top of the conventional economic construction. The methodology of the economist has little to do with scientific methodology. What is science after all? I would simply say that science is a form of knowledge free from dogma, aiming to extrapolate general laws from the observation of empirical phenomena, drawing from this extrapolation the ability to predict what will happen next. Science is also able to transcend causal determinism, and to understand the types of changes that Thomas Kuhn labeled "paradigm shifts."[9] That means scientific innovation is essentially a transgression of the established limits of knowledge.

As far as I know, economics does not correspond to this description. Economists are obsessed with dogmatic notions such as growth, competition, and gross national product. They profess social reality to be in crisis only if it does not conform to the dictates of these notions. Secondly, Economists are incapable of inferring laws from the observation of reality, as they prefer instead a reality that harmonizes with their own presuppositions. As a consequence, they cannot predict anything; experience has often shown Economists' inability to predict change or its contingencies. Finally, Economists cannot recognize changes in the social paradigm, and they refuse to adjust their conceptual framework accordingly. They insist instead that reality must be changed to correspond to their outdated criteria. Physics, chemistry, biology, astronomy, and so on conceptualize a specific field of reality, while in schools of economics and business, the subject of teaching and learning is itself a technology, a set of tools, procedures, and pragmatic protocols intended to twist social reality to serve practical purposes. Economic reality does not exist. It is the result of a process of technical modeling, of submission, and of exploitation.

The theoretical discourse that supports this economic technology can be defined as ideology in the sense proposed by Marx (who was not an economist, but a critic of political economy). Ideology is in fact a theoretical technology aimed at advancing special political and social goals. Economic ideology, like all technologies, lacks self-reflection and therefore cannot develop theoretical self-understanding. It cannot reframe itself in relation to any paradigm shift.

The Economist is the entangler of the Engineer. Engineering as a technology can be linked to Art and Science, can transform conceptual creation into technical *dispositives* for the organization of social life. But over the last century, engineering has been subjected to the dictates of economics, and the technical potencies of machines have been single-mindedly reduced to those of economic determination.

When the Engineer is linked to the Artist, he is producing machines that might emancipate time from work for maximum social usefulness. When the Engineer is controlled by the Economist, he is producing machines for the entanglement of human time and intelligence in the iteration of profit maximization, capital accumulation, and war.

When the Engineer is linked to the Artist, his horizon is the infinity of nature and language. When he is controlled by the Economist, his horizon is economic growth, and for the sake of this dogma he destroys nature while reducing language in order to be compatible with the Economist's code.

Capitalism is no longer able to semiotize and organize the social potency of cognitive productivity, as its economic conceptualization is too narrow for the intellectual potency of society, and intellectual potency demands a trans-economic dimension.

The shift from an industrial to a semiotic form of production has propelled capitalism out of itself, out of its ideological self-conception. Economic semiotization has become a tangled trap for the potencies of the General Intellect.

The problem is: Can knowledge be disentangled from the semiotic grip of the economic paradigm? Has the Economist totally subjugated the Engineer, who previously captured the Artist, or can the Engineer get free from economic limitations and reframe technology according to the intuitions of science and sensibility?

Architecture of disentangled knowledge

We may define architecture as the intentional conjunction of building elements into a system. From this point of view the Economist can be seen as the Architect of the capitalist system: he inter-links social elements according to rules of profit, growth, and competition. As long as political action could govern the complexities of social elements, politics could be the intellectual activity utilized to govern social dynamics. But political reason was based on the possibility of deciding among possibilities, and the acceleration of the infosphere and the complexification of the space of possibilities have made political government an impossible task.

Unable to process the complexity of networked society, politics—the art of conscious and voluntary government—has been replaced by governance, which is the architecture of the techno-linguistic automatisms that result in the financial exploitation of cognitive labor.

As the complexity of knowledge escapes into the sphere of political action, what is necessary now is the disentanglement of knowledge from the entangling architecture of power. This is a challenge for a post-political actor, specific to the dynamics of networked knowledge, able to disentangle this dynamic from the rule of the Economy. What is needed is essentially an Architect of disentangled knowledge.

July 2014

Notes

1. Mario Savio, quoted in Frederick Turner, *From Counterculture to Cyberculture* (Chicago: University of Chicago Press, 2006), 11.
2. See: "Fragment on Machines," in Karl Marx, *Grundrisse: Foundations of the Critique of Political Economy*, trans. Martin Nicolaus (Harmondsworth: Penguin, 1973 [1858]), 690–712.
3. Savio, quoted in Turner, 11.
4. Herbert Marcuse, *Eros and Civilization* (Boston: Beacon Press, 1955); *One Dimensional Man* (Boston: Beacon Press, 1964).
5. Marcuse, preface to *Eros and Civilization*, xxiii.
6. Ibid., xxv.
7. Marcuse, *One Dimensional Man*, 7.
8. Ibid., 14.
9. See: Thomas Kuhn, *The Structure of Scientific Revolutions* (Chicago: University of Chicago Press, 1962).

Chapter 2

White night before a manifesto
Metahaven

White night

Surface
0:00 A.M.

We are designing surface. Surface multiplies, beyond any measure of necessity, beyond the laws of demand and supply, beyond reason. The multiplication of surface, formerly called information overload, is the new reality of design. Its unit of measurement is virtual.

Surface is not territory. Territory, which is actual and geographical (for that reason limited in supply), can be contested and may become the site of an actual conflict, a physical confrontation. This cannot happen on, or to, a surface. Surface is to territory what speculative capital is to gold. Surface may be multiplied without encountering the physical limitations imposed by someone else's terrain, opinion, presence or personality. If surface is a kind of place, or site, the designer is its geographer.

Surface is folded out in order to produce value, while it is folded in to secure it. The production of surface is design's equivalent to the production of space; surface in the generic sense means flat space to display. Surface is anorexic, hyper-thin architecture.

Surface, representing no particular meaning or message, is the precondition for virtual capital, projected revenue and speculative value. Advertising surface in public space initially is merely an add-on to the already existing historical structure of a city. Gradually, surface replaces the primacy of historical structure and its territoriality. The city becomes the profit base of a virtual spin: the multiplication of surface accounts for the exponential growth of value extracted from its public space. By our being in public, by simple existence, we already automatically affirm the exposure which grants the surface infrastructure its right to the city. The inhabitants of cities are, through this mechanism, directly inscribed into the means of value production.

Mute (passive) surface is classified by the informational properties of the materials it is composed of. Titanium informs differently from plastic, while seamless, uninterrupted black marble informs differently from fractured and broken pieces of stained cardboard. A plastic credit card which says "Gold" or "Platinum" has understood correctly that the informational properties of surface do not need to correspond to its material worth. Surface is a transformation of the valueless into the valuable by means of psychological deception.

The image of a stock market crash is a bursting bubble, the moment when the virtual character of the capital base of virtual counterparts and derivative value is exposed.

The surface equivalent to the stock market crash is the Hollows. The Hollows is surface without surface, the exposure of the naked infrastructure or root level system language which precedes surface itself, surface without its effects.

The American Express "black card" is a piece of surface only available to the ultra privileged. Beyond the symbolism of precious metals, it takes the concept of value to its decisive, post-material (virtual) stage. The black card is made of titanium so it is durable rather than valuable. A world of virtual class distinction inhabits the card with its optional concierge and butler services.

As a masthead for surface, "black is the new gold" declares the structural redefinition of the symbols of elite and luxury (and its opposite: poverty). Black surfaces form a continuum. The black in different kinds of objects for all kinds of different functions is the continuum of the single sign value of "luxury." It disjoints the color black from its material properties in each separate object, transforming surface into information.

Black surface belongs to the city's cultural and financial core, the urban tissue which concentrates decision making and spending capacity and connects to other such cores. The victim of surface is the periphery (in virtual terms: off surface) which is declared nonexistent. Peripheries start where the surfaces begin to crack. The resulting logic is that a periphery, which is thus deprived of virtual assets, is gradually also denied of its infrastructural facilities. This process runs exactly parallel to the ranking systems which favor the well-connected virtual spheres on the internet over the detached twins at the outer limits.

The immaterial workers were positioned around an open-air swimming pool on the top floor of a multi-story private members club in the most trendy area of a global capital of finance and creative services. The laborers were sipping cocktails (Flirtinis) to the electronic heartbeat of anonymous synthi-house of unending duration. The workers, "dressed to kill" in black Comme des Garçons, black Prada, black Jilsander, black Burberry, black Balenciaga and black Dior, had bought themselves into their belief. That belief was that they were the elite. Nowhere else had a city been so profoundly transformed by the intricate workings of capital. Skyrocketing real estate prices had made mere living here an impossibility. The creative class of immaterial laborers had responded to this by a great leap forward; they had financialized their own appearance, virtually bridging their class gap. The immaterial workers were designers. They made surfaces. They consumed and produced on the same plane, which was the surface. The motionless water surface of the rooftop pool. The bare, concrete, Miesian surface of the walls.

The black bags. The shiny black leather of clothes and shoes. The Blackberry phones (black, of course). The screensavers and desktops on the screens of the Blackberries.

The new elite was founded on debt, was into black, and lived in the former social housing estates. The old elite (now stuffed) was founded on gold, diamonds, noble titles and fox hunting, and used words like "preposterous." It inhabited monuments.

Communicative (active) surface, or screen, is classified by its capacity to reveal and open up doorways to virtual worlds. In the absence of message, it maintains a system of placeholders and default images. Mobile phones—which physically resemble minimalist jewelry—are inhabited by complex worlds appearing on the surface of their screens. In fact a phone is no longer a phone, as it performs the functions of an email tool, a web browser, an agenda, a calculator, an alarm clock, a video player, a camera and a game console. There is no principal difference between the "phone-as-surface" with its inherent capacities to organize information and social relations, and the "credit card-as-surface" with its capacity to order concierges and butlers.

Active surfaces are inhabited by worlds in worlds. This is a matter of calculus and inner complexity; mobile phones have surpassed the threshold between a dedicated machine (designed to perform a single task or series of tasks) and a machine which appropriates the functions and tasks previously assigned to other machines, resulting in the emptying out of the objects that were formerly machines (like the wristwatch). The system which inhabits the object with the most active surface—the more informational, complex, all-inclusive one—has surpassed a degree of complexity, so that the tasks it performs can no longer be related to its size, its form or its weight.

Design has become the creation and management of virtual assets attached to objects (like tags, or services) or existing within objects (like worlds, or doorways).

"User-generated content" is a common internet term referring to what began as the add-on to a given piece of content that is rooted in the old-fashioned producer-consumer dichotomy. After the early internet, which had "home pages" to "surf to"—distinct locations within a geography—the social networking site and its user-generated content transforms and includes the formerly dispersed home pages into a single surface. Inside this surface, worlds exist in worlds, scenes in scenes, friends in friends, based on the reciprocal addition of more surface and more doorways to your friends and your friends' friends surface as a mutually empowering social act. On this form of organized activity rests the macro-scale corporate appropriation of its projected revenues.

Surfaces extend everywhere, recuperating the potentiality for conflicts by offering more space for the uncontested expansion of self-referential opinion. The actual confrontation between adversaries is prevented from taking place, thus suspending the political. The potentiality for a conflict to occur directly produces production—that is, it perpetuates the immanent breeding ground for new spheres and strata, new identities, new aesthetic needs and thus new spaces for production, combined with a permanent process of tagging. Precisely the tags, or names (which have passed through preceding stages of evaluation) enable the transformation of cultural clashes into capital accumulation. This is the true power of surface, as the multiplication of virtual surfaces is a frictionless event. This mechanism maintains itself only because endless coexistence equals the permanent potential for conflicts. This is the opposite model to the real and the physical, where the natural rule perpetually refuses the territorial coexistence of incompatible alternatives.

Surface is the reincarnation of neutrality. Default friends, default faces, default desktops, default writing. In the world of surface, the confrontation with harsh realities, such as having no face, or no friends, becomes mediated and softened by the presence of placeholders, which become the new symbols for absence. Placeholders also possess the surface capability of gradually overwriting original structures and original texts.

> Lorem ipsum dolor sit amet, consectetur adipisicing elit, sed do ut labore et dolore magna aliqua. Ut enim ad minim veniam, quis nostrud exercitation ullamco laboris nisi ut aliquip ex ea commodo consequat. Duis aute irure dolor in reprehenderit in voluptate velit esse cillum dolore eu fugiat nulla pariatur. Excepteur sint occaecat cupidatat non proident, sunt in culpa qui officia deserunt mollit anim id est laborum.
>
> (Text in placeholder Latin, 2008)

Software does precisely what its name spells out: it softens the relationship between man and manufacture. Writing, visiting friends, searching, finding, saving: what once required at least some physical activity becomes extremely light, pleasant and effortless.

Such a soft regime presents itself as unconstrained and plural. While it seems to cross all territorial boundaries, software rather functions as escapism and synchronizes employment and pleasure over, and against, labor and life. It is because software presents itself as a neutral matter, as a non-directed and infinite open space, that the question of access and circulation in such an infinite void of potentiality arises. The spectacle of participation calls upon an undifferentiated behavior where egalitarian enactments often smell like indifference and tend to obey rules of engagement that explicitly remain unwritten. Far from a no man's land, the matrix of virtual tools, it independently establishes new relations and hierarchies among people, which are inevitably paired with impossibilities and hegemonies.

In the continuum of surfaces, the mechanisms that define the relations between products, needs and values are transformed. The point of no return is the vanishing of those categories as separate entities and the construction of a continuum where any object (material or immaterial) may have a threefold incarnation as product, need and value. The result is the simultaneous abolition of distinctions between production and consumption: when products generate needs, when needs trigger speculative value and when values are embodied by products, we can no longer speak of pure consumption, as consumption itself becomes a productive force, as was already the case for Marx. Consumption directly creates new needs, calls for continuous re-evaluation (financial or symbolic), and motorizes production.

Whether recognized as labor, as entertainment, or as social interaction, the activities of consumers, end-users, designers and managers all are non-dissociable from their corresponding value as producers. The invention and subsequent emergence of a "creative class" marks the transition to a genuinely "post-work" understanding of labor, where laborers and consumers are invited to double their potential in value accumulation. The speculative value of this incentive equalizing production and consumption is used in various ways: to create and sustain new systems of management, to revamp derelict city quarters, or to justify operations evacuated from political choice. What becomes key is the designer's most imaginary reach; to exceed any material limitation, which enables him or her to dismiss function and to redirect the evaluation procedure to a new domain. "Added value," after function, becomes the battle zone of a new regime that capitalizes on speculation. The flight toward the "new" is paralleled with an ever-growing distance to the immediate needs of the designer's direct environment.

We have moved from mediation—operating between products and consumers—to a much wider suppression of the legitimacy of direct relations to the point at which it seems that designers would rather gain credibility through their disconnection and distance from the physical. Relationships reach the designer as images; just as a brand manages the relationships that we have with objects through their image. Nevertheless we see this distance not as a burden, but rather as privileged ground where ideas may come to life, and so forth. This imaginary take on reality immediately produces new phantasms that can be interpreted as valid needs and beginnings for the production of surface. Designers—either by marketing or by fiction—perpetually innovate the seductive regime of surface, which stimulates other designers to do the same thing, disconnected from the non-negotiability of the brutal material ground, historical structure and political struggles on which, originally, surface itself was premised.

White night

Value
0:00 A.M.

We are not useful.

Some examples: at the 2007 Millionaire Fair in Moscow a diamond-plated Swarovski Mercedes Benz was unveiled. It looked monstrous.

The Wenger Swiss Army Knife—a symbol of functionality and minimalism—now comes in a new and expanded version. The Wenger Ultimate Swiss Army Knife has no less than eighty-five tools. It looks bizarre.

Use value and exchange value are not absolute, but eventually relative phenomena. An absolute exchange value, actualized through the excess of material worth in a design object, is so ostensibly valuable that it is cheap. An absolute use value, achieved by cramming every imaginable functionality into a tool, is so obviously useful that it is useless.

Rob Walker wrote in the *New York Times Magazine* on the diverging paths of function and value, using "nonfunctional watches" as an example. Here function and value separate as there are now such a wide variety of devices with which we can read the time, such as the mobile telephone. This condition does not lead to the disappearance of the watch, but to a redefinition of its value. The watch, or its remainder, becomes a piece of jewelry dedicated to a phantom function. Now that we already know what time it is, the watch can dedicate itself completely to aesthetics, celebrity, poetry and water resistance. The Timeless

Bracelet, designed by Ina Seifart in 2006, is a watch without a watch, a metal bracelet that consists of an empty, watch-shaped metal frame. This "timepiece" captures how design may reflect upon large-scale changes (and incoherencies) in its function and its value. Its designer, who worked at Louis Vuitton before starting her own studio, uses the disappearance of use value to anticipate a new need for another level of added value.

We embrace the realm of added or speculative value that is attached to objects. It is not the objects themselves, but the values inhabiting them that are fundamentally reshaped or reinvented. Objects are inhabited by values, and are at the same time, plastered or covered by them. While a laptop or a mobile phone may be "inhabited" by new values through the actions that are performed with them, those values are not registered in the objects' titanium shells, which curiously mimic a Dieter Rams-style simplicity from the era in which an apparatus was a dedicated machine. Compare a laptop or mobile phone that is made in China, which is inhabited with transgression and plastered with an impeccable surface, to the outer shell of the Guggenheim Bilbao—a surface inscribed with all kinds of values but inhabited by a conventional museum program. The categories of inside and outside have become completely disconnected; like the arrival and departure gates of an airport, they register the global flows that design is now part of. The difference between outside and inside, and between form and content, administers these flows. There is little coherence in the insides and outsides of design objects and the ways in which they are programmed. As with the templates and placeholders for web 2.0-style internet pages, they may be inhabited by all kinds of values that account for the endless transformation of surface.

Design philosophies that treat form and content as a coherent set have trouble in explaining what is going on today. We tend to design so that form and content may obey different regimes. Every part of "surface architecture"—with its structurally identical insides that cater to the desires of the real estate market—is bargained over with different contractors in order to achieve the cheapest possible deal on materials and construction. These buildings contain kilometers of fiberglass cables in order to secure a vital lifeline to the information highway. Finally, the surface, which poses as the building's sign value, is intended to obscure the standardized template. These processes that are vital to the physical and virtual creation of design, register forces which go beyond factors specific to local situation and context. Every designed artifact bears witness to the large scale incoherence of its productive conditions.

It is clear that design is not just political, but primarily geopolitical; the new shapes and forms may arise haphazardly and by chance, but they register (in a quite formidable way) the geopolitical forces of the globalizing world.

Categories like "good design" have become less valid as a way of speaking about objects which all have a hardware and a software aspect to them, an inside and an outside, a modality of inhabitation and a modality of surface, which each obey different rules. Addressing these categories as the incoherent parts of a coherent whole means overcoming the contradistinction between form and content. Coherence in design today exists primarily in the recognition of large-scale incoherence.

An exhibition in a design hotel.

At first the hotel was completely designed (by designers).

Now the exhibition consists of changes to the hotel's design. The changes are made by artists.

A given situation, once it has been designed, turns out to be unsatisfactory simply because it is there; it is, among other things, no longer "new." Then a change has to be incorporated into that situation without rejecting it completely. It must be "altered"—customized—not destroyed, by which our desire to reject the situation is "bent" into implementing a "satisfactory" change into the material reality. So design becomes the apparatus that informs value with the energy of its opposite. "Value" can still be recognized, but there is also value accumulated in the apparent rejection of it.

Think of the Louis Vuitton bag in both its authentic and fake versions. Even though on a physical level they are yet to be differentiated, what matters is that the bare existence of the fake points to the actual reason for the outrageously high exchange value of the authentic. If it were purely a matter of logic evaluation, the gap between the respective exchange values of the authentic and the fake could never peak so high. Without the fake we cannot detect any reason for the price being substantially higher than the sum of all the (material and immaterial) labor that it relies upon. To take the fake seriously literally means to denounce the fakeness of the market value of the authentic model. The mold of the fake bag is virtual. Sealed off from any recognized realm of production, fabricated under the radar of the white market hierarchy, the copy of the authentic only needs to operate as an image, as a container of virtual attributes that are literally a bag of tags. The value of the copy is the virtual value of the original.

In the documentary *Carla's List*, prosecutor Carla del Ponte of the UN International Criminal Tribunal for the former Yugoslavia travels to Belgrade and Montenegro to put pressure on local authorities to hand over war criminals. The camera accompanies Del Ponte and her colleagues on the airplane. It's a tiny business jet and the view is blocked by two huge bags. One is the Coco Chanel bag of the Tribunal's spokesperson, Florence Hartmann, the other is Del Ponte's Louis Vuitton bag. In this brief fragment of video the ostentatious display of French fashion brands interrupts the carefully constructed image of international justice hunting down Ratko Mladic and Radovan Karadzic. The bags are not just expensive, their brand value (which is imaginary and speculative) is written all over them. Thus as a view one may become suspicious of the nature of an alliance between values and values.

The infrastructural channels that connect cities play a major role in the construction of identities in the upgrading of certain areas and in the marginalization of others. A myriad of brands, brand remakes, unethically cheap city trips, massive torrents of entertainment file downloads, and a multiplicity of clothing and food brands, first function supplementary to, but then gradually wipe out, historical structure. The visualized utopias designed for and within real estate advertisements—the powers that turn cultures into markets—create corridors between city centers that outgrow their territorial relationship with peripheral countryside and villages, as if they were part of another realm, which, from a virtual point of view, they really are. The installation of an infrastructure of long-range connectivity, and the simultaneous degradation of short-range (intra-national) transportation and communication networks, can have disastrous consequences. While globalization lands differently in each "destination," the reconfiguration of urbanism into center-to-center channels only sharpens the rupture between center and periphery, creating new walls that can be seen as constituting inner borders.

As cities apply surface branding methods to build ever more channels in the name of cultural diversity, only the so-called cultural cores of cities get to enjoy the privileges of a cross-cultural exchange. These will remain trapped in their own self-valorizing spheres. The onslaught of city branding tags the wealthy inner cores with the seductive labels of the virtual in service of global competitiveness. This regime is carried out using names borrowed from emancipatory politics, which are used to the opposite end: what it directly services is the annihilation of pre-existing social bonds. New class divisions appear whose buying power is mobilized by and transformed into the production of surface.

"Third Way" (post-Left and Right) politics have replaced the social body by an endless spectrum of individual identities that no longer present themselves as "we," and can no longer be represented by the state or addressed by politics (which progresses toward management and benchmarking). As active consumers, individuals can account for their existence and the relevance of the state purely through their economical and virtual transactions. Sociologists in previous years had already drawn the shapes of a post-Fordist political economy based on added value. Ulrich Beck and Anthony Giddens—inventors of the Third Way—have done so with a focus on the changing role of the individual and the self. Scott Lash and John Urry summarize:

> The thesis of the postmodern political economy is one of the ever more rapid circulation of subjects and objects. But it is also one of the "emptying out" of objects. For Giddens modernization is a process of "time-space distanciation" in which time and space "empty out," become more abstract; things and people become "disembedded" from space and time.

For Beck, contemporary society is a risk society which has shifted from the distribution of "goods" to the distribution of "bads." These bads—risks and threats—do not respect the old borders and divisions of race, nation and class. Beck regards those globally distributed risks as unpredictable events which equally affect rich and poor. For him the continuation of modernity is the attempt to deal with these risks rationally now that much of the former core structures of society have disappeared. Giddens sees the project of individual identity as reflexive and in motion, continuously integrating emerging information into the individual's self-conception. His nation state is one of "reflexively monitored systems."

In all these transformations, an economy of design objects is implied; objects are simultaneously lifted from their origin, tradition, space, time, use-value, and exchange-value, in order to assume maximum agility in the aggregation of new needs.

Design must be invested with the potential, the intelligence and the tools to break down the new borders it has created by being borderless. It must be invested with the energy to break through the seamless surfaces of fictitious virtue which have become the new walls of the free world.

Before a manifesto

We, the undersigned.
    This sounds like a manifesto.
    We take the manifesto to be a Utopian form.
    Fredric Jameson distinguishes between Utopia as a genre (as, for example, a written text, or a building, or a Utopian program of revolutionary change) and a Utopian impulse in daily life.
    The "Online Etymology Dictionary" traces the word "manifest" back to 1374, as "clearly revealed," coming from *manifestus*—"caught in the act, plainly apprehensible, clear, evident"—and *manifestare*—"to show plainly." It refers

to *manifesto,* 1644 Italian, as a "public declaration explaining past actions and announcing the motive for forthcoming ones"—"originally 'proof,' from the Latin *manifestus*."

Manifestos are publicly stated decisions. They are written by those who have made up their minds and shall now do as they have openly declared. To write a manifesto is to put all of one's cards on the table. To write a manifesto is to draw up and sign a covenant with a self-declared truth.

This is easier said than done. If a manifesto is a decisive political act, its writers are out for some kind of power, even if such power is quite minimal and temporary. As a manifesto is a statement of principle, it demands a complete loyalty on the part of the undersigned. If the writers diverge from the manifesto's proposed path to the future, they are either disloyal to their own text or they reveal that pragmatic action has simply prevailed over principled decision. This weakens the impact and credibility of a manifesto. If a manifesto is an attempt to gain power by means of writing and publishing, it risks failing because of its potential conflictuality with the *hidden agenda* which comes naturally to the successful exercise of power.

Niccolò Machiavelli stated that "everyone realizes how praiseworthy it is for a prince to honor his word and to be straightforward rather than crafty in his dealings; nonetheless, contemporary experience shows that princes who have achieved great things have been those who have given their word lightly, who have known how to trick men with their cunning, and who, in the end, have overcome those abiding by honest principles."

A printed object may carry the manifesto's text in an efficient way, so that people can either read it or hear about it, or both. Manifestos are bound to the technology that provides their most effective mode of dissemination. Régis Debray calls the historical period when socialism, printed matter and the manifesto prevailed the "graphosphere." For all of its hubris and ambition, a manifesto is a shared text which exists in the public domain as a printed original. In hopes of achieving action, a manifesto usually relies on the frequent usage of commanding phrases like "we must," "we shall" and "we will."

But what happens to the manifesto in the age of television and the internet, the "videosphere," in Debray's words? Does the manifesto have any future when the paradigm of print has come to a close, which does not mean the end of print but the end of the *primacy* of print? As Marshall McLuhan says with regard to the passage from manuscript to print culture: "print multiplied scholars, but it also diminished their social and political importance." In the same way, the internet multiplies publishing, resulting in the diminishing of the status of what is published.

A manifesto is a text with political consequences; it seizes power, but cannot be about power alone. One reason is that a manifesto's writers have usually not yet acquired much power; another reason is that as a carrier of peaceful political violence, a manifesto depends as much on poetry and song as it depends on argument. Formal issues are integral to the aesthetic event that is a manifesto. Because the manifesto's aim is to interrupt, not to affirm, its mode of speech must differ from common speech, to the extent that it allows for new words, new terms and analogies, to render the established ones obsolete.

There are two principal typologies for manifestos.

The fortified structure of arguments, and the assembly of poetic decoys.

In 2000, the Canadian designer Bruce Mau wrote a manifesto about design, printed it in a book, and published it on the internet. It is called *An Incomplete Manifesto for Growth*. It is a numbered list of sentences and process wisdom, not unlike the well-known type of statement which says that "the first rule is that there are no rules."

The *Incomplete Manifesto for Growth*'s forty-three points include:

> (1) Allow events to change you. (2) Forget about good. (5) Go deep. (9) Begin anywhere. (10) Everyone is a leader. (12) Keep moving. (13) Slow down. (14) Don't be cool. (15) Ask stupid questions. (19) Work the metaphor. (18) Stay up too late. (25) Don't clean your desk. (27) Read only left-hand pages. (28) Make new words. Expand the lexicon. (35) Imitate. (40) Avoid fields. Jump fences. (41) Laugh. And (43) Power to the people.

This is a manifesto of the poetic type, allowing for internal contradictions and ironic deception. It places no emphasis on design as a professional activity but instead pursues mistakes, nights without sleep, uncool work, messy desktops, and laughter. (The dictum about the left-hand pages comes from Marshall McLuhan). In doing so, it simultaneously taps into Utopian form and Utopian impulse; Mau's manifesto becomes a program centered on the transgression of program.

The political consequence is that the commonly accepted separations between professional and personal engagement are overruled. Design is taken out of its limited mandate of professional operations, and is brought into the realm of imagination, possibility and contradiction. The manifesto promises that the most interesting ideas will arise out of the lunatic reserve of the white night. This is the signal feature of artistic manifestos; a most famous example, the *Futurist Manifesto* written in 1909 by Filippo Marinetti, mentions it right away:

> We have been up all night, my friends and I, beneath mosque lamps whose brass cupolas are bright as our souls, because like them we were illuminated by

the internal glow of electric hearts. And trampling underfoot our native sloth on opulent Persian carpets, we have been discussing right up to the limits of logic and scrawling the paper with demented writing. Our hearts were filled with an immense pride at feeling ourselves standing quite alone, like lighthouses or like the sentinels in an outpost, facing the army of enemy stars encamped in their celestial bivouacs. Alone with the engineers in the infernal stokeholes of great ships, alone with the black spirits which rage in the belly of rogue locomotives, alone with the drunkards beating their wings against the walls.

The *Incomplete Manifesto*'s hidden agenda is not without corporate appropriation; the recommendation to perform night labor (preferably for Bruce Mau's studio) carries its hidden agenda in an unstated (thus Machiavellian) alliance with the post-Fordist practice of flexible labor and maximized economic productivity.
"We, the undersigned, are graphic designers, art directors and visual communicators who have been raised in a world in which the techniques and apparatus of advertising have persistently been presented to us as the most lucrative, effective and desirable use of our talents. Many design teachers and mentors promote this belief; the market rewards it; a tide of books and publications reinforces it."

The *First Things First 2000 Manifesto* (hereafter *FTF*) was signed by thirty-three graphic designers and was issued in 1999. It was printed in design magazines and put on the internet. Re-reading *FTF* more than eight years after its release, it appears like a covenant of respectable professionals offended by the degrading standards of their trade. In comparison, *The Communist Manifesto*, first printed in 1848 by Karl Marx and Friedrich Engels, had more brutally stated: "Let the ruling classes tremble at a Communistic revolution. The proletarians have nothing to lose but their chains." *FTF* made clear that it had no such modality of sacrifice to offer, rather the opposite: nearly all of its authority was based the professional achievement of the signees, who included Gert Dumbar, Ken Garland, Tibor Kalman, Rick Poynor and Erik Spiekermann.

The manifesto continues: "Many of us have grown increasingly uncomfortable with this view of design. Designers who devote their efforts primarily to advertising, marketing and brand development are supporting, and implicitly endorsing, a mental environment so saturated with commercial messages that it is changing the very way citizen-consumers speak, think, feel, respond and interact."

What do the undersigned offer instead?

There are pursuits more worthy of our problem-solving skills. Unprecedented environmental, social and cultural crises demand our attention. Many cultural interventions, social marketing campaigns, books, magazines, exhibitions, educational tools, television programs, films, charitable causes and other information design projects urgently require our expertise and help. We propose a reversal of priorities in favor of more useful, lasting and democratic forms of communication—a mindshift away from product marketing and toward the exploration and production of a new kind of meaning.

While there is no doubt about *FTF*'s sincere intentions, none of the signees publicly refrained from well paid or commercial work after its release, none set out to make some sort of professional or personal sacrifice that would purport realization of the aims stated, and none changed the trade of advertising from without or within. Simply put: nothing changed. *FTF*'s text, of the fortress type, proved easy to conquer and dismantle for critics. Some of them hit home by targeting the misrepresentation of commercial practice, pointing out that none of the thirty-three undersigned, with the exception of Milton Glaser, had any real experience in advertising and therefore were professionally unqualified to attack it. Michael Bierut, a New York-based designer and partner at Pentagram, writes that they "have resisted manipulating the proles who trudge the aisles of your local 7-Eleven for the simple reason that they haven't been invited to." Michael Rock, partner at the New York-based graphic design firm 2×4, takes a more subtle approach. Eventually he cites the theorists Michael Hardt and Antonio Negri, targeting *FTF*'s simplifications as "lite-radicalism": "The identification of the enemy is no small task given exploitation tends no longer to have a specific place and that we are immersed in a system of power so deep and complex that we can no longer determine specific difference or measure. We suffer exploitation, alienation, and command as enemies, but we do not know where to locate the production of oppression."

Indeed *FTF*'s enemy is simplified, but so is eventually every enemy. The point is that it is hesitantly and politely simplified. So that its signees are not outraged, but "increasingly uncomfortable." Not laborers but "art directors." Not selling one's soul to the devil but "devoting one's efforts primarily to advertising." And so on.

Some conditions at the time of writing of *FTF* were not put to the right use. With regard to the manifesto's general ties with printed matter and the graphosphere, the authors of the *FTF* omitted to realize that in order to historically make sense it must relate to the internet, despite the fact that in 1999 online advertising had hardly developed.

With regard to ideology, 1999 was as post-manifesto as one can get. As British designer and writer Robin Kinross wrote about two years after *FTF*, "the days of manifestos are over. In politics, no one much believes in any sharp polarity of left and right. The difficulties of action are immense. Keeping the boat afloat and away from the rocks seems all we can do." Kinross accounts for the ideological tabula rasa of the post-manifesto world and design's general departure from "socially engaged practice," typical for the world after the fall of Communism and the so-called crisis of the Left. The empty place left by the collapse of the Left-Right opposition has been taken by a new concept, the "Third Way," crafted most prominently by the sociologists Ulrich Beck and Anthony Giddens and implemented by New Labor in the United Kingdom. Critics argue that the Third Way conceals hegemony by advocating the nonexistent possibility of a rational consensus.

Can a design manifesto still be written from the ideological void? Now that the principal tools of design—the computer and its software—have been homogenized among practitioners and democratized among people, professional distinction is an unlikely perspective for a future design manifesto to gain support. User-generated content accounts not for an amateurish supplement to a stable, professional core, but for a fundamental transformation of the workforce and the value it creates. The professional core of designers will not regain the central role it once could claim based on its mastery of tools and services unavailable to users. It seems instead more probable that *among* those professional designers, a gap will increase between those who design as celebrity, and those who design as laborer. Such a gap has already appeared in the architectural profession. Subsequently, for a design manifesto, a new alliance between designers and users may be a potentially more successful way forward. At the key of such a potential alliance is the concept of immaterial labor.

Hardt and Negri define immaterial labor as producing "an immaterial good, such as a service, a cultural product, knowledge, or communication." For the sociologist Maurizio Lazzarato, the immaterial labor of advertising, fashion and software development, comprises "intellectual skills, as regards the cultural-informational content; manual skills for the ability to combine creativity, imagination, and technical and manual labor; and entrepreneurial skills in the management of social relations (...)."

A new common ground for designers and users is provided by the changing links between production and consumption, of which immaterial labor is the "interface." The products of immaterial labor not only materialize "needs, the imaginary, consumer tastes, and so forth," but also generate and produce new needs, imaginaries, and tastes, so that the act of consumption is not the destruction of the commodity but the establishment of a relationship which links production and consumption (read: designer and user) together. Lazzarato holds the social, aesthetic and communicative aspects of immaterial labor (which for him extend into the act of consumption) capable of producing direct social and political ties which escape traditional capitalist appropriation.

An example of the actualization of such ties is provided in *The GNU Manifesto,* written by Richard Stallman in 1985: "I consider that the golden rule requires that if I like a program I must share it with other people who like it. Software sellers want to divide the users and conquer them, making each user agree not to share with others. I refuse to break solidarity with other users in this way. I cannot in good conscience sign a nondisclosure agreement or a software license agreement."

This manifesto (GNU being the acronym for "GNU's not Unix") stands at the beginning of free software, open source and file sharing movements. While different from Marinetti and Mau's white nights, it crosses similar boundaries. It declares the relationship between software developer and user a social one.

Manifestos may require multiple decades of incubation time, as Régis Debray accounts for with regard to the *Communist Manifesto*. On the internet, a manifesto is no longer contained within a printed artifact that protects its integrity. One may choose to read a manifesto only partially, and one may encounter it while searching for something entirely different. This should not harm the manifesto; ideally it should work equally well from each of its sentences, so that in some ways, its fortified structure of arguments becomes a distributed network.

References

Bierut, Michael. "Ten Footnotes to a Manifesto," in *Seventy-Nine Short Essays on Design* (New York: Princeton Architectural Press, 2007).

Bruinsma, Max et al. "First Things First 2000: a design manifesto." http://www.xs4all.nl/~maxb/ftf2000.htm (accessed April 27, 2008).

Debray, Régis. "Socialism: A Life-Cycle," *New Left Review* 46 (July–August 2007).

Hardt, Michael, and Antonio Negri. *Empire* (Cambridge, MA: Harvard University Press, 2000).

Jameson, Fredric. *Archaeologies of the Future: The Desire Called Utopia and Other Science Fictions* (London: Verso, 2005).

Kinross, Robin. "More Light! For a Typography that Knows what It's Doing," in *In Alphabetical Order. File under: GRAPHIC DESIGN, SCHOOLS or WERKPLAATS TYPOGRAFIE,* ed. S. Bailey (Rotterdam: NAi Publishers, 2002).

Lang, Peter, and William Menking. *Superstudio: Life Without Objects* (Milan: Skira editore, 2003).

Lash, Scott, and John Urry. *Economies of Signs & Space* (London: SAGE Publications, 1994).

Lazzarato, Maurizio. "Immaterial Labor," in *Radical Thought in Italy: A Potential Politics*, eds M. Hardt and P. Virno (Minneapolis: University of Minnesota Press, 1996).

Machiavelli, Niccolò. *The Prince* (London: Penguin, 2004).

Marinetti, Filippo. "The Futurist Manifesto." Accessed 27 April, 2008. http://www.cscs.umich.edu/~crshalizi/T4PM/futurist-manifesto.html.

Mau, Bruce. "An Incomplete Manifesto for Growth," in *Life Style*, eds B. Mau, K. Maclear and B. Testa (New York: Phaidon, 2000).

McLuhan, Marshall. "Joyce, Mallarmé, and the Press," in *Essential McLuhan*, eds. E. McLuhan and F. Zingrone (London: Routledge, 1997).

Mouffe, Chantal. *On the Political* (London: Routledge, 2005).

Rock, Michael. "2 x 4 Essay: Save Yourself." http://2x4.org/ideas/4/save-yourself/ (accessed 27 April, 2008).

Stallman, Richard. "The GNU Manifesto – GNU Project – Free Software Foundation." http://www.gnu.org/gnu/manifesto.html (accessed 27 April, 2008).

Chapter 3

The capitalist origin of the concept of creative work

Richard Biernacki

For the moment we seem to inhabit an era of "creatives," the modish term that assembles into a class the urban professionals whose engagements in architecture, design, graphic arts, and more seem to unfold from individual artistry. If creativity is a term of ambiguous application, many of us trust that it captures nonetheless some natural dimension of undertakings. In historical perspective, however, the concept of creative work is a peculiar and recent concoction. It did not yet exist in the Renaissance, a period commemorated for its artistic and architectural imagination.[1] Where was the modern concept of creativity first disseminated, and what does its value reveal about the contemporary "creatives" to which, perhaps, many architects belong?

This chapter excavates the hidden origin of our notion of creativity from its sustaining source in the exceptional labor conditions of eighteenth-century Germany. The term "labor" is associated all too generally with service industries or industrial manufacturing. The social critiques of degrading exploitation, bodily exhaustion, and stultifying specialization may be associated with blue-collar movements, but they actually germinated as an ensemble diagnosing wage work by German intellectuals in the eighteenth century. In particular, elite but miserably situated German writers, working for the book market, who referred to their own undertakings by a derogatory term for crude "day labor,"[2] promoted the notion of creativity (*geistige Schöpfung*) as they adapted to regimented production.

What changed with modern creativity

When German *litterateurs* in the late eighteenth century theorized artistic creativity as productive of new worlds, they broke with centuries of classical reflection. Classical aesthetics had acknowledged that the artist or writer took on the role of craft producer (one who uses rhetorical tools) but not that of what we would call a creator, who gives birth to new models of writing. Within the classical tradition a piece of literature could be recognized as an original for its individuality. But it is telling that even the "genius" that comprised a work, in the first half of the eighteenth century, referred to writing from inward inspiration, rather than to the unveiling of exciting departures through revolutionary exemplars.[3]

There is a sure index for the transition to the modern concept of creativity: the transition is accomplished when borrowing and reworking of any sort becomes suspect. Immanual Kant illustrates this condition in his legendary *Critique of Judgment* of 1790. He felt compelled to clarify the obvious point that a creative art could incorporate prior linguistic forms such as rhymes: "Some new educators believe that free art is best promoted when all necessity is put aside and work is transformed into unencumbered play," Kant acknowledged. "It is advisable to recall however that in all free arts something compulsory ... remains requisite (for example in poetry the treasury of words and grammar, in line with prosody and syllable length)."[4] It was possible for reliance on linguistic convention to seem deserving of defense only in an era in which artistic creativity was likened to God's original deed of commanding, "Let the world be." Creativity had moved beyond mere individuality to equal the paradigmatic unveiling of previously unexplored principles.[5]

If one considers only the history of ideas, it might seem that favorable preconditions for crystallizing this notion of creativity were in place in eighteenth-century Britain, where literary uniqueness earned rich praise.[6] Why then did the launch of the modern concept of creativity take place in Germany?[7] Today it appears difficult to distinguish works that are inventively variant (say, adept "two-part inventions" for harpsichord) as opposed to those that are creatively paradigmatic (Picasso's *Demoiselles d'Avignon*). Since even Picasso's brushwork cited past idioms to accentuate what was new in his unveiling of cubism, his techniques remind us how the creative is shadowed by dependent reference to tradition.[8] A skeptic can analytically decompose brilliant departures into ever smaller, technical steps until each appears as a combinatorial variant on prior models as much as a creation *de novo*.[9] How then did an ideology arise for which the divide between skillful ingenuity and inspired creativity was reified as absolute rather than acknowledged as perspectival?

Intellectual work as wage labor

A trove of exceptional documents addresses creativity's riddle. German authors in the eighteenth century engaged in constant correspondence with counterparts as they worked their manuscripts. The highbrow Friedrich Schiller illustrated his marketing savvy when he discussed management of a journal with a collaborator, noting "for the founding of a magazine intended to reach many hands, your plan is obviously too serious, too respectable—how should I say? Too refined."[10] Schiller advised that a writer process "fashionable stuff," like ghost stories or anecdotes "from remote pastures." Schiller testifies that with the growth of the book market beyond the confine of educated elites, writers in eighteenth-century Germany confronted an explosive demand for entertaining trash.[11] As the novelist Georg Friedrich Rebmann complained in 1793, "The public whose voice rules over our authors, not from an intellectual but from an economic viewpoint to be sure, consists of young ladies' hair dressers, valets, commercial apprentices and the like."[12] Difficult literature now ranked low in value, prompting authors to cultivate the same dismissive attitude toward readers that Jonathan Franzen has articulated in our day.[13] Increasingly liberated from wealthy patrons, authors dismissed the market even as they lived off it.

Everyday correspondence reveals three features distinct to the German manner of producing for a market. Together they suggest that the differential cause explaining the inception of modern creativity was not the array of philosophies on tap in Germany, but how writing was organized as labor.

First: writerly practice was organized around the minutely timed expenditure of effort, a result of publishers' system of exchange. In the second half of the eighteenth century, most publishers in Germany distributed their books by journeying with their wares to the national book fair at Easter time or in the fall.[14] Publishers from all German lands sold to each other in a few days the work they had printed throughout the preceding year. In exchange, they acquired works to be resold to consumers in their home districts. The wares were traded unbound, priced per printed page—or more accurately, by the *Bogen*, the standard-sized sheets folded up for stitching into covers. To ease the calculation of manufacturing costs in relation to sales price, writers were also paid per *Bogen*.[15] In pay disputes, writers haggled over the size of the typeface, which in turn determined a printed work's physical length, length being the unit of remuneration.[16] The age of treating print as sheer "content" was launched long ago in Germany, for as Johann Merck wrote cavalierly to his publisher in 1771, "I write wonderful junk."[17]

If the book fairs established the *Bogen* as a metric for decomposing writing into its exchange value, it additionally imposed severe time discipline. Publishers and authors sought to complete work by the spring or fall fairs to quicken their returns. Since no publisher could typeset on the very eve of the event, most expected authors working during the prior season to deliver a fortnightly, or even weekly, quota of text.[18] The need to meet deadlines for the fair, or else wait months for publication and payment, lent writers a sense of now-or-never in their daily scribbling. In his younger days, Johann Wolfgang von Goethe, the best known of Germany's classical writers, demanded of himself each day a quantity of writing to fill one printed *Bogen*.[19] For later works, such as *Wilhelm Meister,* Goethe still promised his publisher a weekly delivery.[20] This deadline set up a cycle of five-to-seven days of work, within which Goethe subdivided his tasks.[21]

Whatever an author churned out in a week became the final page proofs, since the opening pages of a book were sent off and printed before an author had penned the middle.[22] The writing thereby comprised an ongoing stream of bits of material, not the controlled reworking of an edifice. The so-called "factory owner," a frequent term for the publisher, required the writer to feed the printing presses reliably once the first installment of a work was at the compositor's office. As German authors in the late eighteenth century fretted about being reduced to the status of "day laborers"—*Tagelöhner*—their reckonings of daily pay for daily output constantly enacted that nightmare. In contrast to their English or French counterparts, elite German writers often spoke of organizing for productivity.[23]

Second: in practice authors reductively equated fractions of qualitatively unique texts and the inspiration with which they were composed by the expenditure of time they required.[24] In 1772 Gotthold Ephraim Lessing wrote to his brother that "in the same time which it costs me to write a theater piece of ten *Bögen*, I could happily and with less effort write a hundred *Bögen* of another kind."[25] Schiller wrote to a prospective publisher in 1795 that:

> If I am not to suffer obvious damage, I must have the time that I would apply on the revision of my poems and on the preparation of some new ones paid at least so well as it would be remunerated through composition of another essay during this period. Therefore I propose that you credit me four *Louisdors* per *Bogen* as the honorarium.[26]

Everything affiliated with Schiller, from his writing desk to his skull, became sacred for German cultural identity. But his business letters referred to labor time as the remunerated object rather than the literary composition. Likewise, from public gatherings of writers in Weimar in 1796, the novelist Jean Paul quoted time calculations so precise, "Everyone says, 'I receive pay by the hour.'"[27] Authors justified their requested compensation per *Bogen* by calculating average hours deposited on each.[28] They equated fresh composition, translation, and proofreading with "time expenditure" per *Bogen*.[29]

Third: writers rationalized their offices as "work rooms," conceiving of writing as a bodily process. The monetization of this process led quickly to interior design and furniture intended to increase efficiency. Initially, mercantilists advocated the establishment of writing factories, in which labor would be divided and goods churned out for export. The *Hannoverisches Magazin* in 1764 detailed how writers could be assembled for production with a joint library and shared assistants.[30] Although these industrial plans went unrealized, eighteenth-century authors still discussed forming unions so publishers would not "hold them as daily wage laborers."[31] The term "Factory Author" became widespread, as one sees from Friedrich Jakob Tromlitz's engraving of 1800 (see Figure 3.1).

Figure 3.1 Friedrich Jakob Tromlitz after Karl Moritz Berggold.
Source: From Christian Friedrich Traugott Voigt, *Triumph des deutschen Witzes* (Leipzig: Baumgärtner, 1800), 58. Beinecke Rare Book and Manuscript Library, Yale University.

The factory author in this portrayal wore night clothing for round-the-clock production and occupied a brick cell where time was marked by mechanical clock rather than by a view upon movements of the sun or moon. The industrial-size jar of ink reflected the transition of the inputs of writing to factory production, down to tens of millions of quills.[32] Unlike portrayals from the early eighteenth century or before, there is no suggestion writing is of solemn importance.

If Tromlitz's engraving was composed as critique as much as depiction, it nevertheless captured the transition in office design that coincided with the move to writing for a market. In his engraving, Tromlitz lampooned the writer for resting his feet on giant bundles of *Bögen*, as if physical comfort prevailed. But the writer's body as the machine of output indeed became a pivot of furniture design. According to physicians who attended to writers, concentrated hours spent at a desk disrupted the body's needs for rhythmic change. As one expert reported,

> A man full of genius who set to work with exaggerated eagerness recently told me that after he had worked vivaciously for several hours, as he felt his powers of mind lifted, he suddenly sensed faintness in his head, his ideas became confused, he could no longer focus, he became ill, and he repeatedly vomited.[33]

The solution, physicians determined, was to equate writers with craft workers at a bench, since writers benefited similarly from variation in physical action.[34]

Concern for health and efficiency turned sales of desks and stools with mechanisms for altering heights and postures into a fad. "For men who write a lot continually, a writing desk at which they can work while standing, for pleasant change and for maintenance of their health, is indispensable," a literary review opined in 1786. It recommended an accompanying saddle chair for "half standing."[35] Goethe had an ergonomic stool designed that permitted him to sit astride a tilted lectern and to vary his position.[36] Reading chaises came equipped with book stands that were advertised as "fully adjustable in every direction" to match varied body posture.[37] For Monticello, Thomas Jefferson had designed a similar kind of *chaise longue-bureau* for working while reclining, but his was unadjustable.[38] By crowning the productive agent as its center point, physically adaptive furniture in Germany united the contradictory circumstances of intellectual labor: regimented scribbling of *Bögen* for a market under the command of a solitary free agent.

The rationalization of the writing process can also be glimpsed by contrasting a German writer's workroom with the studio of the Renaissance humanists. The desk, chairs, and book holders of the studio were imposing pieces that encased the writer.[39] For inspiration, the studio was elaborately decorated, often adjoining the intimate sphere of the bedroom. In the German writers' workrooms, by contrast, furnishings were of utilitarian simplicity. "Surroundings with soft refined furniture override my thoughts and shift me into a cozy, passive state," Goethe complained.[40] He put his office out back, in relatively cramped quarters away from the bright house, effectively separating work from home. Rather than being enclosed by their furniture, as in Renaissance Italy, German writers tailored their furniture to their body. "Just as a potter, a cabinetmaker, a turner, a boot maker, a tailor and so forth needs a shop to suit him and his labor, so a writer and tradesman needs an office corresponding to his individual affairs," a popular art magazine explained. "Our writing desk must be as individually fitting for us as our coat."[41]

The novelist Jean Paul confirmed the awareness of writing as timed manual efficiency when he said that the most important topic of an author's autobiography was "the writing hour, the corporeal relation to his work."[42] Small wonder eighteenth-century commentators on furniture spoke of time as a productive resource, the "scarcest" of all.[43] Correlatively, pen and ink holders were molded to hold watches, and writers expressed a demand for eighteenth-century cabinet makers to pre-fit desks with receptacles for clocks.[44]

The aesthetic predicament of work

This sketch of labor conditions allows us to appreciate how commercial work infused the development of aesthetic ideology. Before the emergence of a mass market for writing, even the noblest writers were likened to craft workers in so far as both were masters of a traditional corpus of techniques. When writers gave birth to a composition that was out of the ordinary, their achievement was attributed to a higher force—to God or to a muse. These pre-capitalist versions of the writer—as craft worker and as conduit of divine intervention—shared a hidden premise.[45] Neither of them credited the artist personally for a spiritual outpouring. The *Economic Lexicon* of 1753, prior to the commercialization of the publishing market, had grouped authors together with other manual workers in the manufacture of a book:

> Many people work on this ware before it is finished . . . the scholar and the writer, the papermaker, the type founder, the typesetter and the printer, the proofreader, the publisher, the binder, occasionally the gold gilder and the *Gürtler*, etc.[46]

This merging of manual and intellectual labor, sustained by pay per *Bogen* for both printing and writing, remained professionally inconsequential, since almost no one in this era conceived of writing as a career.

With the development of a corps of professional writers for an explosive market, however, authorship as commercial labor entered the light of day. New booksellers in small towns hung out their shop signs like "dealers in victuals."[47] Traditional aesthetic ideology was not designed to shield writers from joining the ranks of other suppliers of materials. Since writers "sold wisdom and humor like cubit wares,"[48] they were said to earn their keep the same as "dyers and wool makers."[49]

Johann Gottfried Herder, who celebrated the infinite play of language, complained in 1784 that he had written for weeks as if he were "an ass" controlled by "external proddings."[50] Jean Paul complained at his romantic height of "working like a cattle cow."[51] In sum, the combination of tight schedules under the guidance of the publisher, the calculated delivery of abstract work time, and the acute awareness of writing as a regulated corporeal process lent German writers an experience of dependent wage work as much as of independent commodity production.[52]

At the same time, writers gloried in their newfound autonomy as market agents emancipated from the constraints of courtly patronage. Dedications to noble financial supporters became increasingly fraught. Book reviews in Germany, many times over more numerous than in France or England, were distinctive for discussing only the book itself, a ware separate from the author's character in polite society.[53] "The single good thing I have is freedom and autonomy, which I prize at every moment," Herder wrote.[54] Under German conditions that freedom could be protected only if writing were an extraordinarily creative act in a universe untouched by the regularities of material labor.

It is indicative therefore that the inception of the modern concept of creativity seems to have crystallized first in the reflections of a writer who experienced the paradoxes of mercenary artistry most acutely. Karl Philipp Moritz had been apprenticed to a hatter early in life, but progressed to write travelogues, novels, and a stream of ephemera, including an ABC primer, all of it driven by a desire for income. To pad his *Bogen* totals, Moritz copied whole pages of his own words from one publication into the next. "Then he did not even begin to write until the compositor was already waiting for the manuscript," his brother reported.[55] As indicated by his founding of a journal for psychology, Moritz had a genuine intellectual agenda, however. In place of the light tales about Italy expected by his publisher in 1788, Moritz handed in a revolutionary treatise on the formation of beautiful art. Moritz's weighty philosophy sold so poorly, however, most of its copies were pulped, setting off a bitter contractual dispute.[56]

As if to anticipate this failure, Moritz's aesthetic theory (and his reworkings of it for additional output) radically shifted the value of a work from its reception back to its inception. Moritz proposed that the purpose of a composition was simply to achieve its own perfection as a "consummated whole," an ideal high above the increments that Moritz reeled off. No writer or painter as an artist, he said, would sacrifice the internal beauty of a work simply to increase "the pleasant sensations of thousands of people, who have no appreciation for its bounties."[57] This break with centuries of thinking about art as an instrument for eliciting human responses was the dawn of art for art's sake.

More specifically, Moritz's aesthetics rolled the whole value of art into the experience of the labor process:

> The creative genius that brings forth a work remains the most intense engagement of the beautiful; and the beautiful therefore has achieved its ultimate purpose in its creation, in its coming to be. Our later enjoyment of the beautiful thing is only an after-effect of its existence. Generative genius in the scheme of things is there principally for *its own self* and there only secondly for our sake.[58]

If this valuing of productive experience released the artist from the need to germinate work that fitted external popular convention, what was a composition to depict? In artwork, the generative power of a creator, like God, properly "reflected itself," a process Moritz described as if he were prefiguring a Pollock action painting.[59] Goethe remarked on how widely Moritz's theory resonated with German writers and called his own encounter with it "a rebirth."[60]

The demon of mechanical labor drove the eruption and dissemination of ideas about the exercise of creativity as an end in its own right. It is telling that when Kant drew upon Moritz's innovations for his foundational *Critique of Judgment*, Kant insisted that remunerated labor lacked the autonomy necessary to produce art at all. "Fine art," he wrote, "cannot be work as paid labor, whose magnitude by a standard measure lets itself be assessed, enforced, or paid."[61] In Moritz's writing, similarly, art could never exist as an offspring of production for instrumental "self gain."[62] Moritz, unlike Kant, held out the possibility of artistic creation based on the artist's subjective indifference while producing for the market, however. For the writer himself to treat the writing as a useful commodity remained counterproductive, Moritz reasoned. When a writer's ideas "cannot be coaxed out of him with enthusiasm for the project, they covertly go wrong and in each line again destroy themselves."[63]

The insistence that art as such had to be produced freely without a useful end in mind did more than defend the writer's autonomy: it cleaved art from manufacture. The aesthetics inherited until then had been unable to enforce this distinction. To protect their *Bögen* from reduction to physical objects of exchange, exactly that contrast was required by commercial writers. Compared to their British and French counterparts, German writers were unique for reiterating that market dynamics threatened to mechanize authorship: "The writer will never be profaned, writing never degraded into a book factory!" the profession's defenders vowed.[64] Correlatively, German authors insisted that they did not sell products at all; they only temporarily licensed the use of their words as if they were giving a public lecture.[65] "Artistry is differentiated from craftwork," Kant wrote. "The first is free, the second is also salaried skill."[66]

The pursuit of artistic models for their own sake set genuine creation apart from writing as rule-bound assembly. Long before the scourge of computers, German mercantilists asked if writing for sale could be automated with rods and wheels.[67] In truth, many hidebound scholars simply borrowed selections from other works and had a copyist assemble them to fill up *Bögen*.[68] Such output for exchange seemed to execute teachable conventions and therefore proceeded by rules of necessity. Artistic creativity by contrast followed no rules (although it might suggest some afterward) and as play was precisely what labor was not.[69] The notion that an autonomously produced artistic whole created its own universe of meanings let writers claim with qualification that they were creative even as appropriators. If they had a new integrative inspiration, they could draw upon prior works while "creating" an entirely new product.[70]

The self-generative force of an author's creativity let German writers claim magically independent productivity. An author, Moritz wrote in 1793, "is someone who has brought forth something out of himself or the creator [*Urheber*] of his work out of his own vitality."[71] The word *Urheber*, the term reserved in Martin Luther's theology for God as He who produces the heavens out of nothing, strategically distinguishes the author from an earthly worker who merely processed materials.[72] Yet the venue for which Moritz penned these words betrays them as almost a worried necessity. They come from his *Grammatical Dictionary of the German Language*, one of the hack compositions that Moritz undertook for payments of "content" inscribed in *Bögen*.

Into the present

Creativity's meaning continues to evolve in a dance with the valorization of labor as a commodity. As early as 1842, popular journals in Germany explained how difficult it was for creators to obtain compensation for intellectual "productions of the arts" as opposed to material input. At the very least, "the cultivation of talent and the years of preliminary education must be calculated additionally." Yet this calculus culminated by reaffirming that a creative producer introduced value from "the inexhaustible depth of his own spirit."[73] This style of economic analysis outwardly sustained the appearance that creativity made new worlds out of nothing, but more fundamentally it measured that productivity as a kind of surplus value relative to other inputs, exactly as economists examining the "creative class," including Richard Florida, contend today.[74] Economics instrumentalizes creativity as a factor of production. If creativity in a knowledge economy is folded back into the very norms of capitalist labor, we domesticate creativity's meaning by treating it similarly to the craft know-how deemed adequate for artistic excellence until the late eighteenth century.[75] Creativity in the master framework of economics nowadays equals skill at manipulating data, words, or visual components for "creative problem solving" in the manufacture of non-standard products.[76] Among these "symbolic analysts," as the former Secretary of Labor Robert Reich calls them, are "creative accountants," engineers, and architects, all of whom are creative in the restricted sense of customizing products as artisans did in earlier epochs.[77]

The norming of creativity as a job skill, the premise behind talk of "the creatives," takes several forms in architectural work today. Professional curricula designed to cultivate creativity do not recognize the historical irony in the very proposition of a method for inspiring germination. In many accounts of practice, the proliferation of computer-assisted design, by making the parameters of problem-solving choices more identifiable, decomposes creation into a less mysterious or romantic process.[78] In some quarters therefore the meaning of architectural authorship is shifting from the expression of a visionary individual to the merging of resources from multiple contributors, including networks or communities.[79] But the key to the norming of creativity is its duality: not only "should" architects deliver creativity, but they "should" feel fulfilled by that dimension of their work.[80] For the artist is still thought to plumb fundamentals of experience more profoundly than a mere worker, and that desperate conceit of the eighteenth-century commercial authors is the ghost of creativity that lives on.

Notes

1. Donatien Grau, *The Age of Creation* (Berlin: Lukas & Sternberg, 2013); Paul Oskar Kristeller, *Renaissance Thought and the Arts* (Princeton, NJ: Princeton University Press, 1965), 188.
2. Johann Gottfried Herder, *Herders Briefe* (Berlin: Aufbau, 1983), 361.
3. Edward Young, *Conjectures on Original Composition* (Dublin: P. Wilson, 1749), 13, 16.
4. Immanuel Kant, *Gesammelte Schriften* (Berlin: G. Reimer, 1910), 5:304.
5. Ibid., 318; Karl Philipp Moritz, "Über die bildende Nachahmung des Schönen," *Werke* (Frankfurt: Insel, 1981), 2:567.

6. John Mahoney, *The Whole Internal Universe* (New York: Fordham University Press, 1985).
7. Simone Mahrenholz, *Kreativität: Eine philosophische Analyse* (Berlin: Akademie Verlag, 2011), 153–54; Cord-Friedrich Berghahn, *Das Wagnis der Autonomie* (Heidelberg: Universitätsverlag, 2012), 115.
8. From George Steiner's discussion in *Grammars of Creation* (New York: Faber and Faber, 2001), 93.
9. Tony Veale, *Exploding the Creativity Myth* (London: Bloomsbury, 2012).
10. Friedrich Schiller, *Briefe I: 1772–1795* (Frankfurt: Deutscher Klassiker Verlag, 2002), 306.
11. Jochen Schulte-Sasse, *Die Kritik an der Trivialliteratur seit der Aufklärung* (Munich: Wilhelm Fink, 1971), 46.
12. Georg Friedrich Rebmann, *Werke und Briefe* (Berlin: Rütten und Loening, 1990), 1:79.
13. David Kirkpatrick, "'Oprah' Gaffe by Franzen Draws Ire and Sales," *New York Times*, 29 October, 2001.
14. By 1782, few publishers attended the autumn book fair. Johannes von Müller and J. Georg Müller, *Johannes von Müllers sämmtliche Werke* (Schaffhausen: Hurter, 1840), Supplement 4:107.
15. Staatsbibliothek zu Berlin, Deckersche Buchdruckerei 9, Georg Decker, 7 April, 1782 and calculation, 330.
16. Verlagsarchiv Walter de Gruyter, Jean Paul to Georg Andreas Reimer, 19 February, 1817.
17. Karl Wagner, *Briefe aus dem Freundeskreise von Goethe, Herder, Höpfner und Merck* (Leipzig: Fleischer, 1847), 55.
18. Staatsbibliothek zu Berlin, Deckersche Buchdruckerei 9, Georg Decker, 26 April, 1776; Thomas Abbts, *Vermischte Werke* (Berlin: Friedrich Nicolai, 1771), 3:52.
19. Erich Frederking, *Goethes Arbeitsweise* (Darmstadt: K. F. Bender, 1912), 50. Analogously for other writers, Karl Friedrich Bahrdt, *Briefe angesehener Gelerten, Staatsmänner und anderer* (Leipzig: Weygand, 1798), 4:45.
20. Flodoard Woldemar von Biedermann, ed., *Johann Friedrich Unger im Verkehr mit Goethe und Schiller* (Berlin: Bertholddruck, 1927), 71.
21. Frederking, *Goethes Arbeitsweise*, 88. Goethe was partly able to avoid pay per *Bogen*.
22. Gotthold Ephraim Lessings, *Briefwechsel mit Karl Wilhelm Ramler, Johann Joachim Eschenburg und Friedrich Nicolai* (Berlin: Friedrich Nicolai, 1794), 500.
23. Frederking, *Goethes Arbeitsweise*, 51.
24. Jean Paul, *Ideen-Gewimmel* (Frankfurt: Eichborn, 1996), 35.
25. Gotthold Ephraim Lessing, *Gesammelte Werke* (Berlin: Aufbau, 1968), 9:560.
26. Friedrich Schiller and Albert Leitzmann, *Schillers Briefe: Kritische Gesamtausgabe* (Stuttgart: Deutsche Verlags-Anstalt, 1892), 1:287.
27. Jean Paul, *Briefwechsel mit seiner Frau und Christian Otto* (Berlin: Weidmann, 1902), 25.
28. Pamela E. Selwyn, *Everyday Life in the German Book Trade* (University Park: Pennsylvania State University Press, 2000), 347.

29. Karl Goedeke, *Geschäftsbriefe Schillers* (Leipzig: Velt, 1875), 91.
30. *Hannoverisches Magazin*, November 30, 1764, 1524.
31. Siegfried Unseld, *Goethe und seine Verleger* (Frankfurt: Insel, 1991), 116.
32. Claus Maywald-Pintellos, "Das Tintenfaß: Die Geschichte der Tintenaufbewahrung in Mitteleuropa (Deutschland)" (Ph.D. diss., Freie Universität Berlin, 1998), 64.
33. S. Tissot, *Von der Gesundheit der Gelehrten* (Zurich: Füeßlin, 1768), 28–9. Analogously, *Berlinisches Archiv der Zeit* 2, (July–December 1800): 268.
34. Tissot, *Von der Gesundheit*, 148
35. *Journal der Moden*, (May 1786), Table 16.
36. Hans Eckstein, *Der Stuhl. Funktion – Konstruktion – Form. Von der Antike bis zur Gegenwart* (Munich: Keyser, 1977), 146.
37. *Journal des Luxus und der Mode* (February 1799): 107.
38. Élisabeth Pélegrin-Genel, *L'art de vivre au bureau* (Paris: Flammarion, 1995), 19.
39. Elizabeth Currie, *Inside the Renaissance House* (London: Victoria and Albert, 2006), 81; Dora Thornton, *The Scholar in His Study* (New Haven, CT: Yale University Press, 1997), 76; Peter Thornton, *The Italian Renaissance Interior 1400–1600* (New York: Harry Abrams, 1991), 227; Frida Schottmüller, *Wohnungskultur und Möbel der italienischen Renaissance* (Stuttgart: Julius Hoffmann, 1921), 67.
40. Willi Ehrlich, *Goethes Wohnhaus am Frauenplan in Weimar* (Weimar: Nationale Forschungs- und Gedenkstätten der klassischen deutschen Literatur, 1982), 7.
41. *Journal des Luxus und der Mode* (May 1793): 285.
42. Jean Paul, *Ideen-Gewimmel*, 59.
43. *Journal des Luxus und der Mode* (May 1793): 286.
44. Klaus Mölbert, *Als noch Zeit zum Schreiben war* (Stockstadt am Rhein: Klaus Mölbert, 2006), 41; "Intelligenz-Blatt," *Journal des Luxus und der Mode* 12 (1795): CCXXV.
45. Martha Woodmansee, *The Author, Art, and the Market* (New York: Columbia University Press, 1994), 36.
46. George Heinrich Zincke, *Allgemeines oeconomisches Lexicon* (Leipzig: J. F. Gleditschens Handlung, 1753), 1:442.
47. Daniel Jenisch, *Der allezeit-fertige Schriftsteller* (Berlin: n.p., 1797), 73.
48. Adolph Freyherr Knigge, *Ueber den Bücher-Nachdruck* (Hamburg: Hoffmann, 1792), 11.
49. Karl Wagner, *Briefe aus dem Freundeskreise von Goethe, Herder, Höpfner und Merck* (Leipzig: Fleischer, 1847), 244.
50. *Herders Briefe* (Berlin: Aufbau, 1983), 228.
51. Jean Paul, *Briefweschsel*, 177.
52. Wagner, *Briefe aus dem Freundeskreise*, 193.
53. Martin Fontius, "Produktivkraft Entfaltung und Autonomie der Kunst" in *Literatur im Epochenumbruch,* eds. Günther Klotz, Winfried Schröder and Peter Weber (Berlin: Aufbau, 1977), 419.
54. Emil Gottfried von Herder, *Johann Gottfried von Herders Lebensbild* (Erlangen: Theodor Bläsing, 1846), Vol. 1, Part 2:211.

55. Hugo Ebysch, *Untersuchenen zur Lebensgeschichte von K. Ph. Moritz und zur Kritik seiner Autobiographie* (Leipzig: Voigtländer, 1909), 272.
56. Reinhart Marx and Gerhard Sauder, *Moritz contra Campe: Ein Streit zwischen Autor und Verleger im Jahr 1789* (St. Ingbert: Röhrig, 1993).
57. Karl Philipp Moritz, "Über den Begriff des in sich selbst Vollendeten," *Werke* (Frankfurt: Insel, 1981), 2:546.
58. Moritz, *Werke*, 2:564.
59. Moritz, *Werke*, 2:566.
60. Martin Fontius, "Produktivkraft Entfaltung," 517–23. Documenting Moritz's crucial reception: Thomas Saine, *Die Ästhetische Theodizee* (Munich: Wilhelm Fink Verlage, 1971), 17–19; Hans Joachim Schrimpf, *Karl Philipp Moritz* (Stuttgart: Metzler, 1980), 113.
61. Kant, *Gesammelte Schriften*, 5:321.
62. Moritz, *Werke*, 2:566.
63. Reinhart Marx and Gerhard Sauder, *Moritz contra Campe*, 41.
64. Armin Mallinckrodt, *Ueber Deutschlands Litteratur und Buchhandel* (Dortmund: Gebrüder Mallinckrodt, 1800), 47.
65. Richard Biernacki, "The Social Manufacture of Private Ideas in Germany and Britain, 1750–1830," *Wissenschaftskolleg zu Berlin*, ed. Wolf Lepenies (Jahrbuch 1998/1999): 241.
66. Kant, *Gesammelte Schriften*, 5:304.
67. *Hannoverisches Magazin*, November 30, 1764, 1523.
68. Wagner, *Briefe aus dem Freundeskreise*, 349.
69. John Zammito, *The Genesis of Kant's Critique of Judgment* (Chicago: University of Chicago Press, 1992), 145.
70. Rainer Nomine, *Der königlich preußische literarische Sachverständigen-Verein in den Jahren 1838–1870* (Berlin: Duncker & Humblot, 2001), 249.
71. Karl Philipp Moritz, *Grammatisches Wörterbuch der deutschen Sprache* (Berlin: Ernst Felisch, 1793), 1:160.
72. Christian Benedict Gloerfeld, *Der Catechismus D. Martin Luthers* (Berlin: n.p., 1792), 55.
73. *Allgemeine Press-Zeitung*, January 7, 1842, 13.
74. Richard Florida, *The Rise of the Creative Class* (New York: Basic Books, 2002).
75. Andreas Reckwitz, *Die Erfindung der Kreativität: Zum Process gesellschaftlicher Ästhetisierung* (Berlin: Suhrkamp, 2013), 115.
76. Robert Reich, *The Work of Nations: Preparing Ourselves for 21st-Century Capitalism* (New York: A. A. Knopf, 1991), 235.
77. Reich, *Work of Nations*, 177.
78. Mary N. Woods, *From Craft to Profession: The Practice of Architecture in Nineteenth-Century America* (Berkeley: University of California Press, 1999), 177.
79. Hélène Lipstadt, "'Exoticising the Domestic': On New Collaborative Paradigms and Advanced Design Practices," in *Architecture and Authorship*, eds Tim Anstey, Katja Grillner, and Rolf Hughes (London: Black Dog, 2007), 164–73.
80. Magali Sarfatti Larson, *Behind the Postmodern Façade: Architectural Change in Late Twentieth-Century America* (Berkeley: University of California Press, 1993), 143.

Chapter 4

The architect as entrepreneurial self: Hans Hollein's TV performance "Mobile Office" (1969)[1]

Andreas Rumpfhuber

Hans Hollein's *Mobile Office* (1969)[2] has been catalogued as an installation consisting of PVC-foil, a vacuum cleaner, a typewriter (Hermes Baby), a telephone, a drawing board, a pencil, a rubber, and thumbtacks. In fact the *Mobile Office* is a two-minute-and-twenty-second-long performance exclusively produced for television (see Figures 4.1–4. 6). It paradigmatically shows contours of an emerging shift in architectural practice that must be read parallel to the radical transformations in the organization of labor in the post-War years. It is exactly then that Fordist business organization in Western industrialized countries, with its hierarchic structures, becomes fragile in favor of a new workers' society. To read the *Mobile Office* as a paradigmatic project mirroring aspects of this very transformation allows me to understand alterations, shifts, and disruptions in the practice of architecture. It allows me to identify and analyze contours of a possibly new emphasis in the work of an architect. It helps me to trace the implications for the work and the product of architects at the very moment of the alleged shift in western industrialized societies from a Taylorist organization of production toward today's dominant form, the post-Fordist production of immaterial labor. Thus the analysis of the *Mobile Office* makes exemplarily visible the tendency toward today's generalized and proletarized form of the creative entrepreneur and his or her production.

The architect as entrepreneurial self

Figure 4.1 Mobile Office 9'21".

Figure 4.2 Mobile Office 9'40".

Figure 4.3 Mobile Office 10'11".

Figure 4.4 Mobile Office 10'20".

Figure 4.5 Mobile Office 10'33".

Figure 4.6 Mobile Office 10'55".

The becoming dominant of an organization paradigm

The transformation in the 1960s and 1970s of western industrialized societies from a Fordist model and its Taylorist organization of work processes toward a post-Fordist model and its becoming dominant of immaterial forms of production has been widely discussed. Discourses in Gender and Queer Studies have described a transition from the mass worker to the *laborer of society*, Maurizio Lazzarato introduced the concept of *immaterial labor,* expanding the traditional Marxian concept of labor with a multitude of social productions, and finally it was Mario Tronti who originally coined the notion of "the factory of society," in which the formerly confined factory literally spills out into the city.

All of these descriptions imply the implementation of a popular and rather technocratic understanding of cybernetics as the core principle of governance into the work-processes of the post-War years. It conceives of humans as well as machines and automats as autonomous, self-directing entities, whose behavior is understood as coded and thus as being able to be re-programmed. This is made possible by placing the emphasis on information flow within an organization that needs to be optimized. That is, cybernetic logic understands human beings as well as calculating machines and automats as equal entities on the same hierarchic level when it comes to processing information. Calculating machines and automats start to take over repetitive work-processes that are based on known information and routines that can be coded. Within this logic, workers need to take over work-processes that are based on a high degree of choice and on unknown information, which calculating machines, for the time being, cannot process. In this very moment, all the workers left in the factory or in the office get addressed as specialists—as a creative worker, or as a knowledge worker—who need to take on responsibility for their decisions within the organization of a corporation. Simultaneously, teamwork and strict codes of conduct are being introduced in order to secure decision-making processes. This introduction of automation in the factory but also in administration (of companies and the state, on both sides of the Iron Curtain) has been accompanied by the popular promise of dismissing everybody in the near future into an everlasting spare time, the so-called leisure society.

In this sense the transition from Fordism to post Fordism in the 1960s and 1970s anticipates a contemporary condition in western industrialized societies of which the Factory of Society is its precise spatial metaphor. The old dictum of spatial and temporal simultaneity and concurrence of work processes, as well as the functionally distinct, well-defined attribution of spaces of production disintegrates with these new organizations of a labor concept that is becoming increasingly diffuse. Yet this new situation also produces a new kind of worker who adapts and affirms this new organization of labor: he or she needs to exercise knowledge based on creative work, he or she become an entrepreneur and take up responsibility for what he or she is doing, no matter if one is still employed or has already been outsourced. Thus today's modes, as well as means of production, not only require different spatial figurations for work that are permanently and continuously manifest in new and unprecedented formations and figurations, they also require a different workers' subject.

These alterations in the organization of work, accompanied by the popular promise of the leisure society to come, also affected architects and their objects in manifold ways. Noticeable in this context are the many avant-garde projects of the 1950s and 1960s in which labor seems already abolished and life is to circle around the play and self-organization of free subjects in their endless spare time. In this context Hans Hollein's performance is unique. With the *Mobile Office* Hans Hollein portrays himself as a new type of architect, a new type of laborer in a new workers' reality. Hollein anticipates that the new workers' reality is not that of endless spare time, and not even the promised twenty-hour-week. Instead, life is full of work. In front of and with the TV-cameras on he challenges and alters various aspects of the traditional architect's practice: be it the mode of appearance and performance of the architect; be it the drawing as the core of the work of an architect, as well as the status of the drawing itself; or finally be it the status, the representation, and the organization of the architectural object. In a specific way the *Mobile Office* portrays the deferral of society's organizational and technological advancements against the bourgeois understanding of the work of the architect. Inasmuch as Hollein stages the transparent bubble as an envelope for working, and certainly not for leisure, he makes architecture visible, as a specific part of a palpable situation of a new formation of labor. In its presentation via television he relates significant and typical conditions of a nomadic living- and working-formation to architecture and its specific quality and materiality.

2:20 minutes

The 2:20-minute performance starts with a young Hans Hollein seesawing in a rocking chair. He is wearing a woolen pullover, a shirt, and black trousers. Next to him on the floor, and behind him in the shelves, there are piles of books and print-outs. He explains: "The idea of the *TO-CARRY-AROUND-HOUSE* is derived from today's way of living." He goes on talking about the modern nomad, the

The architect as entrepreneurial self

caravan, and his idea of the house that can be folded into a suitcase. *CUT.* A small propeller-driven aircraft rolls along an airstrip. In the far background Vienna's 1964 *Danube Tower* with its radio- and television-masts looms into the summer sky. The cabin door is open. A pilot and two male passengers are sitting in the aircraft. *CUT.* The airplane stands still. Both of the passengers get out of the plane. The one with long, blond hair and sunglasses is the 34-year-old architect Hans Hollein. He is wearing a leather jacket, a white shirt, and light-colored trousers, and carrying a black suitcase. His bearded companion, Franz Madl, is wearing a white shirt and tie. He is carrying a wooden drawing board and a T-square. Both men head for the lawn next to the airstrip. *CUT.* The suitcase is open. An alien-looking, foil-like material glistens in the bright sunlight. The two men start to unpack and unfold the transparent textile. Hollein takes a black tube that is attached to a Hoover-like apparatus suddenly lying around in the grass and attaches it to a latch on the textile. *CUT.* The textile is blown up to a slackish bubble. Hollein crawls into it. He squats in the bubble. His companion passes him the architect's working utensils—the drawing board, the T-square, and paper. Hollein closes the lid to the outside world and sits down in his bubble. Madl turns the apparatus to full volume. Now the bubble stands vertically, like a cigar. It is shiny and transparent. The voice-over explains: "This all might sound somewhat crazy, but is already in use for sport facilities in other countries. For protection against the weather." *CUT.* One sees the bubble with Hollein in close-up. Hans Hollein's hair stands on end. Again an explanation from off screen: "Hollein once wrote: Today Architecture is in exile, on the moon or at the north pole, and all the people are building on and on, just houses, houses, houses, houses ..." *CUT.* Hollein sits cross-legged in the bubble with the drawing board on his lap. His companion stands there curiously looking at him. The architect works in the bubble. He draws with ruler, triangle, and pencil. *CUT.* One sees the same working position from a different angle. *CUT.* The camera frames a close-up of a telephone that suddenly stands there on the drawing board in Hollein's lap. The telephone rings. Hollein picks it up and a dialog unfolds: "Hello, this is Hollein ... Yes, I just arrived at the airfield Aspern ... Yes, I just finished the house. It will be delivered at once. You can look at it in a second." Now one sees the drawing that Hollein has produced: a small villa with a pitched roof, high chimney, and a garden wall. At that very moment Hollein draws the smoke coming out of the chimney, telling his conversation partner on the phone: "Yes, a very modern design, yes. As you ordered ... Good Bye." *CUT and a long shot.* Music. The wide lawn; on the horizon a few bushes; a cloudless sky; to the left of the picture the Hoover-like apparatus to which the bubble is attached; the envelope (*Hülle*) nearly dissolves visually and is barely noticeable.

Only through some interferences and shadows one can vaguely discern the bubble. Hollein still works by drawing. For a moment he looks up from his work. *CUT.* Hans Hollein and his companion again sit in the small plane. This time Hollein will be the pilot and puts on the helmet …

Here the performance of the *Mobile Office*, or the *TO-CARRY-AROUND-HOUSE*, as it was called by Hans Hollein, ends. The performance was produced in the summer of 1969 as a part of a sequel about Hollein on the post-war TV series *"Das österreichische Portrait"* (The Austrian Portrait). The *Mobile Office* is a 2:20-minute segment in the 30-minute portrait of Hollein. It was aired in the early evening on the second Sunday in Advent the same year. Hollein does not represent his intimate space in its conventional meaning or by traditional means. Television allows for experimenting with a different form of representation of architecture, but also gradually shifts the role of the architect. With the help of cameras, an architecture-drawing is produced that depicts a nomadic, cosmopolitan worker's future and its architecture. The architect himself plays different roles: he is the story-teller in the rocking chair; he is the young, dynamic working nomad; he is the architect with commissions all around the world. In this sense the *Mobile Office* is an architecture of information and its message is being transported through a new medium, the television.

The entrepreneur virtuoso and his space

The half-hour portrait constructs Hollein's sentimental relationship to tradition-steeped Vienna and to Austria as a whole. It is an analogue to his revolutionary ideas, as they would be called, to the history of Austria and its architecture, but also to the cozy way of living of the long-gone imperial-metropolis Vienna, to the horse carriages, to the *Riesenrad* Ferris wheel, etcetera.

The cornerstones of his biography are told as follows. He was born and raised in the fourth district of Vienna, where he still lives with his wife. He went to school in the neighborhood, then he studied architecture at Clemens Holzmeister's master-class at the Academy of Fine Arts at Schillerplatz. After graduating, he worked in Sweden and then did his master's degree in architecture in America, in California. With the refurbishment of the candle shop Retti he became famous. And now he is a professor in Düsseldorf, Germany. At the same time he is about to build a bank in Vienna, as well as a gallery on 79th Street in New York City. He is working on a project for the World's Fair in Osaka, Japan and on a project for Olivetti in Amsterdam. At the beginning of the sequel, Hollein is being introduced as the creative architect who thinks beyond the norm(al): "I am not the kind of architect who only builds," he says.

"I am interested in miscellaneous ... Also commercials and things like that. I present products. I am something of an idea man." (0:39)[3] In other words, he is a virtuoso, always a bit crazy, visionary, but still pragmatic, always interested in finding solutions to problems.

Hollein stages himself as a kind of hybrid working subject: he is the cosmopolitan entrepreneur and he is an outstanding creative worker. Yet he is goal-oriented and lives a stable life. He works on a multitude of projects of different scales around the world. Still, he also works in teams. He collaborates, for example, with his wife, who is an haute-couture designer, and designed the costumes and suits for the Austrian Pavilion at the Milan Triennale exhibition in 1968. Hollein is not only an architect. He is also a designer of objects, an art-director, and an artist. But he is also an entrepreneur: he is active and self-employed, he is innovative.

To borrow a term coined by the German sociologist Ulrich Bröckling, Hans Hollein shows the first contours of the *enterprising self*.[4] Published in 2007, Bröckling takes up today's general imperative that everybody ought to become an entrepreneur. He analyzes the societal maelstrom and its discursive diagram that this imperative had released. He speaks of the normative requirements, but also about new choices and opportunities, the institutional arrangements, and about the social- and self-technologies that regulate the behavior of the enterprising self. In doing so, he lays out a grammar for governing and self-governing, describing the currents that carry people away, circumscribing the dynamic of an increasingly economized society.

To read Hollein as an *enterprising self* emphasizes an otherwise underexposed relationship between architecture and economic discourses that go beyond a discussion about building norms and the economic framing that restrains the architect's creativity. Rather, this reading takes into account that the architect, himself or herself, is enmeshed in societal discourses. He or she is shaped by a dominant economic logic and its imperatives. Yet he or she also acts upon this logic by affirming the situation and responding to it.

In general terms the modern architect's work is based on a bourgeois mode of work that primarily comprises communication and produces value by applying knowledge and exchanging services. This is true for two distinct modes of work within the practice of architecture. On the one hand there has always been the architect-entrepreneur. He—as the traditional history of architecture discourse primarily knows males—has always been discussed as a singular master and public intellectual. This part of the practice of architecture is a mode of productivity that today can be described with the neologism *networking*. On the other hand, the work of the architect, or more precisely of the many collaborators and co-workers of the architect-entrepreneur, pursues a more mundane activity, that of the drawing and constant re-drawing of endless variations of a façade, a layout, a section, or a detail of a building. This is the production of communication material for clients, the public, but not least for other professionals involved in the production of the built environment.

Thus, in the words of Maurizio Lazzarato describing the general concept of immaterial labor, the work of the architect, as it is generally understood, needs to be considered to be a specific form of labor that "produces the informational and cultural content of the commodity."[5] Lazzarato refers to changes in companies in the industrial and tertiary sector itself, where skills needed for labor processes increasingly involved skills in cybernetics and the control of computers. On the other hand, he points toward intellectual activities that normally were not recognized as work but generally were understood as the privilege of the bourgeoisie and its children that in the post-war years have become part of the domain that has been defined as "mass intellectuality." Lazzarato argues that these profound changes not only modified the organization of production, but also the function of intellectuals toward a generalization of their activities.

The *Mobile Office* depicts the value-creating form of practice generally known as architecture. Yet it radicalizes the traditional understanding of the work of the architect, as well as its product. On the one hand it is the public figure of the architect-entrepreneur, one who networks, that merges with the architect-worker, who produces drawings. Thus the performance of the *Mobile Office* depicts an act of labor whose purpose lies in itself. It is a work-process that solely exists through communication. In that sense it is work that produces an object, which cannot be isolated from its performance (*handeln*),[6] as the Italian philosopher Paolo Virno had described it. It is not so much about knowledge- and information-based work in its original meaning, where knowledge would present a kind of product, but it is rather labor in that it finds its compliance and its purpose in itself. It is structured like a musician playing a concert. Virtuosity, that is the practice that was formerly attributed exclusively to the artist, has become a generalized category that implies the presence of others. Today we find its generalized form in various guises within the culture industry, in consulting, in information-technologies, in design and advertising, in tourism and finance, as well as in entertainment and research.

Yet there is also a spatial aspect that closely correlates with this kind of labor performance of the *Mobile Office*. As Paolo Virno furthermore pointed out, post-Fordist, immaterial labor takes on the traditional characteristics of political acting (*politische Handlung*). It has become a prerequisite to expose oneself to the gaze of the Other. And this requires a space that is structured like the public.

Metaphorically speaking, it is in the space of television where Hollein appears in order to make his spectacle public. At the same time, one needs to recognize that although the space of television is structured like the public, as is the stage for the musician in a concert, there is a traditionally distinct border or boundary between the one performing and the audience watching. The architecture of the stage produces, simply, a distance. For Virno this distance is being abolished in the new organization of labor. The monologue character of work disappears and the relationship to the Other becomes the constitutive prerequisite for labor that from now on needs to get along without a script. Yet as an architect, Hollein emphasizes not only the need for distance in the performance itself, but also explicitly in the design and use of the bubble. By pragmatically anticipating the new workers' reality he produces architecture for this very situation out of his own experience.

The workplaces of the young architect are "his flat … on the way to his building sites, the airplane, and his third work-place is his atelier." (12:55) His workplaces have no boundaries: his office is not only everywhere and mobile but also extended—living and working become one. The atelier, the airplane, and his flat need to allow all possible programs and a multitude of functions; they are all workplaces and places for living at the same time. Hollein lives and works anywhere, be it in his rocking chair or in his transparent pneumatic construction. The space for living and space for working converge.

Despite and precisely because of the convergence, the pneumatic bubble is an architectonic prototype of a new paradigm of a creative, entrepreneurial subject: the soft and cuddly sphere isolates the architect from his or her immediate surroundings. It produces an insular indoor climate in which the worker is immersed and thus—no matter where—becomes active, and is only then able to work. In other words the bubble is—as design—the precondition for nomadic and precarious modes of working, modulating itself, as Hollein points out, from place to place. As a kind of outstanding element, the iconic design is effective in two ways: on the one hand, the bubble is its own metaphor. It is its own thought bubble and represents the absolute monadic enclosure of the working subject. The bubble is not functionally determined; it is not a production space for a group of people but decidedly an ironically over-subscribed, proto-typic, single workplace of a boundless, world-spanning daily grind.

It is a technologically feasible and socially conceivable vision that Hollein presents on television. The above-mentioned two-minute clip that represents the *Mobile Office* is part of a series of utopias at the end of the 1960s that, as the art-historian and art critic Helmut Draxler states, are composed by technological and social utopias. Draxler argues that the pre-condition of these projects had been a stable and secure economic prosperity attributable to Keynesian economic policy. Next to technological and constructive innovations, this was accountable for conceiving feasible utopias for the near future—but not necessarily utopias of hope and salvation.[7]

The *Mobile Office* is a decidedly pragmatic vision of a workers' society. Hollein uses everyday objects that are—more or less—trivial and petty items accompanying modern life in 1969, emphasizing and demonstrating the normalcy and actuality of the project. In using these objects in a twisted way, he then also asserts their difference: the Hoover as compressor, the airplane as everyday vehicle, the suitcase to transport one's own dwelling, or the mobile phone. The portable bubble in which Hollein sits and works is introduced on television as something that everybody is familiar with in a more conventional form: the trailer, the caravan. Still the *Mobile Office* is not architecture in a conventional sense, but is part of a series of early projects of Hollein's that deal with the radical extension of the concept of architecture and design. By using and adopting artistic means and strategies, Hollein reacts to various social (but also technological) developments to make them, on the one hand, visible, and, on the other hand, possible to pursue and research, to extend and radicalize by means of architecture and design. The projects *Extension to the University of Vienna* (1960), the architecture capsule series *Nonphysical Environmental Control Kit* (1967), or the *Space-Spray Svobodair* (1968, with Peter Noever), to name just a few, deal with media and immaterial aspects of a man-made environment as architecture. Instead of built architecture, Hollein conceives an immaterial architecture of pure affect—a kind of excessive atmospheric simulation: the TV-set as an extension to the university, the Architecture pill to construct a non-physical environment, or, in collaboration with the Austrian office-furniture producer Svoboda, a spray that immediately changes the workers' atmosphere as a revolutionary way to improve the office.

These projects illustrate Hollein's singular approach to architecture: a system going beyond the three-dimensional object and extending everywhere as he emphasizes in his famous, manifesto-like text *Alles ist Architektur* (All is Architecture). The *Mobile Office* traces *Alles ist Architektur* in its full radicalism as Craig Buckley observes in his discussion of Hollein's manifesto:

> Between these images one begins to pick up an alternate repetition present in the manifesto, one that shifts from the image of the body to its extensions. Citing the "telephone booth," the "helmets of jet pilots," and the "development of space capsules and space suits," the expansion of the human environment proceeds by becoming smaller, departing from a "building of minimal size extended into global dimensions" to approach the contours of the subject. The

dynamic of extension and contraction stretches the paradoxically inclusive logic of the manifesto, which expands architecture to be identified with all things but regrounds this manifold in one thing: architecture.[8]

The Mobile Office takes up the postulation that everything could be architecture, and returns to architecture. In contrast to all immaterialized experiments, the Mobile Office is tangible architecture. The inflatable bubble is a radical design for a nomadic work-life that is able to modulate itself from place to place. It is a hybrid object between the arts: it is architecture, it is installation. And, most importantly, it is being broadcast on television—it is pure communication.

Instantaneous programming

In his texts, Hollein stresses the effects of architecture, the impact that the environment has on people. For him this environment is always already man-made, in his sense, an artificial environment. In *Alles ist Architektur* he describes a topologic situation: men and women are part of an environment that they themselves construct, but it conditions every single one of them, as well as society (the individual is always and already part of a group, a society). At the same time, people act on this environment; they extend it and re-create new artificial environments. Thus Hollein writes: "Again and again, physically and psychologically, the human being extends his physical and psychological area, affects his environment in the broadest sense."[9]

Thus, the vast plane on which the bubble is staged is already constructed as an environment made by people and already structured as a world-spanning (cybernetic) infrastructure. The field is an open, extensive plane that is not yet functionally determined, yet is equipped with all the technology needed to blow up a bubble or to plug in a telephone. Furthermore, it neither follows a visible grid, nor has a quantitative, observable order. The infrastructure and its knots are just there, they are assumed, do not require highlighting, or even definition. They are just there, as Hollein would relate: "and everywhere … I can blow up this thing." (09:35)

The bubble is the extreme version of an enclosed minimal environment. It is, in Hollein's terms, a better contemporary dwelling, architecture that goes beyond mere function, that ensures physical protection but also offers psychic shelter and at the same time acts as a symbol. It is a kind of architecture that is, on the one hand, an apparatus that isolates one from inhospitable (man-made) ambiances, as do the space suit and the space capsule, and at the same time it also allows for communication with others far away. It is an architecture that adapts itself to every single place.

As an envelope conceived for an individual, the pneumatic construction actualizes itself in each and every situation and with each new program. It is, in a twofold way, programmatically open. First, it is its relationality toward the outside. It ideally can constantly adapt itself to its context, as Hollein emphasizes. Secondly, it is in itself a functionally open interior. Depending on its use, the portable house—as Hollein would call his design in the 1969 television broadcast—becomes a nomadic dwelling or a workplace, finally becoming the Mobile Office. Similar to simple objects of minimal art—as the German philosopher Juliane Rebentisch points out—that are simultaneously readable as thing and as sign, that addresses the observer not only as producer of meaning, but at the same time always already subverts the production of meaning,[10] the bubble of the Mobile Office allows a constant programming of the functions of its space.

The dwelling becomes what one uses it for. In the specific case of the TV performance it becomes a workplace—the Mobile Office. If Hollein had slept in it, it would be probably known today as the "Mobile Bedroom." The bubble's distinct quality is to adapt itself to every situation, as the contemporary worker needs to adapt him- or herself to every situation. The design takes up the dictum of a continuously required adaptability, of an architecture of maximized flexibility. But the design does not simply produce a flexible object that adapts itself to functions that are assigned in advance, but, more in the spirit of structuralism, it produces an object without attributes, that, depending on use, is in the process of becoming.

With his design of the Mobile Office Hollein affirms a specific situation in which the modern, flexible, working nomad is thrown out into the inhospitable, sheer endless spaces of non-places (to use a phrase from Marc Augé) that is part of an even larger infrastructure that guarantees the same standards worldwide. Hollein's design, however, withdraws from an idea of efficiency that would describe space through a dense catalog of requirements, and creates an object, that is—due to its material qualities and its figuration—able to house a multitude of programs. At the same time the practice of the architect alters in order to become performative: be it the acting out of the architect him- or herself, or be it the drawing.

Notes

1. This research was funded by the Austrian Science Fund (FWF): P 22448-G21.
2. Other examples that I discuss elsewhere are: the Invention of Office-Landscaping by Eberhard and Wolfgang Schnelle, the Fun Palace by Cedric Price and Joan Littlewood, Herman Hertzberger's Centraal Beheer, or the Bed-In Performance by

John Lennon and Yoko Ono. See: Andreas Rumpfhuber, *Architektur immaterieller Arbeit* (Architecture of Immaterial Labor) (Vienna: Turia und Kant, 2013). Open Access Version: http://www.oapen.org/search?keyword=rumpfhuber

3. The numbers in brackets depict the timecode of the DVD I received from the Austrian Broadcasting Company, ORF Kundendienst, that was broadcast on December 7, 1969. See: Dieter O. Holzinger, "Das österreichische Portrait," DVD Archivs des Österreichischen Rundfunks ORF, 2008. Hollein's original statement is, "Ich bin nicht so ein Architekt der nur baut. Mich interessiert Verschiedenes. Auch die Werbung und dergleichen. Ich mache Produktvorschläge. Ich bin so etwas wie eine *Idea-Man*."
4. See: Ulrich Bröckling, *Das unternehmerische Selbst, Soziologie einer Subjektivierungsform* (Frankfurt: Suhrkamp, 2007), particularly Chapter 3.2.
5. Maurizio Lazzarato, "Immaterial Labour," in *Radical Thought in Italy: A Potential Politics*, Paolo Virno and Michael Hardt, eds (Minneapolis: University of Minnesota Press, 2006).
6. Paolo Virno, *Grammatik der Multitude* (Vienna: Turia and Kant, 2005), 67. Italian original edition, Madrid: Traficantes de Sueños, 2001.
7. Helmut Draxler, *Die Utopie des Designs, Ein archäologischer Führer für alle die nicht dabei waren*, exhibition catalogue (Kunstverein Munich: 1994, no pagination).
8. Craig Buckley, "From Absolute to Everything: Taking Possession in 'Alles ist Architektur,'" *Grey Room* 28 (Summer 2007): 114.
9. Hans Hollein, *Alles ist Architektur*: "Physisch und psychisch wiederholt, transformiert, erweitert [der Mensch] seinen physischen und psychischen Bereich, bestimmt er ›Umwelt‹ im weitesten Sinne." "Construction" magazine for architecture and urban planning, 23 year, Issue 1/2 1968 Vienna. Edited by Central Association of Austrian Architects, eds. Hans Hollein, Oswald Oberhuber, and Gustav Peichl, in "All Things Architecture – An Exhibition on the theme of Death" 27 May to 5 July, 1970, Municipal Museum Mönchengladbach.
10. See Juliane Rebentisch, *Ästhetik der Installation* (Frankfurt: Suhrkamp, 2003), 55ff.

Part II

The concept of architectural labor

Chapter 5

Work[1]
Peggy Deamer

At a recent symposium, a young audience member asked the distinguished panelists what she could expect from a career in architecture. One of the panelists answered fervently: "Architecture is not a career. It is a calling!"

Prologue: How did we get here?

For a profession that seems to have it all—architects' creativity, unlike artists, is professionally sanctioned; we make things that matter to the world—how could we be victims of the same capitalist ideology which, in the form of Christianity, asks the poor to feel righteous about their poverty?

My first answer is—we don't believe we do work. We go to the office, we get a paycheck, but as a profession architecture produces designs, neither mere products nor services. We know we are producing an object (indeed, a big one) but we don't like to think that we produce a "commodity." We compare ourselves to doctors and lawyers, but believe our work is too creative and culturally significant to be properly filed under "service sector." Consequently, we fail to conceptualize our work *as* work.

In comparison to manufacturing jobs, we lack security structures—unions, guilds, or institutionally sanctioned labor laws—that prevent architectural staff from being fired with no cause, working for no pay, or enduring oppressive hours. Considering that the majority of architectural staff are asked to work 70-hour weeks at an average of $55K a year, we earn $15 an hour, roughly the same as my daughter earns babysitting, and are no better off than factory workers. In comparison to service professionals, the starting salary for architects, with comparable years of education at a top school like Yale, is less than a third of that of lawyers and doctors; six years out, that percentage rises but lingers just above 45 percent.[2]

My second premise is—we have a pathetic notion of design that isolates it from work. Architects design, constructors build; we do art, they do work. This division, which is both conceptual and contractual, keeps architecture from not only achieving the above described financial and monetary rewards, but also social relevance and personal satisfaction.[3] It precludes social relevance because we do not see ourselves in the class of workers. In discussions about minimum wage, in reading about the strikes of non-union food-service providers, in producing designs that are built by indentured labor in Asia and the Middle East—we don't relate. More than this, Marx has made clear that labor is a social issue, not merely because it relates worker to worker, but because it permeates every aspect of our home and psychic life.[4]

The first two parts of this chapter attack architecture's "work-aphasia" from these two observations. Part I exposes polemics about art and creativity that

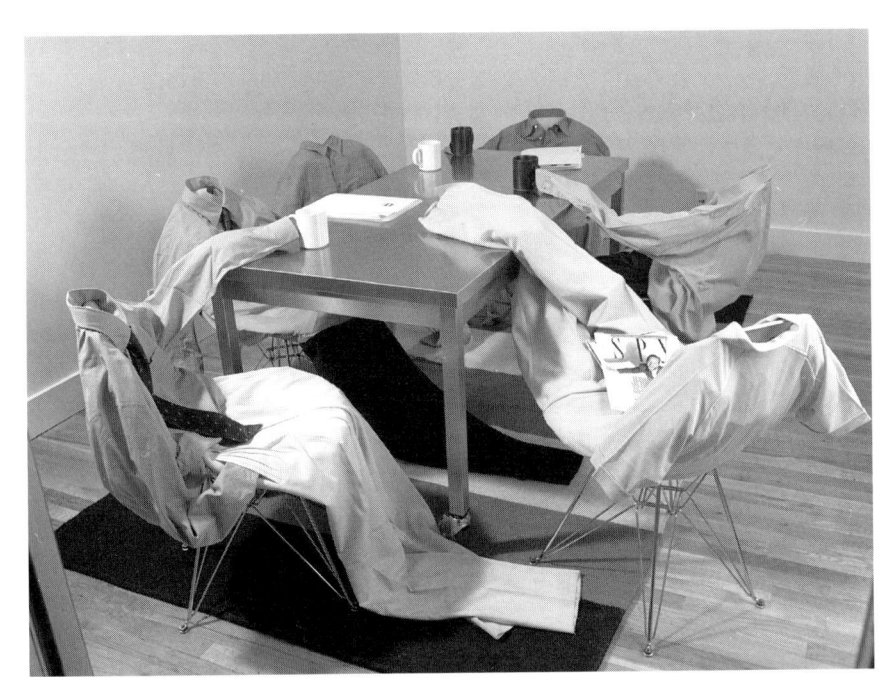

Figure 5.1 *Casual Fridays, Table Top*, 2002, Maureen Connor. Image one of three from PowerPoint presentation. Although adherence to workplace dress codes has long been an aspect of "performance evaluation," Casual Friday has brought about a transformation of identity and self image within the corporate structure. Fearful of what appeared to be the breakdown of the implicit rules of dress that helped define social and economic boundaries, institutions suddenly needed to find new ways to represent their internal hierarchies and power structures by actively controlling employees' appearance. This included the publication of official dress codes that were then interpreted by self-appointed image consultants, seminars, and self help publications. Bringing together found materials from all sides of the Casual Friday negotiations, this installation used PowerPoint presentation, the technology of corporate communication, to continue the artist's ongoing study and analysis of the aesthetics of power and the power of aesthetics in the contemporary workplace.

refuse to be divorced from issues of work/labor,[5] value, and money. Art practices are instructive because, if architects think we do art, not work, it's surprising to show that artists *do* think they do work. Part II attacks positions claiming that work in general is inherently not fun, creative, or aesthetic. Theorists, both utopian and practical, who espouse the creative nature of work, offer liberating perspectives on reconstituted and re-managed formulations of work. After this, the implications for architecture are explored.

Part I: Art as work/labor

I've always held the belief that art is labor that deserves proper compensation. It is often difficult to assert this, in all levels of the art system. I'm sure that all involved would agree that art has 'value,' but where the work lies, and who is paying for it becomes a very clouded issue. I have issues with the premise that art is its own reward.[6]

Christine Hill

While aesthetics tends to hold itself apart from issues of labor, the two are historically intertwined. The appearance of labor as a concept distinct from feudal obligations in the late 1400s depended on the artisans who supplied the goods for export trade; the fact that goods came from "free" work allowed it to be conceptualized as exchange value.[7] Even if artisanal work was not transmitted from workers to employers or exchanged among independent traders, it was central to the mercantile system foreshadowing capitalism.[8] When industrialization broke the hold guilds had on "free" artisans, they became autonomous workers; at the same time, their work, like all work, became exchangeable as labor-power. With this shift, the distinction between artists and artisans took hold, as artisans were subsumed by assembly production. Yet even within this distinction there are shades; writers, for example, like assembly-workers, were paid by the piece, the delivery of manuscripts being analogous to the weavers' delivery of a bolt of cloth.[9]

Marx suggests that mental production such as art has the potential to escape capitalist ownership of labor. Indeed, we are all potentially artists, the term "artist" existing only in societies framed/defined by the division of labor.

> The exclusive concentration of artistic talent in particular individuals ... is a consequence of division of labour. Even if in certain social conditions, everyone were an excellent painter, that would by no means exclude the possibility of each of them being also an original painter, so that here too the difference between "human"

and "unique" labour amounts to sheer nonsense. In any case, with a communist organisation of society, there disappears the subordination of the artist to local and national narrowness which arises entirely from division of labour.[10]

But art work is *not* free, he says, when it plays into the hands of capitalism. "A writer is a productive laborer in so far as he produces ideas, but in so far as he enriches the publisher who publishes his works, he is a wage laborer for the capitalist."[11] While Marx clearly doesn't enjoy this capitalist bracketing of occupations, he nevertheless points to its inevitability.

In the early twentieth century, Russian Constructivists added another spin, pressing to prove that art *was* labor. Given the political atmosphere, they had to prove that art was proletarian, not bourgeois, and did so by emphasizing its kinship to manufacturing. Vladimir Mayakovsky, in the journal *Contemporary Architecture* (1928), lists the necessary requirements for poetry:

> 1. Poetry is manufacture. A difficult, very complex kind, but a manufacture.
> 2. Instruction in poetical work doesn't consist in the study of already fixed and delimited types of poetical objects, but a study of the means for executing all kinds of poetical work, a study of productive procedures that help us make new things.
> 3. Innovation in material and devices is the basis of every poetical product. ...
> 9. Only by approaching art as manufacture can you eliminate chance, arbitrariness of taste and individual judgment ... instead of mystically pondering a poetic theme you will have the power to tackle any pressing problem accurately with full poetic qualifications.[12]

Likewise, Alexander Malinovsky, aka Bogdanov, wrote:

> Creation, whether technological, socio-economic, political, domestic, scientific, or artistic, represents a kind of labour, and like labour, is composed of organizational (or disorganizational) endeavours. It is exactly the same as labour, whose product is not the repetition of a ready-made stereotype but is something "new". There is not and cannot be a strict demarcation between creation and ordinary labour; not only are there all the points of interchange, but it is even impossible often to say which of the two designations is more applicable ...[13]

These inspiring pronouncements, while forced by communist conformism, demonstrate a commitment not only to art as labor, but also to co-existence within a work-defined social fabric.

This attitude was shared by German Marxists of the same period, although they, unlike Russian artists, were looking at socialism from the outside. Certain members of the Frankfurt School, Walter Benjamin principal among them, picked up on the idea that work could be the model for art; others, including Herbert Marcuse, found that art was the model for work. As is well known, Benjamin, in his "Work of Art in the Age of Mechanical Reproduction," links mental, artistic production to material, technical production. In this he followed Bertold Brecht's instructions for "Epic Theatre" which negated the divisions between author and actors, actors and stage-hands, and actors/stage-hands and audience; all were seen as creative workers. Marcuse, on the other hand, while incorporating Theodor Adorno's belief in the autonomy of art, nevertheless espoused that the aesthetic dimension, in which freedom is imagined, prefigures material labor.[14]

Like the Constructivists, certain art practices in the late 1960s and 1970s explored the infiltration of work into art practice. To escape any effete notions of art, the Artist Placement Group (APG) staged events that were equally performance and financial negotiation.[15] Making sure that art was not held apart from systems of value, labor, and social change, they put union representatives on their "board," placed their artists in industry, and sought and achieved positions in the government.

More recently, in this same tradition, Relational Aesthetics, the name given to a particular trend in art of the 1990s by the French art critic Nicholas Bourriaud, has promoted artists who present "models of action" in the real world and respond to "contemporary precariousness" with a "regime of aesthetics" "based on speed, intermittence, blurring and fragility."

> [Contemporary] art presents itself as an editing console that manipulates social forms, reorganizes them and incorporates them in original scenarios, deconstructing the script on which their illusory legitimacy was grounded. The artist de-programmes in order to re-programme, suggesting that there are other possible usages for the techniques, tools and spaces at our disposition.[16]

In her 1996–7 "Volksboutique" in Berlin, Christine Hill, who "always held the belief that art is labor that deserves proper compensation"[17] and who is associated with Relational Aesthetics, managed a thrift shop/sculpture where tea was served, inexpensive clothes were available, and discussions were encouraged. When she franchised her boutique in 1997 for Documenta X in Kassel, she ascribed the role of thrift shop salesgirl to stand-ins. In another piece, she made an audio guide "tour" for which she charged $12. In yet another, to the outrage of the museum/gallery owner, she included a vending machine that yielded a profit.[18] Also associated with Relational Aesthetics, artist Andrea Fraser, in her 1989 "Museum Highlights," took the role of docent at the Philadelphia Museum of Art and described not the artifacts but the history of social difficulties experienced by the Museum.[19] Another, Pierre Huyghe, directed other artists to make videos of a purchased Japanese manga figure he and partner Phillipe Parreno named Annlee, then transferred the copyrights of those videos to the figure's private "association."[20] Another, Rirkrit Tiravanija, cooked and served food to the visitors in his exhibition "Untitled" 2002—a work bought by the Guggenheim Museum with the aid of American Express who handled its programming in its PR department and created subsequent programs and events.[21]

Bourriaud's Relational Aesthetics has been criticized by artists who operate outside the museum/gallery system for its pseudo-social engagement with a rarified audience. Nevertheless, the "Relational Aesthetic"[22] artists operate with complete confidence that their work functions within a system of value that can be toyed with. However, an alternate view of that value-cum-art relationship is offered by Jacques Rancière. Rancière stresses that work is shaped by the logic of art, not the other way around.[23] In his *The Politics of Aesthetics: The Distribution of the Sensible* (2004), the "aesthetic regime" of art (in contrast to the more trivial "ethical regime" or "poetic regime"), being "formal" and "sensuous,"[24] shapes our political identities and with it our attitude about work. Democracy, for example, is not simply a form of government; it is a specific mode of symbolic structuring only performed by art, whose forms "life uses to shape itself."[25] He suggests that Benjamin was wrong in saying that mechanical reproduction/art made available a new visibility of art to the masses; rather, the aesthetic regime was in place before the mechanical/reproductive mode of thinking could begin. In *The Nights of Labour*, Rancière contends that workers in the 1830 French Revolution were not fighting against the hardships they experienced, but against the constricted nature of their lives. At night, instead of recuperating for the next day's work, they read the works of poets and writers who spent their nights producing a language of liberation. After appropriating this other language and performing these other lives, the workers had the strategies needed for rebellion. Art practice "anticipates work because it carries out its principle: the transformation of sensible matter into the community's self-representation."[26]

Whether art precedes its connection to labor (Marcuse, Rancière) or succeeds it (Constructivism, Benjamin, APG, Relational Aesthetics), artists and aestheticians have historically probed the thin line between the two. Why has architecture not listened? Not noticed?

Part II: Work as art/play

A spider conducts operations that resemble those of a weaver, and a bee puts to shame many an architect in the construction of her cells. But what distinguishes the worst architect from the best of bees is this, that the architect raises his structure in imagination before he erects it in reality.[27]

(Karl Marx)

Just as the tradition of art-as-labor suggests that architecture as a profession should consider "labor value," the tradition that sees human work as inherently imaginative, creative, and self-realizing should be equally embraced by architects. Creativity in architecture rests not on an ever-expanding categorical inclusion of form-making but rather on an imaginative approach to problem solving.

The essential writing for nearly all who explore the liberating, play-structured aspects of work is Friedrich Schiller's *Letters Upon The Aesthetic Education of Man* (1794). Schiller himself does not address "work," but he does examine play/art's essential role in civil society. Civilization, Schiller posits, has suppressed the "sensuous impulse" to serve the "form impulse," such that when the sensuous emerges out of its repressed state, it is destructive. Art and play, Schiller argues, overcome this negative eruption by transcending the false dichotomy between sense and form. Art, as the "reasonable" realm of the sensual, brings together the sensuous and the formal.[28] Play, allowing art to be deployed, makes both the sensuous and the formal "contingent" and hence capable of synthesis.[29] In a defense against the possible attack that art, in being aligned with "mere" play, is degraded, Schiller writes, "But what is meant by a mere play, when we know … that it is play which makes man complete and develops simultaneously his twofold nature? What you style limitation … I name enlargement."[30]

Working from Schiller, Gottfried Semper justified his aesthetic position in his "Prolegomena" to *Style in the Technical and Tectonic Arts; or, Practical Aesthetics* (1860) by appeal to pleasure and play. As he writes,

> On a more exalted plane, what we mean by terms like 'sense of beauty,' 'delight in beauty,' 'enjoyment of art,' and 'artistic instinct' is analogous to those instincts, pleasures, and gratifications that govern the way in which we maintain our telluric existence … Surrounded by a world full of wonder and forces whose laws we may divine … we conjure up in play the perfection that is lacking … In such play we satisfy our cosmogonic instinct.[31]

As has been described, Marx's ideal socialist society, shaped by his readings of Schiller and other German Romantic philosophers,[32] envisions all workers as creative and everyone as an artist. "In a communist society there are no painters but only people who engage in painting among other activities."[33] But when work serves capital, "freedom" is only found *outside* of work. Marx, in other words, sets out the negative image of labor imposed by capitalism that subsequent, more optimistic theorists have striven to revise.

Utopians go back and forth between espousing Marx's negative view of industrial production and endorsing a hoped-for society where all work is imaginative. For example, where Welsh social reformer Robert Owen, in his "Report to the County of Lanark" (1820), structured his New Lanark mill town to limit work to eight hours—leaving time for reading, gardening, and exercise—French socialist and phalanx theorizer Charles Fourier, in his *Theory of the Four Movements and the General Destinies* (1808), insists that, if "industry is the fate assigned to us by the Creator, how can one believe that he wishes to force us into it—that he does not know how to bring to bear some nobler means, some enticement capable of transforming work with pleasure."[34] Where American socialist Edward Bellamy, in his utopian novel *Looking Backward: 2000–1887* (1888), describes a regime dictating the strict division of work tasks and the division between work and leisure,[35] English textile designer and Marxist/socialist William Morris, in his *News from Nowhere* (1890) rebuttal to *Looking Backward*, describes how people in his ideal community live out Marx's vision to "hunt in the morning, fish in the afternoon, rear cattle in the evening, criticize after dinner,"[36] changing jobs for the pleasure of edification. Ebenezer Howard's precise division of private work and public pleasure in his *Garden City* was countered by Frank Lloyd Wright's insistence, in "Broadacre City," that "our leisure, our culture and our work will be our own and as nearly as possible, One."[37] Le Corbusier, not necessarily in disagreement with any particular previous architect/utopian but nevertheless insisting on the essential value of (real) play, says, "Only those who play are serious types …. The mountain climbers, the rugby players and the card players, and the gamblers, are frauds, for they do not play."[38]

If these utopians, in giving a picture of *ideal* work, only underscore its actual unpleasantness, twentieth century philosophers of work, who fall into one of two camps—neo-Marxists and pragmatists—look at creative aspects of work within capitalism. Herbert Marcuse picks up Marx's philosophic probing of Schiller's emphasis on the role of play in a civil society; Marcuse contests the labor/leisure divide dominating the discourse of German sociologists such as Max Weber. Equating Schiller's dichotomy of the sensuous versus formal instincts with Freud's pleasure versus reality principles, work is elevated by Marcuse to the pleasure principle. In *Eros and Civilization: A Philosophical Inquiry into Freud* (1955), he writes:

> [T]he abolition of toil, the amelioration of the environment ... flow directly from the pleasure principle, and, at the same time, they constitute *work* [his emphasis] which associates individuals to "greater unities"; no longer confined within the mutilating domination of the performance principle, they modify the impulse without deflecting it from its aim. There is sublimation and, consequently, culture; but this sublimation proceeds in a system of expanding and enduring libidinal relations, which are in themselves work relations.[39]

This condition is not pervasive, but individuals are capable of tapping into their libidinal energy to transform production. "The biological drive becomes a cultural drive."[40]

Recent neo-Marxists emphasize the communal, cooperative, and collaborative nature of contemporary work. Antonio Negri and Michael Hardt's *The Labor of Dionysus* (1977 Italian; 1994 English) and Maurizio Lazzarato's "Immaterial Labor" (1996) analyze "labor that produces the informational and cultural content of the commodity." In the transition from a service to an information economy, Negri and Hardt say, "cooperation is completely immanent in the labouring process itself."[41] As Lazzarato puts it, work is now the domain of "mass intellectuality" and,

> can be defined as the capacity to activate and manage productive cooperation. In this phase, workers are expected to become 'active subjects' in the coordination of the various functions of production, instead of being subjected to it as simple command. We arrive at a point where a collective learning process becomes the heart of productivity, because it is no longer a matter of finding different ways of composing or organizing already existing job functions, but of looking for new ones.[42]

Because the old model for describing production and consumption is no longer useful, one should turn to the aesthetic model involving "author, reproduction, and reception:" if "author" loses its individuality, "reproduction" becomes organization, and "reception" is also communication.[43]

Alexander Galloway, speculating about post-capitalism, sees play—the ultimate goal—as already embedded in our capitalist production structures.

> After trying to understand how to imagine a life after capitalism, and seeing how this is both done and undone in everything from *World of Warcraft* to the stratagems of Donald Rumsfeld, what one sees is how two of the hitherto most

> useful tropes for communicating a life after or outside capitalism—networks and play—are slowly shifting from what Rumsfeld calls the unknown unknowns … to the known unknowns, and perhaps simply to the known. … What is clear is that the possibility of life after capitalism is often articulated today through a utilization of the very essence of capitalism. Play is work and networks are sovereigns.[44]

Like Lazzarato, Galloway insists that the play-oriented side of work can wreak havoc on the existing system.

The pragmatist trajectory of work-play-art centers on the writings of John Dewey who, in his analysis of education, valorized play as essential to development. In holding a view of education that was playful and child-like while also encouraging a Protestant work ethic, he redefined work to mean something like play—spontaneous, voluntary, fulfilling. Dewey writes:

> What has been termed active occupation includes both play and work. In their intrinsic meaning, play and industry are by no means so antithetical to one another as is often assumed, any sharp contrast being due to undesirable social conditions. Both involve ends consciously entertained and the selection and adaptations of materials and processes designed to effect the desired ends. The difference between them is largely one of time-span, influencing the directness of the connection of means and ends. In play, the interest is more direct.[45]

Play passes into work when "(t)he demand for continuous attention is greater, and more intelligence must be shown in selecting and shaping means."[46]

Donald Schön, whose doctoral thesis in philosophy at Harvard was on Dewey's theory of inquiry, applied Dewey's pragmatist philosophy to his theories of organizations. Arguing that "change" was a fundamental feature of modern life and recognizing that companies, social movement, and governments were essentially systems of change, he explored them as learning systems of "groping and inductive process(es)." His interest in jazz linked work to improvisation and "thinking on one's feet;" through a feedback loop of experience, work, like art and music, is "practiced." Famously, he also said that an organization, to stimulate change, must create conditions in which the individual practitioner is committed to an action because it is intrinsically satisfying, not because it provides external rewards.

Peter Drucker, "the man who invented corporate society" and who was the guru of corporate management from the 1950s through the 1980s, forecasts, like Schön, capitalism's decentralization, privatization, and marketing. But in his *Post-Capitalist Society*, Drucker goes farther than Schön in describing the nature of work in late capitalism. In the eighteenth century, Drucker says, the worker's knowledge was applied to tools; in the nineteenth and early twentieth centuries, it was applied to productivity (Taylorization); today, he says, it is being applied to knowledge itself. Today, "knowledge workers" *own* the means of production: that is, knowledge. Because the skills held by these workers—research, product design, fabrication, marketing, advertising, customer consulting, financing, contracting—allow technical insights to be linked to marketing strategy and financial acumen, the traditional distinction between goods and services breaks down. Moreover, the traditional factors of production—land, labor, and capital—are restraints rather than drivers; indeed, no class, he points out, has risen or fallen as quickly as the blue-collar worker. Emphasizing here and in earlier writings that organizations have been "too thing focused" and produced too *many* things, he advocates "planned abandonment," non-infatuation with yesterday's successes, stream-lining, and embracing destabilization. In addition, the goal of organizational management is to recognize that the most valuable resource is the worker (the most flexible and intelligent component of the system); to construct alternative, specialist-based models of organizations; and to acknowledge that the real business of business is "not how to do things right but how to find the right thing to do."

Work of this sort, which architecture epitomizes—not because it makes form but because it organizes itself so fluidly—sounds pretty fun.

Figure 5.2 *Casual Fridays, Exhausted*, 2002, Maureen Connor.

Part III: Architecture

The two trajectories followed here yield remarkably similar projections for post-Fordist work: creativity applied not to object-making but to process; destabilization; organizational flexibility; planned obsolescence; empowering the autonomy of the worker. Architecture increasingly operates this way even if its overt structures do not yet reflect it. Design today is not merely the conjuring of an object, but a problem-defining, problem-solving, information-structuring activity that, on the basis of understood conditions and rules, defines a specific course of action.[47] Instead of it being done by "an architect," architectural work is the creative manipulation of specialized design developed by a socially diverse panoply of contributors. Increasingly, architectural work is distributed and dispersed, collaborative and entrepreneurial, knowledge-based and open-sourced, specialized and flexible.

The benefit for architects—if we endorse the idea that our knowledge/service is spatial, material, and organizational innovation—is a reconception of our compensation and our place in the social fabric.

A reconception of compensation begins with the elimination of percentage-of-construction fees that reinforces the disastrous idea that our value resides in the object we produce and not in the knowledge that produced it. It not only wrongly places value on the one-offness of the object but also, as piece-work, aligns us with the most degrading form of compensation. Marx is clear on this: "Piece-wages therefore lay the foundation of … the hierarchically organized system of exploitation and oppression."

> The quality of the labour is here (in piece-work) controlled by the work itself, which must be of the average perfection if the piece-price is to be paid in full. Piece-wages become, from this point of view, the most fruitful source of reduction of wages and capitalistic cheating …
>
> Given piece-wage, it is naturally the personal interest of the labourer to strain his labour-power as intensely as possible; this enables the capitalist to raise more easily the normal degree of intensity of labour. It is moreover now the personal interest of the labourer to lengthen the working day, since with it his daily or weekly wages rise.[48]

If you are an architect, this likely sounds familiar.

Alternatives to this not only resist the piece-work model of compensation but also its architect-as-subordinate-to-owner framework. The most obvious option is to *be* the developer-owner. But more crafty and less financially demanding approaches exist. In the Integrated Project Delivery use of the Special Purpose

Entity, a type of limited liability company, the owner puts aside an agreed-upon amount of money determined to be the project's worth; the architect and the contractors (and others) provide services at cost so they, in any case, do not lose money. It is agreed that there can be no lawsuits. If and when the work costs are lower than the target cost, there is a three-way split of savings. Likewise, pay by percentage-of-profit, a calculation used to pay independent project managers, would identify the value added by architectural intervention, a figure that would not be difficult to identify if records were sought. Another fee alternative is the formation of a publicly traded company that, like tech start-ups, relies on investor banking on the intelligence architectural firms can bring to the beauty, procurement, performance, and maintenance of the built environment. Skepticism regarding the ability of an architectural corporation to produce consistent shareholder profits is alleviated when one considers the expertise—environmental, material, economic, structural, procedural—available to the architect via parametrics and building information modeling (BIM). [49] The spread of expertise and the invasion of architectural intelligence into areas once divorced from the discipline—for example, BIM management, facilities management, or construction management[50]—are potential architectural domains.

Models of compensation other than the existing hourly or yearly salary present themselves for architectural staff as well. Knowledge-based organizations compete for the best and the brightest and hence consistently refine their modes of compensation to balance appeal to and retention of top prospects with firm profitability. That architecture firms sadly do not yet approach their hiring and compensation in this manner is surely related to the fact that architecture school graduates, despite seven years of expensive education, present themselves as cheap labor. Be that as it may, in lieu of flat compensation rates, incentive-driven wages should be considered. Co-ownership, performance-based compensation, "pay-at-risk," employee stock options, or other firm owner-employee contracts sharing value creation and profit are common in new-economy, knowledge work compensation models. In *Capital*, Marx adds this footnote in his discussion about piece-work:

> Even Watts, the apologetic, remarks: 'It would be a great improvement to the system of piece-work, if all the men employed on a job were partners in the contract, each according to his abilities, instead of one man being interested in overworking his fellows for his own benefit.[51]

If we never again want to hear a potential architectural employee say that they understand why they will get paid next to nothing since they know the firm they hope to work for earns next to nothing, we also need to look to unions. Unions—the modern incarnation of the guild system so admired by architecture for its designer/maker integration but totally overlooked as a human resource apparatus for the profession—have traditionally served creative organizations. The Screen Actors Guild (SAG, now combined with the American Federation of Television and Radio Artists (AFTRA) to create SAG-AFTRA), was founded in 1933 to stop exploitation of Hollywood actors signed by major studios to multi-year contracts that had no restrictions on work hours or any required breaks. Actors Equity, founded in 1913 representing American actors and stage managers, negotiates wages and working conditions and provides health and pension plans for its members. In the same vain, the Freelance Workers Union, formed in 1995, offers health, disability, and life insurance and has recently opened a Brooklyn walk-in health clinic for its members. Their resources include corporate discounts, job postings, and contract deliberation tutorials.

These unions, traditionally militant organizations whose members have been willing to strike, are today less anti-management and more communities of support and promotion. As Lowell Peterson, the director of the Writers Guild of America, East writes,

> I do not have the wisdom to proclaim whether a national economy can be sustained on the basis of moving around pieces of paper representing capital, or on the basis of creating and selling innovative ideas without actually making physical products. But I do think the economy will be based on services for quite some time. The Writers Guild of America, East knows how to represent knowledge workers … (who) build … stories for television, radio, movie screens, and the internet (and for whom) employment is contingent, job-to-job, script-to-script, show-to-show.[52]

These alternate forms of compensation and security operating in the heart of capitalism should not be held as perfect solutions for humanist, aesthetic production. But the discomfort we surely feel when trying on these other models of organization indicates the inexcusable conceptual distance between architectural work and other labor structures. The scary thing is not the unfamiliarity of these structures; it is our righteous ignorance of them.

The social benefit of labor lessons for architecture is being social identified *at all*. Workers identify with workers. While many of the artists associated with Relational Aesthetics refused to have their work exhibited at the Guggenheim Museum in Abu Dhabi—a building built by indentured labor—architects remain unmoved. Pleas by Human Rights Watch for architects designing buildings in the Emirates and China to pressure their clients to reform bad construction practices have fallen on deaf ears. Architects rightly claim that they are not at the negotiating table, but sadly refuse to reflect on how their disengagement impacts this tragedy. Architecture, either in the form of the American Institute of Architects (AIA) or the office structure, needs to shed its work-aphasia and identify as an organization of workers. Only then will its cultural caché have real social value.

At this transitional moment in the profession, when design responsibility and financial savvy are shared amongst various players, the constitution of a new model for architectural practice is entirely open. Now is the time to think expansively about what we want this new practice to look like and how its organization might be linked to larger social, political, and economic formations. As newly enlightened players in the labor game, architects are free to move directly toward an imagined ideal.

Notes

1. Reprinted with permission of *Perspecta*, Yale School of Architecture. "Work," *Perspecta 47: Money* (2014): 27–39.
2. See Phil Bernstein's article "Money, Value, Architects, Buildings," in *Perspecta 47: Money* (2014): 14–20. I am indebted to him for sharing and expanding on the indignation expressed here about the profession of architecture.
3. While the division between design and construction has existed since the Renaissance, work-aphasia and the unhappiness it causes has not. Between the Renaissance and the Industrial Revolution, drawings produced by the architect were intentionally incomplete to allow for the input of the constructor's craft. The drawings described the effect to be achieved and were considered objects of beauty in their own right. During the Industrial Revolution, when craft in construction was at risk of being spread out over a number of trades, architects and craftsmen together fought the effects of the division of labor by turning to the interior as the provenance of synthesized design and industrially produced craft. In the twentieth century, in keeping with the (popular?) turn in economic concern from production to consumption, architects saw themselves as producing not just the modern, clean, unsentimental building but the modern, healthy, unsentimental citizen. While this concern for the client as opposed to the constructor/laborer was initially ethical and public in nature, it quickly became practical and private as architects aimed to please their clients, not educate them. The architect's social concern, having shifted from builder to owner/user, disappeared all together.
4. James Surowiecki describes how low-margin enterprises like McDonald's, depending on cheap labor for its 6-cents-on-the-dollar profit, need to be re-conceived. It is not merely that McDonald's needs to pay more, "It isn't enough to make bad jobs better. We need to create better jobs." One can't dismiss the similarity between architecture and McDonald's as low-margin industries. How many times have we heard the excuse

of the under-paid staff member: "How can I ask for more money when I know the boss isn't paid properly either?" James Surowiecki, "The Pay Is Too Damn Low," *The New Yorker*, 12 August, 2013. http://www.newyorker.com/magazine/2013/08/12/the-pay-is-too-damn-low (accessed 9 September, 2014).

5. If the term "labor" has a negative connotation—work indicates use-value, labor indicates exchange value; work is distinctly human while labor is bestial, never-ending, animal-like—it also correctly insists that production is organized by a system of value that is socially constructed.

6. Regine, "Interview with Christine Hill," *We Make Money Not Art Blog*, 4 July, 2007. http://we-make-money-not-art.com/archives/2007/07/interview-with-20.php#.UgRUaxbq2Do (accessed 5 May, 2012); see also Lucy Lippard and Barbara Steiner, eds., *Inventory: The Work of Christine Hill and Volksboutique* (Ostfildern, Germany: Hatje Cantz, 2004).

7. Richard Biernacki, *The Fabrication of Labor: Germany and Britain 1640–1914* (Berkeley: University of California Press, 1997), 215. Biernacki continues on the following page:

> As early as the 1470s, Italian administrators who wrote on government policy identified labor as the primary source of a state's wealth. A century later, the noted economist Giovanni Botero reaffirmed the centrality of labor when he said that neither the gold mines of the New World nor the landed estates of the Old produced so much wealth as "the industrie of men and the multitude of Artes."

8. Ibid, 235. Biernacki continues:

> During the first century of liberal commercialism in Britain, the belief persisted that workers delivered their labor only under the compulsions of law and hunger. Many enterprises in pottery, mining, and textiles bound their laborers by servile terms of indenture that held them to the same employer for terms of one to twenty years. After the middle of the eighteenth century, employers began to rely upon cash rather than coercive stipulations to secure labor. The opinion slowly and tentatively took hold that workers could be stimulated to work harder by the promise of higher earnings.

9. Biernacki, in *Fabrication of Labor*, shows that in Britain and Germany weavers were paid by the quantity of production, but what was quantified was different in the two countries. In Britain, the piecework rates were based on the number of weft threads per inch. In Germany rates were calculated by the number of shuttle moves across the warp, i.e., by the time required to produce a given length of cloth. In other words, in Britain, the commodification of labor was understood as "the appropriation of workers' materialized labor via its products," (88) while in Germany, it was understood as the timed appropriation over workers' labor activity. Biernacki outlines how these differences in piece-work compensation for weavers led Germany and Britain to have radically different ideas about what constituted a copyrightable literary "work." Britain, with a tradition of paying by the manuscript (labor materialized in a product),

determined that copyright protection was based on possession of the physical document produced by the author, implying that there was nothing to distinguish an "author" from any other person—a critic, a commentator, an accountant—who could deliver a document. Germany, on the other hand, with a tradition of paying by the page (labor materialized by the movement of the pen), struggled to determine what ultimately held together the pages as a "work," deciding it was the originality of the authors' ideas. Originality, in other words, was granted the privileged copyright condition in Germany, not in Britain. Richard Biernacki, "Contradictory Schemas of Action: Manufacturing Intellectual Property" (lecture, Havens Center at the University of Wisconsin-Madison, 2004).

10. "The German Ideology of Marx and Engels," Marxists.org, http://www.marxists.org/archive/marx/works/1845/german-ideology/ch03l.htm (accessed 9 September, 2014).
11. Karl Marx, "Productivity of Capital/Productive and Unproductive Labor," in *Theories of Surplus Value*, pt. 1 (London: Lawrence and Wishart, 1969), 401.
12. Quoted in Catherine Cooke, *Russian Avant-Garde* (London: Academy Editions, 1995), 100; translated by the author from *Sovremennaia arkhitektura*: *SA or Contemporary Architecture* 6 (1928): 160–6.
13. A. Bogdanov, "puti proletarskogo tvorchestva" (Paths of proletarian creative work), *Proletarskaia kui'tura*, 15/16 (1920): 50–2; translated in J. Bowlt, ed., *Russian Art of the Avant-Garde: Theory and Criticism 1902–1934* (London, New York: The Viking Press, 1976), 178–82.
14. See Marcuse, *An Essay on Liberation* (Boston: Beacon Press, 1969); *Counterrevolution and Revolt* (Boston: Beacon Press, 1972); Larry Hartwick, "On the Aesthetic Dimension: A Conversation with Herbert Marcuse." http://www.marcuse.org/herbert/pubs/70spubs/78InterviewAesthDim.htm (accessed 5 May, 2012), also *Contemporary Literature 22* (Madison: University of Wisconsin, 1981): 417–24.
15. Founded in 1966, this artist-run organization in London redirected art away from the gallery and toward business and government.
16. Nicholas Bourriaud, "Precarous Constructions:Answers to Jacques Rancière on Art and Politics," *Open* 17 (2009): 20–37. http://www.skor.nl/_files/Files/OPEN17_P20-37(3).pdf (accessed 16 July, 2010).
17. Biernacki, *The Fabrication of Labor*.
18. Lippard and Steiner, eds, *Inventory: The Work of Christine Hill and Volksboutique*.
19. Andrea Fraser, *Museum Highlights* (Boston: The MIT Press, 2005).
20. The collaborative project known as "NO Ghost Just a Shell and the film, *One Million Kingdoms*," was one of the first venues to display Annlee.
21. See Walead Beshty, "Neo-Avantgarde and Service Industry: Notes on the Brave New World of Relational Aesthetics," *Texte Zur Kunst* 59 (September 2005), http://www.textezurkunst.de/59/neo-avantgarde-and-service-industry
22. The artists who Bourriaud enumerates under the Relational Aesthetics designation do not, themselves, so identify. It is a descriptive category that he uses to describe a contemporary zeitgeist.

23. The territorial disagreement between Rancière and Bourriaud goes like this: the emphasis that Bourriaud puts on empirical acts of art making is seen by Rancière as keeping intact, despite Bourriaud's espousal of a participatory audience, a traditional and passive view of art consumption. The emphasis that Rancière puts on historical examples, in Bourriaud's view, misses the changing nature of both aesthetic consumption and production in today's open source, transitory society.
24. These are Friedrich Schiller's terms. In the second part of this chapter, Schiller's view of art is elaborated. Rancière should be seen in the long lineage of aestheticians reworking Schiller's view of art in civil society.
25. Jacques Rancière, *The Politics of Aesthetics: The Distribution of the Sensible*, trans. Gabriel Rockhill (London: Continuum, 2004), 23.
26. The quote goes on, "The texts written by the young Marx that confer upon work the status of the generic essence of mankind were only possible on the basis of German Idealism's aesthetic programme, i.e. art as the transformation of thought into the sensory experience of the community" (Rancière, *The Politics of Aesthetics,* 44). And farther on, he continues: "(T)he cult of art presupposes a revalorization of the abilities attached to the very idea of work … What ever might be the specific types of economic circuits that lie within, artistic practices are not exceptions to other practices. They represent and reconfigure the distribution of these activities" (Rancière, 45).
27. Karl Marx, *Capital*, Vol. I (New York: New World Paperbacks, 1967), 178; quoted in David Graeber, *Toward an Anthropological Theory of Value* (New York: Palgrave, 2001), 58.
28. J. C. Friedrich Schiller, Letter 25, *The Harvard Classics, Vol. 32: Literary and Philosophical Essays* (New York: P. F. Collier & Son, 1909–14).
29. Explicitly, Schiller says:

    The instinct of play … in which both (the formal and the sensuous) act in concert, will render both our formal and our material constitution contingent, accordingly, our perfection and our happiness in like manner…(I)t will place (feeling and passion) in harmony with rational ideas, and by taking from the laws of reason their moral constraints, it will reconcile them with the interest of the senses.

    (Ibid. Letter 14, 27–8)

30. Ibid, Letter 15, 30.
31. Gottfied Semper, *Style in the Technical and Tectonic Arts; or, Practical Aesthetics* trans. Harry Francis Mallgrave and Michael Robinson ed. Willy Boesiger,rom work." er 2014, (Santa Monica, CA: Getty Research Publication, 2004), 81–82.
32. For a description of Marx's faith in the classical imaginary, see George E. McCarthy, *Classical Horizons: The Origins of Sociology in Ancient Greece* (Albany, NY: SUNY Press, 2003).
33. "The German Ideology of Marx and Engels," Marxists.org, http://www.marxists.org/archive/marx/works/1845/german-ideology/ch03l.htm (accessed 9 September, 2014). In the ideal society, as the above quote continues:

nobody has one exclusive sphere of activity but each can become accomplished in any branch he wishes, society makes it possible for me to do one thing today and another tomorrow, to hunt in the morning, fish in the afternoon, rear cattle in the evening, criticize after dinner, just as I have a mind, without ever becoming hunter, fisherman, herdsman or critic.

34. Quoted in Herbert Marcuse, *Eros and Civilization: A Philosophical Inquiry into Freud* (Boston: Beacon Press, 1966), 217n. 31.
35. In *Looking Backwards*, Bellamy's work model is the following: the nation has become the sole capitalist; work an obligation for every citizen; work from age twenty-four to forty-five ("industrial army"); people choose their own career based on talents; everyone pre-twenty-four is educated about all the trades; adjust the appeal of popular and unpopular work by shortening the length of the unpopular and lengthening that of the popular; but there are also some second choices; healthy conditions for all; a class of unskilled, common laborers, made up of the first three years you do work; whether it is white collar or blue collar is up to the individual and there is no prestige to one or the other; schools of both are nationalized; since the government owns and distributes all, there is no need for trade, and with no need for trade, no need for money; a credit card is issued corresponding to his share of the annual product of the nation, with which he procures from the public storehouse.
36. See note 21.
37. Frank Lloyd Wright, *When Democracy Builds* (Chicago: University of Chicago, 1945). Quoted in Robert Fishman, *Urban Utopias in the Twentieth Century* (Cambridge, MA: The MIT Press, 1982), 129. On the previous page, Wright imagines a Broadacre City life that is remarkably similar to Marx's post-revolutionary one. "Everyone would have the skills to be a part-time farmer, a part-time mechanic, and a part-time intellectual. Only drudgery would be absent from work."
38. Le Corbusier, *Last Works*, ed. Willy Boesiger (London: Thames and Hudson, 1970), 174. Quoted in Vikramaditya Prakash, *Chandigarh's Le Corbusier* (Seattle: University of Washington Press, 2002), 20.
39. Marcuse, 212.
40. Ibid. As he continues, "The pleasure principle reveals its own dialectic. The erotic aim of sustaining the entire body as subject-object of pleasure calls on the continual refinement of the organism, the intensification of its receptivity, the growth of its sensuousness. The aim generates its own project of realization" (18).
41. Michael Hardt and Antonio Negri, *Empire* (Cambridge, MA: Harvard University Press, 2000), 294.
42. Maurizio Lazzarato, "Immaterial Labor," http://wordpress.anti-thesis.net/projects/notes/labour-lazzarato.txt (accessed 20 August, 2012).
43. Lazzarato insists that this is not "utopian" because this form of work still describes capitalism's operations, as the subjects need still to conform to the demands of "production for production's sake." Critics of immaterial labor point out that labor

always had an immaterial side—Marx's argument was never to stress the physical nature of work but rather the social and subjective construct in which work operates—and immaterial labor always will have a material side—sweating through our time in front of the computer, the kitchen sink, or the shopping counter.

44. Alexander Galloway, "*Warcraft* and Utopia," *1000 Days of Theory, ctheory.net,* http://www.ctheory.net/articles.aspx?id=507 (accessed 15 July, 2011). The quote continues,

    And finally that virtual worlds are always in some basic way the expression of utopian desire, and in doing so they present the very impossibility of imagining utopia; … the very act of creating an immaterial utopian space at the same time inscribes a whole vocabulary of algorithmic coding into the plane of imagination that thereby undoes the play of utopia in the first place. The key is not to mourn this transformation, but to examine cultural and media forms themselves and through them (borrowing a line from Jameson) to pierce through the representation of social life both how it is lived now and (how?) we feel in our bones it ought rather to be lived.

45. See Chapter 3 of John Dewey, *Democracy and Education* (New York: Wilder Publications, 2009 [1916]).
46. Ibid.
47. See Paolo Tombesi, "On the Cultural Separation of Design Labor," in *Building in the Future: Recasting Labor in Architecture*, Peggy Deamer and Phillip G. Bernstein, eds (New York: Princeton Architectural Press, 2010), 117–36, for an excellent discussion on architecture's confusion over its labor practices.
48. Karl Marx, *Capital: A Critique of Political Economy*, Vol. 1, Part II (New York: Vintage Books, 1977), 605–6. If this scenario only seems to speak to the architectural firm partner in relationship to the client/owner and not to the salaried worker that makes up the bulk of the profession, Marx covers that, too. As he continues:

    [The hierarchical organized system of exploitation and oppression] has two fundamental forms. On the hand piece-wages facilitates the "sub-letting of labor" … On the other hand piece-wages allows the capitalist to make a contract for so much per piece with the head labourer … at a price for which the head labourer himself undertakes the enlisting and payment of his assistant workpeople. The exploitation of the labourer by the capitalist is here effected through the exploitation of the labourer by the labourer. (606)

    The initial problem swims downstream.
49. Caudill, Rowlett, Scott (CRS), at one point the largest architectural firm in the country, was the first architectural corporation to appear, in 1971, on the U.S. stock exchange. While their move to public ownership has been criticized as the beginnig of the decline of the firm as it changed from "one ambitious but still service-oriented (and) imbued with humanistic ethos" to one that was merely profit oriented (see Paolo Tombesi, "Capital Gains and Architectural Losses: The Transformative Journey of Caudill

Rowlett Scott (1948–1994)," *The Journal of Architecture* 11:2, 145–68), the structure of public ownership itself is not to blame, as many tech companies today demonstrate. Equally noteworthy for contemporary practice is CRS's "marketing through research" which preceded the public offering and is linked to it by the desire to escape a merely client-driven reputation. As Avigail Sachs describes in her "Marketing through Research: William Caudill and Caudill, Rowlett, Scott (CRS)," (*The Journal of Architecture* 13:6, 737–52), "Presenting the work of the firm as research, and not only as design, created a link between architects as professionals and scientists," a valuable asset in the Cold War, tech dominated economy of the 1950s and 1960s. It also solved, Sachs says, the paradox of needing to impress both clients (marketing) and peers (research). Current firms that are publicly held corporations are AECOM and URS (formerly United Research Services).
50. SHoP's three organizations (SHoP Architecture, SHoP Construction, HeliOptix) are precursors of this type of organizational entity.
51. "Economic Manuscripts: Capital Vol. 1 – Chapter Twenty-One," Marxists.org, http://www.marxists.org/archive/marx/works/1867-c1/ch21.htm (accessed 9 September, 2014).
52. "Representing Knowledge Workers in the New Era," *AFL-CIO Blog*, 11 April, 2011, http://www.aflcio.org/Blog/Economy/Representing-Knowledge-Workers-in-the-New-Era (accessed 6 April, 2013).

Chapter 6

More for less: Architectural labor and design productivity

Paolo Tombesi

Work and labor in architecture

Discussions around work in architecture tend to fall within two separate domains: one concerned with the theoretical, socio-cultural definition of the intellectual pursuit; the other preoccupied with the operative, managerial, and eventually (under-)remunerative aspects of the metier. The difference in focus implies a different framing of the architect as the subject at the center of the analysis: individual political agency on the one side, service provider collective on the other.

One could say that this duality is entrenched in the understanding of the term "work"—i.e. the mental and physical effort deployed in order to achieve specific results, and the professional nature of architectural activity. As a creative technical practice, architecture is defined by the integration of conceptual and material exploits and thus the generation of intangible and tangible outputs—or reflective decisions and communicative supports.

But would it be useful to try and do justice to both the intellectual and the productive character of the association architect/worker? Is there any merit in bringing the thought processes ontologically embedded in the practice of architecture to bear on the job routines of the building enterprise and vice versa? In the belief that the proper merging of intellectual and productive spheres in architecture is critical and central to any discussion of the future of the profession, because its focus on "work" ultimately serves to speculate on the possibility for design, this chapter favors an affirmative answer.

In constructing the argument about what sort of workers architects are, can, or should be, two terminology clarifications are in order. The first is that work differs from labor. Etymologically, the Greek "work" (εργου) signifies external "acts" done by people, whereas "labor" (κοπου) does not focus on the "thing" itself but in the "effort" behind it. Hannah Arendt's famous distinction in *The Human Condition* (1958) builds on this effort/deed contrast by defining labor as repetitive, never-ending, borne out of necessity and carried out under submission, in contrast with the instrumental, temporally defined, enduring, result-producing freedom of work.[1] These two characterizations can be (and have been) seen as evocative of the traditional social structure of the architectural industry, internally divided between professional conception and vocational execution roles. "Work" does indeed define architecture's intellectual objectives while "labor" reminds us of the salaried workforce necessary to articulate them. Yet, neither set provides help in determining the natural product of both. Is it the building as the result of project(ive) work? The documentation as the physical output of a professional service agency? Or the conceptual advice embedded in the latter and hopefully embodied in the former?

Architectural work as labor

A further distinction, this time internal to labor, clarifies the challenges and the importance of making such a determination. Its terms are defined in Chapter 1 of Marx's *Critique of Political Economy* (1859), where human labor is presented as "abstract" and "concrete".[2] Abstract labor is the economic time spent to add value to productive enterprises. Concrete labor is a particular activity with a specific useful effect in producing particular tangible products or results that can be used or consumed by others. Labor, in other words, can be considered in a double guise: as an abstract function that, if deployed efficiently, can help create value to its promoters, or as an activity that, in concrete, helps create particular kinds of products.

Similarities in the terms employed should not generate confusion. The difference between "abstract" and "concrete" in Marx's human labor does not relate to the distinction between "conceptual" and "material" in architectural work. Rather, it suggests that human activity can be motivated by the advantages of producing and distributing artifacts or by the revenues generated by engaging in a particular line of work.

Lack of symmetry notwithstanding, the connection between labor and architectural work helps frame architectural practice. If we took architectural practice as an economic activity that services the industry of building whilst having to sustain itself, the whole of architectural work could be reconfigured as "abstract labor"—that is, the embodiment of an enterprise that generates value through the provision of services paid above their cost to the producer. The same work, however, also contributes to the conceptual development of a spatial construct as well as to the actual manufacturing of a building product with specific procurement and consumption patterns; this makes it acquire "concrete labor" connotations that can refer to both intangible and tangible artifacts: designs as well as buildings.

Such double take is useful to highlight the multiple and concurrent conditions to which architectural work is subject: as a professional undertaking, it has public and cultural obligations; yet in fulfilling them it must be mindful of its own exchange values and production costs and it must also adapt to its functional use and subsequent timing within the building process. Work in architecture is not only an activity required to facilitate the translation of social readings and determinations into physical assets but also one made possible by the allocation of resources that are limited by the ultimate exchange value of what is produced and the constraints of the production cycle.

Bringing disciplinary autonomy into contact with the industrial dependence flagged by construction is critical in raising the design issue alluded to earlier. If the applicative context of architectural work responds to parameters that are external to architecture and functional to other endeavors, can architectural workers be put in the condition "to work", where the verb implies not only the application of professional routines but also the effective development and delivery of thorough disciplinary advice? Can the system grant the workers enough resources to perform?

Abstract labor and economic time in architectural practice

At the base of these questions lies the interpretation of labor as a factor of production that can be employed in combination with technology upon capital investment. In keeping with the abstraction that informs the classical critique of labor, "time" can be used as a proxy for the work carried out, its degree of complexity, and the socio-technical milieu in which it takes place.

A survey conducted almost twenty-five years ago in the United States involving data from over seven hundred architectural firms with up to ten employees exemplifies the extent to which time matters in architectural practice.[3] The study found that community centers, hospitals, churches and individual residences were the building types requiring the longest time to design per surface measure of one thousand square feet. Hospitals took fifteen times the number of hours invested for a supermarket and 2.5 times those for a shopping mall. Hospital design and documentation time doubled that of a bespoke single family residence, which, in turn, required four times more than a new model of tract housing. Times per drawing sheet showed less variance: the difference between the most cumbersome task (hospital) and the lightest one (tract house) was a factor of six. But, in general, if one took out simple ancillary buildings at the one extreme and medical/research facilities at the other, drawing sheet production time would never double across building types. Specialized facilities, community buildings and private client residential commissions still took the longest.

In terms of the relationship between amount of documentation and average program size, single family housing design was easily the most labor-intensive task for architects: it took four times more documentation than hospitals and theaters, three times more than schools, and two times more than retail; yet it was only marginally more demanding than institutional buildings such as churches and community centers.[4]

In theory, architectural practice should measure work (and its subsequent remuneration) in line with the information contained in studies such as the one described, through the time and effort it takes to provide the services contracted (insofar as they are necessary for a satisfactory result). In reality, economic quantifications relate to it only notionally since, independent of their levels, professional fees are calculated mainly by association with building budgets. In the (few) jurisdictions around the world where they can still be applied or recommended, fee scales ostensibly reflect the nature of the design problem, the skills and knowledge of the workers involved, and the relationship between decisions and the extent of their application.[5] Ways of distinguishing between types of work vary as do the relative increments associated with particular types of projects, job size, or work settings. (See Figures 6.1 and 6.2.) In the end, however, fee scales merely indicate the parameters contracting parties ought to employ to arrive at defining what percentages of construction costs should be deemed appropriate as compensation for professional labor under given circumstances.

This is a cultural custom that, irrespective of whether or not official scales are used, carries significant implications and conditions the way in which we look at design as "work" within the building process. In fact, connecting compensation for professional work to construction investment privileges the relationship between architectural labor and building systems: the more elaborate the systems—in terms of engineering, manufacturing, material components, assembly—or intensive their use, the higher the cost of the building, the higher the professional effort ostensibly required and the relative fee. By extension, the same link suggests that the recognizable output of architectural labor is

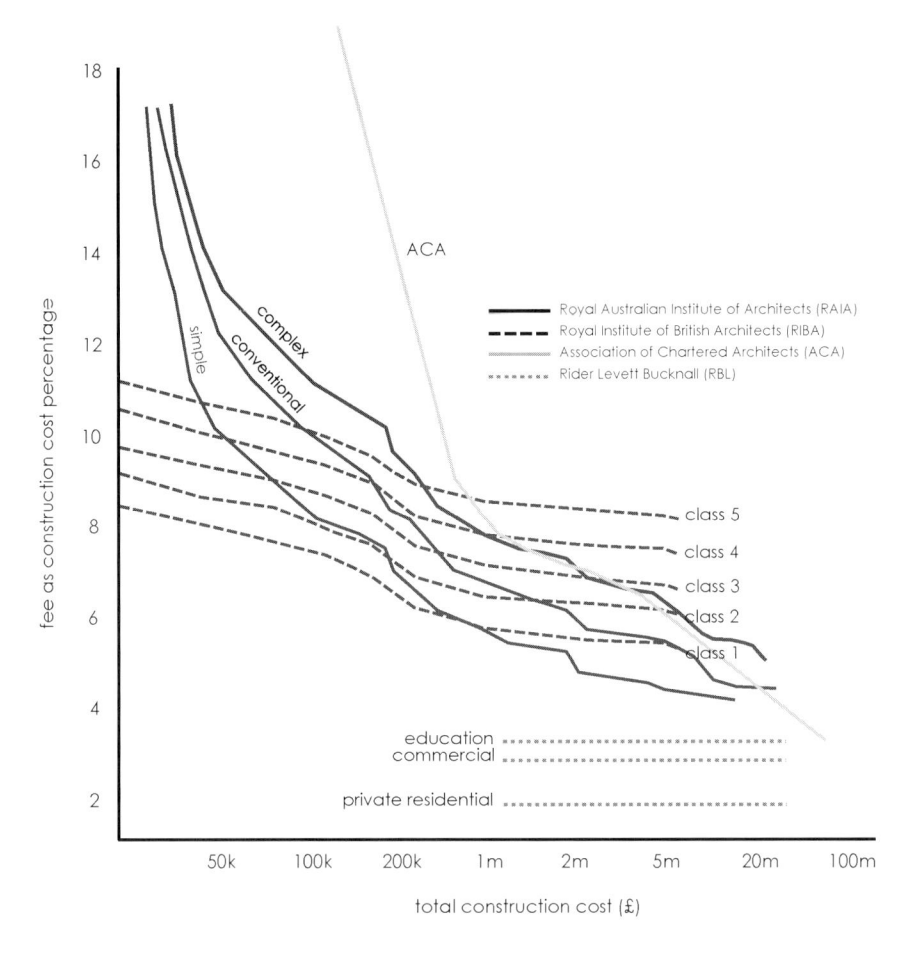

Figure 6.1 Comparison between nominal fee scale structures and fees actually charged or due, all indexed at 2011 construction costs. The now defunct Royal Institute of Architects (RIBA) "fee graph" (from 1990) is divided into five "classes" of complexity that go from barns and sheds (class 1) to warehouses, stables, and hostels (class 2), housing, commercial and community infrastructure work (class 3), specialized housing, high retail, institutional and healthcare facilities (class 4), high-tech, R&D, performance centers, and custom housing (class 5). The Royal Australian Institute of Architects (RAIA) scale (from 2001) reduces these classes to "simple" buildings (various forms of sheds), "conventional" buildings that make the urban fabric, and "complex" buildings that "involve special or prolonged study and calculation, require the application of special skills or experience," or increase the work normally provided by the practice. The Association of Chartered Architects (ACA) graph (2011) is the result of a survey asking architects to quantify and translate into a fee percentage the number of hours required to resource projects of a specified value. It essentially coincides with the remuneration theory behind fee scales other than for smaller projects. But the data provided by cost consultants Rider Levett Bucknall (RLB) on average architectural fees in the United Kingdom in 2010 shows the dislocation between work and payment.

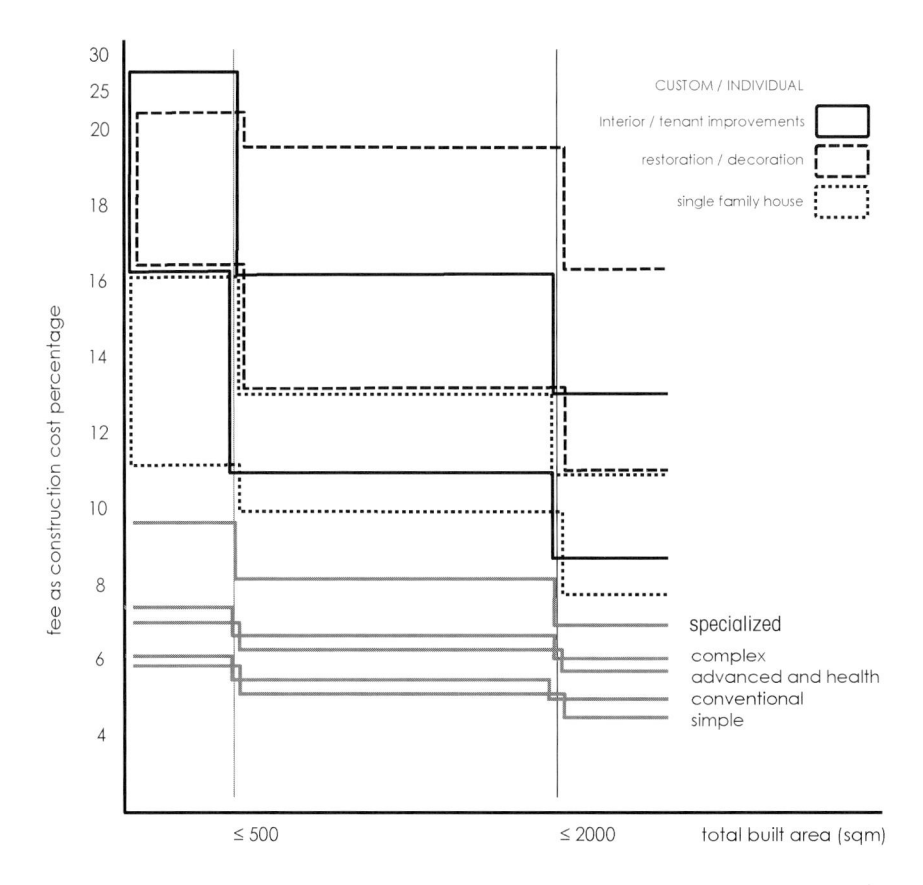

More for less: Architectural labor and design productivity 87

Figure 6.2 Example of the surface-based Tariff of Fees for Architectural Services recommended by the Architectural Institute of British Columbia (AICB). Divided into multiple "classes" of complexity (ten overall) it acknowledges the significant marginal investment required to custom design small spaces by defining bands of remuneration well above the threshold of "specialized design."

Source: Image by Paolo Tombesi based on: http://www.aibc.ca/wp-content/uploads/2013/11/tariff_feb091.pdf (accessed July 20, 2014).

something built rather than something conceived (and eventually validated through construction). Its "concrete" and directly instrumental dimension, in other words, relates to building more than it does to design. This not only ties the architect's work to the resolution of material technology challenges (rather than, say, spatial, social, or cultural ones); it also inevitably discounts (at least economically) the conceptual side of architectural practice. (Note: Switzerland is possibly the only place in the world where the standard contract for professional services by the institute of architects includes a detailed spreadsheet analysis of the challenges of the project and the strategy adopted to overcome them, accompanied by annually updated coefficients and formulas to calculate subsequent hours and rates.)[6] And given that building costs can fluctuate depending on market locale, conditions, and competition, exactly the same type and amount of design work can be paid differently due to circumstances that are entirely external to it.[7] Besides, levels of investment in building are also a function of the availability of resources, which not only depends on construction commodity indexes but also on access to capital or cost of money as well as financing parties' ability or willingness to spend.[8] (See Figure 6.3.) So, different parties, communities or financial environments can determine how any given design program is valued and subsequently resourced, i.e. how work is remunerated independent of the labor expended.[9]

The now only vestigial use of fee scales around the world makes the relativity of the entire business even more evident in the face of market pressures: private negotiations in regimes of competition have indeed succeeded in lowering actual work rates below rational thresholds, with plenty of evidence to prove that the payment of architectural labor is detached from the specific measurement of economic time. If firms in Australia could document the losses produced by working at both market and government rates in the 1990s,[10] the ACA in Australia and Britain have recently released data showing that actual fees have now come all the way down to 1 percent to 3 percent of construction costs (depending on the size of the project), and that architects systematically undercharge.[11]

This does not mean, of course, that architectural services are never paid at the rate they should be. It does suggest, however, that by and large abstract labor (i.e. practice billings) is independent from concrete labor (i.e. task development).[12] Pushing the significance of this point to the extreme could make us say that the practice of architecture is in danger of becoming disconnected from its professional theory.

Fees as labor boundaries

If the remuneration of work represents what is obtainable in a given market rather than the level of resources somehow conventionally accepted as necessary to fulfill specific obligations, it may be useful to consider whether the terms of this relationship can be adjusted to facilitate the preservation of professional agency capacity with the architect.

What if one moved away from the fee levels issue (which in itself is a cultural problem, not a technical one) and instead considered any billable amounts as the economic boundaries architectural work has to adapt to by defining,

More for less: Architectural labor and design productivity 89

```
                    construction budget
                          │
                          │   SIA indexed
                          │   remuneration base
                          │         │   complexity factor
                          │         │         │   project adaptation
                          │         │         │   factor
                          │         │         │         │           group factor
                          │         │         │         │                 │

Tm      =        ( $        p        n        r  )      ×        ( i )
```

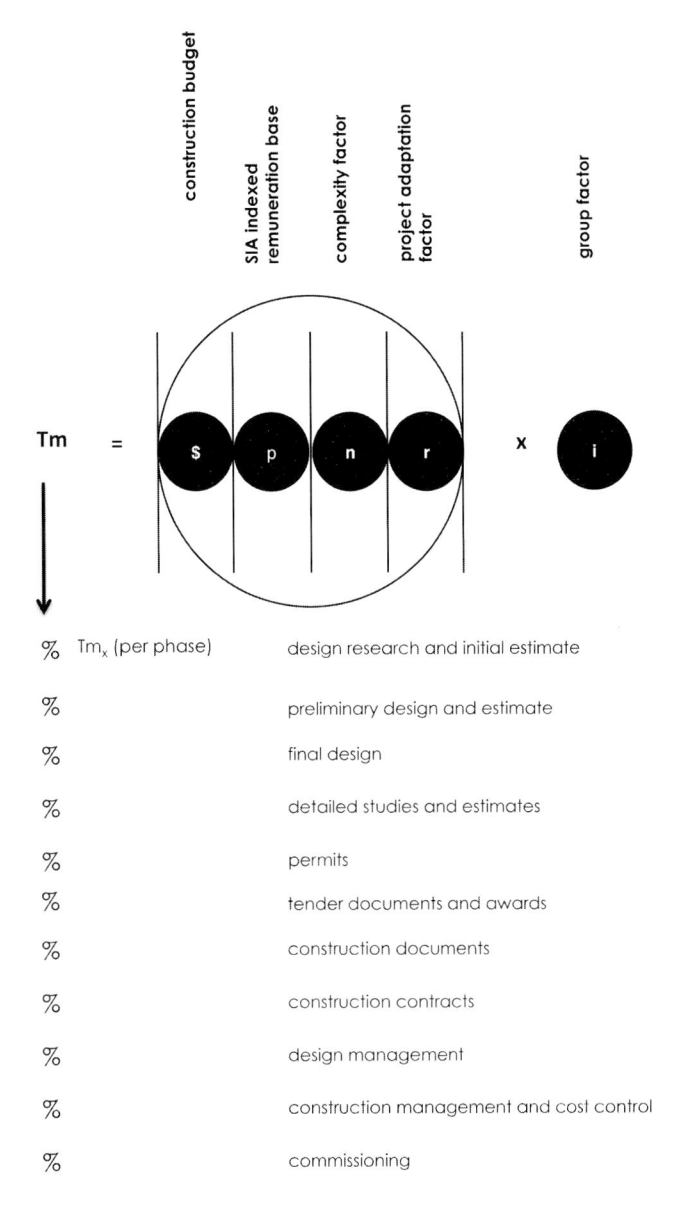

%	Tm$_x$ (per phase)	design research and initial estimate
%		preliminary design and estimate
%		final design
%		detailed studies and estimates
%		permits
%		tender documents and awards
%		construction documents
%		construction contracts
%		design management
%		construction management and cost control
%		commissioning

Figure 6.3 The time-based logic of the contract agreement for professional services (1002/2003) of SIA, the Swiss Society of Engineers and Architects, where construction budget is translated into "average time required in hours" (Tm). This on the basis of a calculation that includes indexed remuneration coefficients set by the Society (p), degree of complexity of the work (n), adaptation required to these coefficients by the project (r), and a group factor (i). As indicated in the image, the contract enables explicit negotiations with the client on the importance of each service stage and the subsequent allocation of hours. (The list of activities is not complete.)

Source: Image by Paolo Tombesi based on: http://www.sia.ch/fileadmin/content/download/sia-norm/vertraege/e1002_2003_e.pdf (accessed July 20, 2014).

contingently, the terms of the design problem, the strategic allocation of time, and the possible combinations of salaried workforce? Would adjusting "scope" to "remuneration" rather than the other way around alter the nature of architectural work or the way we look at it?

Accepting the possibility of a "design to (design) budget" proposition certainly brings abstract and concrete labor closer together because it introduces productivity as a variable. The idea of working within means, in fact, cannot possibly be about accepting that an under-resourced job must result in under-par output; rather it should posit that, in circumstances where resources are finite, design objectives and tactics can or should be weighed carefully against their development needs and impacts. Architectural work, that is, must be efficient, i.e. employ available resources economically to achieve most useful results (where "useful" inevitably relates to the most thorough development and sound realization of the design under the circumstances). Within such perspective, the productivity of architectural labor can be recast as a measure of design efficiency—a quality that could be described as the ability to minimize the resources required to reach design decisions, curb the probability that such decisions were reverted through the building development process, and maximize their impact on the final artifact.

Design efficiency and architectural work

At this point the question becomes whether the conventional use of architectural labor within the building process permits its efficient design deployment. Here the differences between types of work, cultural settings, socio-technical environments, or endowment contexts become significant, particularly in light of the relationship suggested earlier between professional fees, architectural labor and building systems. One can consider this relationship by using construction budget as a generic marker.

In projects where budget must be kept to a minimum, building design strategies have to favor the selection of materials and components that can be treated as commodities: simple, available in large quantity, manufacturer generic, preformatted yet technologically adaptable, and so forth. The task of professional labor is to give them meaning by organizing their architectural integration in keeping with design intent generally constrained by speed of building procurement time, spatial and structural conventions, and materials' mechanical properties. Aesthetic preferences cannot disrupt conventional detailing patterns or existing supply chains lest they dissipate the economic advantage embedded in their selection; for this reason, language choices either concern components' assembly and juxtaposition or are embedded in the initial component manufacturing process.

Formal/spatial/environmental decisions and variations, in a sense, exist within the nature of the system put together from essentially autonomous elements; and, given that this system must be kept simple production-wise, modifications to the work in progress are possible provided that they fall within the set of elementary permutations built into the technological palette. The building process hardly interferes with the design or its eventual variations because, in order to be viable, the latter must already incorporate production constraints. As such, the degree of uncertainty built into it is minimized whilst the ability of labor to intervene on the work and its results is relatively high: by and large, what gets properly conceived under conditions of clear economic limitation has a good chance of being implemented. This suggests that, in principle, the efficiency of the architectural resources invested in such contexts is pronounced: the provision of design labor must and can be kept to a minimum, while its conceptual contribution and the quality of it are not only critical but also evident in the finished product that is informed directly by them. Low-cost buildings use and display any particle of architectural thinking (or lack thereof) put into them.

One could say, of course, that work scenarios such as the one described are not necessarily the result of capital scarcity; they can also reflect a particular design ethos or cultural approach to building—which can incorporate levels of material craft without undermining the economic premises of the design enterprise.[13]

Albeit for different reasons, much custom housing design reflects a similarly efficient ratio "expended labor/resulting work." To start with, it deals with a product that is well understood in its general lines and possibilities (and tested by the structures at work on it); it is served by a mature building component supply industry that permits endless fine-grained combinations of parts and materials. It is also the province of unmediated relationships between the parties involved in its development; thus, functional needs and future building characteristics can be defined, validated, and, if necessary, modified through effective information and communication loops. Since the resulting buildings are procured through traditional methods of delivery, design work can be completed, costed, and adjusted before the start of construction and tendered as a lump sum on the basis of estimates that are generally reliable. If detail design variations (or replacement of parts) are required, the characteristics of the "fabric" allow them to be implemented throughout the construction process without affecting overall product lines. Within this work context, the relationship between cost and level of professional services in the form of bespoke solutions

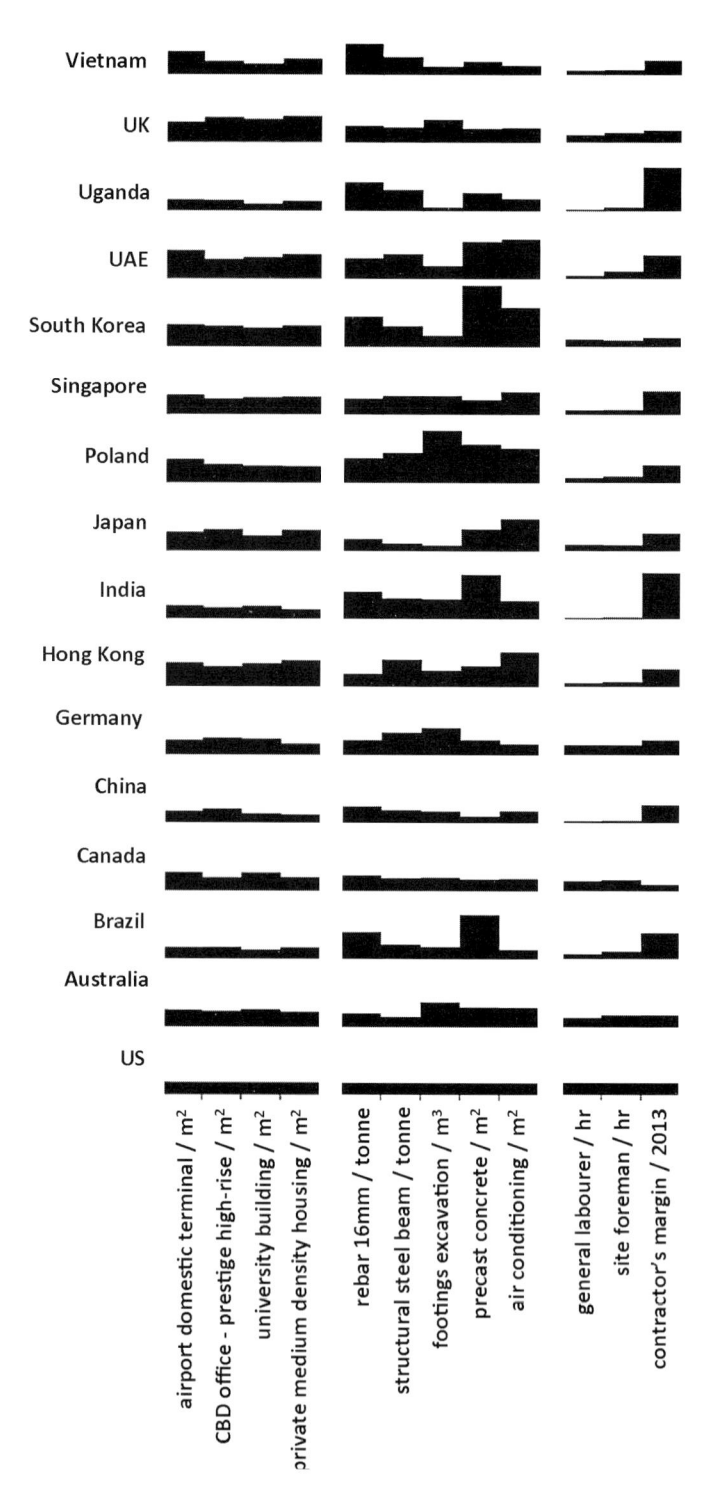

Figure 6.4 International comparison of percentage differences in building costs in PPP dollars per square meter of internal area in 2013. The U.S. column provides the 100 base. It is easy to see how similar types of buildings require different amounts of investment depending on where they are designed and constructed, and how specific items contribute to their cost. The double logical inference is that very similar building projects can command different building cost-related professional fees, and that buildings with the same program, costing the same amount of money, can present very different technical challenges.

Source: Image: Paolo Tombesi, from data contained in: Turner & Townsend, "A Brighter Outlook—International Construction Cost Survey 2013," http://www.turnerandtownsend.com/ICC-2013/_21145.html (accessed August 20, 2014).

and design development needs is generally recognized—even because, as noted earlier in this text, the output required from architectural labor in terms of product specifications and instructions is normally visible: project documentation practice makes the use of (abstract and concrete labor) resources tangible. All this defines an information-rich open market where, on the basis of their purchasing power and preferences, commissioning parties have the ability to determine scope of work, level of investment, technological framework, and amount of professional service required, essentially within the same product class. In Australia's major cities, residential design-for-a-client work can result in architects' professional remuneration that ranges, in theory, from approximately $80 to over $1,000 per square meter (with consequent, although not proportional, increases in labor resources and project documentation output).[14]

Design efficiency becomes more challenging as the program complexity or building budget grow—and so does the possibility/need to be more "inventive" and/or to use more technology-dense systems. This is due to three main reasons. The first is that, with buildings, design tends to generate more design. The physical creation of any environment responds to fractal mechanisms, always open to further levels of resolution. This means that the moment a particular aspect of a project is magnified, design issues that lay dormant become active. And if the emphasis also includes modifications to the conventional characteristics of any spatial or material system, the architectural interface with all other systems in place must also be re-examined. The second reason is that, on top of this, product sophistication generates an incremental need for design input into areas connected with sheer technology: building system development, building system integration and building fabrication. As technological scope increases, building performance naturally becomes more sensitive while part of project-based work tends to move into product-design territory—today largely controlled by specialized design-and-build actors. Through this simple mechanism, the work environment of the project changes: the social division of design labor expands beyond its boundaries, and concurrent product development cycles are created that are at least partially autonomous from the original overall design intent. Thirdly, as buildings grow in scope and size, so does the opportunity cost of the capital required to develop them as well as the risk involved in the investment. This normally generates pressure to compress the development cycle, overlap design and construction, break design documentation into packages, and allocate decision-making responsibilities with actors willing to bear the consequences of project participants' actions.

When combined, these last two factors generate a work environment where projects are procured through methods chosen for reasons other than design facilitation, where design tasks must be carried out in relation to construction sequences and against the constraints produced by supply chains, where proliferating architectural decisions are compressed toward the front of the project, where detail design moves away from the architect and toward manufacturing, and where the marginal cost to production of design variations to earlier decisions is too high to contemplate.[15] This last point acquires significance against cost control practices as, under such circumstances, contract scope adjustment at any given stage can only be concerned with what remains yet to be done (the relationships of which, though, cannot be redesigned)—most likely envelope, finishes, and fit-out.

The consequences for the deployment of architectural labor are substantial. The shortening of the traditional architectural design phase to the advantage of product engineering stages places pressure on early design development and resolution. And this calls for a concentrated and strategic allocation of high-skill personnel, capable of anticipating the demands of the building manufacturing process or making the qualitative aspects of the project adaptable to their repercussions. At the same time, the number of design problems such personnel must look into grows exponentially, thus requiring a larger skilled workforce.[16] Unfortunately, profiles that imply a deep understanding of architectural goals, intents, values and correlations between systems carry market value and thus higher wages. For this reason, "abstract labor" structures are not organized as such in architectural practice. They tend to be more skewed toward design production than conceptual labor.

Lack of design efficiency, then, appears when the development of a design solution generates additional design problems that put pressure on work resources and task implementation, or makes it likely for "concrete labor" work already carried out not to be brought to fruition. This can happen when earlier design decisions are made under conditions of imperfect information, either in relation to the characteristics of the problem as eventually defined or the characteristics of the industrial context eventually validating decisions by proceeding with construction. In most cases, they end up being ineffective, voided or altered.

Resources as hindrances to productivity

In short, the input-output efficiency of architectural labor depends on the ability to limit, isolate, and circumscribe design-related tasks and to control the social allocation of decision-making. With low budgets, constraints exist before the project and are used as starting points for the work; manageable resources tend to be used expediently to make the most of the process and the technical means available. In low-technology environments, this may mean developing the building system; in industrialized settings, it may require narrower concentration on visual and topological relationships.[17]

As budgets increase, work emphasis naturally shifts toward construction and manufacturing as markers or enablers of design quality/performance. Constraints in this case exist because of the project and need to be resolved within its space. Labor allocation and time consequently move toward building system documentation and development, leaving complex, qualitative non-construction aspects comparatively less resourced.

Against this scenario, the relative design disadvantage embedded in generous construction budgets is paradoxical but clear: higher building costs per square meter enable higher amounts of abstract labor; but they carry "structural" technological conditions that increase the scope of work more than proportionally while making the control of concrete labor and the management of design intent more difficult. More expensive construction does not necessarily produce better buildings and, while technology may make production more efficient, it does not necessarily render the architect's work more productive or effective.

This situation is exacerbated by the degree of formal inventiveness and system innovation: the more idiosyncratic the building proposal and bespoke its industrial procurement, the more taxing, rigid, and unforgiving its design resolution becomes. This creates a tension between the work required to develop a large bespoke building and the work required to complete it well throughout its whole spectrum of design dimensions.

Labor strategies and technological trajectories

If the cumbersome demands placed upon architectural labor by the building industry and investments have been correctly identified, a critical reflection on the evolutionary trends of the context in which contemporary practice exists is in order: no matter its alleged increases in production efficiency, some of its features may in fact run counter to the effective management of work and workers within the design process. The narrative developed in these pages suggests that any analytical agenda that looks at architectural practice and labor strategies against retainment of professional control and resource outlay must consider at least five issues.

The first one is the approach to the definition of building parts. As suggested, reliance on engineered systems compresses design decisions toward the start of the process, thus putting pressure on the allocation of skilled labor while reducing the resilience of building design to the modifications that can be brought about by the development of the same process. For this reason, there are architectural advantages in keeping building assembly components functionally integrated yet independent from a production perspective: more time remains available to build up workforce levels gradually in the project and to design integrative solutions; if needed, architectural labor can be used efficiently later on to respond to unforeseen problems. In the end, while system design and manufacturing can perform proficiently within established programs or under exceptional project circumstances, the dis-integration of any building system in terms of actual procurement is likely to lead to more flexible, sophisticated, and, eventually, successful building applications in most cases, particularly when formal innovation or environmental specificity are part of the challenge. Indeed, the way in which direct manufacturing can absorb or diminish the rigidity built into system engineering developed under design-and-build provisions—and still lead to effective monitoring of product development—will be a critical element in the inevitable discussion on design development and supply chains.

Building assemblies provide a lead into the second issue—the way in which design and construction components integrate. There is little doubt that the sequential staging of the building process is the best way to reduce risk and maximize the final yield on the resources expended; yet since growth in financial exposure in building calls for the compression of the cycle, the transfer of risk, and the exploitation of the cost advantages of competitive tendering, it is also true that the so-called "special features building" projects, of larger-than-average size and developed by firms with a significant salaried workforce, are likely to show a tendency to overlap design and construction, break tender documentation down into separate packages, and have design responsibilities or decision-making partially allocated with contractors. In this case, is it better for design to migrate toward construction or for construction to enter the design process? Surely, a way for architectural work to acquire certainty of outcome under these circumstances is to address construction challenges—i.e. incorporate industrial constraints—in the conceptual stages of design. This can be done autonomously or by letting expertise in through various forms of contractors' design assistance (early contract negotiation, fully integrated forms of project procurement, etcetera). The issue, of course, is the extent to which commissioning clients are willing to renounce the cost advantages of competitive tendering and bring contractors in at the beginning of the process, or capable of seeing through the actual challenges of schematic design documentation release under contractual novation or bridging mechanisms, or courageous enough to forsake building parts warranties in favor of planned design flexibility.

Perhaps the underlying solution to the productivity of architectural labor in such design-contested and time-pressed environments could be not to design (i.e. to work on) what is likely to be modified by others in the course of the process. Blunt though it may seem, there is value to this proposition, not only because it would trim down professional responsibilities or tasks underutilized (and thus at risk of being undervalued) but also because it suggests that there are marginal benefits to be found in concentrating the same design resources onto defining what cannot be changed or what can be prescribed.

This leads to the third issue: work on building performance. In spite of the seemingly accepted association between architecture's concrete labor and building systems, professional agency should ultimately reveal itself in the spatial and environmental performance of the built work.[18] If logically conducted, the delineation of the characteristics leading to such performance cannot but constitute the privileged professional domain of the architect—if anything because it is a difficult design domain to enter from outside architecture. While engineered systems can contribute to aspects of the spatial performance of the building, they are not in a position to instigate it or to replace architectural instructions about the intangible qualities of the overall space. Value engineering practices are in a similar position: once desired environmental outcomes are explicitly set and agreed upon, building cost adjustments should only relate to their construction alternatives.

For this reason, the ability of architectural workers to conceive and communicate the inhabitation qualities of a built object is strategically more important (and economically more efficient) than the desire to specify the physical composition of its constructive elements: the first sets the bar for the work of others; the second is by and large constrained by it. Yet, the definition and communication of spatial goals beyond what can be inferred through architectural rendering does not occupy a prominent position in the general output of architectural practices: it is a difficult activity to charge for in the accepted fee structure model and, when engaged with occasionally rather than as part of an office's culture of work, it requires multi-skilled, reflective professional labor—naturally drawing higher wages.

This could be something that the fourth issue, digital modeling capabilities, could take up with multiple advantages from both an architectural work and an architectural labor perspective. In spite of their endless applicative potential, BIM technologies remain largely Ruskin-ian in their cultural understanding and use, particularly in their almost fetish-like pursuit of streamlined fabrication opportunities (and the consequent pre-selection of otherwise unyielding technologies). The literal focus on the modeling of building information puts pressure on the design process: BIM environments have an effect on work resource allocation similar to that of non-sequential building procurement methods, as they call for the shift of the project labor bell curve toward the beginning of the process. Be that as it may, the emancipation of architectural BIM from manufacturing, leading to the architect's concentration on establishing and communicating the qualities of a space rather than the integration of its construction systems, could be an effective way to divide conceptual and material design responsibilities between parties, thus shedding off cumbersome labor activity. Architectural modeling capabilities could be used to simulate and verify spatial behavior whereas contractors' modeling capabilities could be used to simulate and plan construction assembly.

In spite of all this, at the end of the day, the most efficient way to economize on labor resources is to reduce the scope of work. And this, for enterprises like architectural companies that trade on informed advice, can be done by moving decisions outside the specific work environment or by importing into the same environment decisions already made somewhere else; in other words, by sourcing applicable knowledge produced outside the work domain on which remuneration is based. Such knowledge can be of different origin: it can come from the discipline (and take on typological traits at different scales), the industry (in the form of codes, conventions, or technological availability), the project (through proper development of briefs), or the firm (via work libraries or tested decision routines). Irrespective of the channel selected and the opportunities generated, the logic is the same: the more one can take advantage of previous work the less new work (and labor) is needed.

The integration of project-specific work and contextual knowledge in architecture represents the fifth issue in this discussion and raises important questions related to both the profession's management (and benefits in terms of project productivity) and its future. On the one hand, the ability to rely on project-external material suggests that specialization has value for practice for, by narrowing focus and reducing job variables, it allows prior labor expenditure to flow on and available design resources to be allocated efficiently where the specific occasion needs them. On the other hand, being able to externalize relevant knowledge means that product design input is available beyond (or before) the professional architectural sphere; and this reveals the natural tension that links, on one side, professional advice (i.e. intangible work) to traditional construction (i.e. socialized knowledge) and, on the other side, professional advice to industrial development and efficiency (i.e. sophisticated routine solutions available within an open system).

How these five issues actually intersect or economically define the practice of particular sections of the architectural profession would be a revealing exercise to undertake in detail and through the analysis of hard office project data sets; yet, within the flow of the argument laid out in these pages, a couple of remarks can suffice to complete it.

Apart from the use of digital modeling devices, the speculations just offered are remarkably descriptive of the operational strategies behind good architectural work (i.e. effective and efficient) in environments that are either resource-constrained or culturally integrated. In different ways and distant parts of the architectural world, there is plenty of built evidence demonstrating how professional expediency and industrial awareness can jointly contribute to the crafty production of inspiring spaces on the basis of modest labor structures, limited material palettes and constrained project budgets. In this context, architectural agency is important and shows that cultural assertiveness can be maintained even against seemingly overwhelming odds.

Yet the same issues, this time perhaps with reduced emphasis on the value of inhabitation experience, also characterize the work strategies of architectural firms that have become both famous and commercially successful for the distinctiveness of their design output. By themselves or together, the externalization of tasks and liabilities to network allies, internal specialization on labor-efficient tasks, project-independent selection of technological palettes and approaches, indication of preferred work delivery and contractual methods—all these can be found with firms that enjoy strong market positional rents and are thus in a position to choose how to work.

From labor to work—the education of architects

The possibility for different professional interpretations of similar cost-reduction strategies indicates that labor models are not, in themselves, architecturally prescriptive. Working in a particular way does not define the architectural boundaries of one's work, although it may define the ability to sustain it.

But regardless of the degree to which labor-conscious practices will be in a position to overtake or subsume more traditional practice environments, there is no doubt that they imply a specific understanding of what constitutes work in architecture. This makes the question that runs beneath the surface of this book emerge clearly at this point: is the culture of professional education in place at the moment conducive to the creation of the right class of workers, for the job as it were?

As Marx suggests, it is "intent" that separates manual laborers from intellectual workers. After all, "a bee puts to shame many an architect in the construction of her cells. But what distinguishes the worst architect from the best of bees is this, that the architect raises his structure in imagination before he erects it in reality."[19]

Clearly, the acquisition of intent is not a matter of training but one of cultural understanding and acceptance. Can we make architecture students understand the relationship between design and construction socially, beyond the obviousness of their chronological order? Can we make them question the idea of the architect as a generalist, or at least reflect on its viability? Can we expose the dangers of creativity as opposed to critical knowledge? Can we teach the value of project constraints, professional discipline and discerned tradition? Can we make future practitioners reconsider the dogma of technology as the compass, moral, and signifier of architecture? Can we acknowledge and celebrate the ambitious humility required to use labor and the world of practice as a lever for action rather than a justification for ineffectiveness? On the face of curricula, prevailing debates and official positions, the work to be done is in academia.

Notes

1. See, in particular, Chapter III, "Labor," in Hannah Arendt, *The Human Condition* (Chicago: The University of Chicago Press, 1958).
2. The distinction is first introduced in Part II of "The Chapter on Money," Notebook 1 of *The Grundrisse* (1857) as "particular" labor and "general" labor. It is then further articulated in "The Twofold Character of the Labour Embodied in Commodities," Chapter 1, Section 2, Volume 1, of *Capital* (1867).
3. *Small Architectural Practice: Statistics and Profiles—Problems and Solutions* (Orinda, CA: Guidelines, 1991).
4. Practice methods and tools have of course changed. The numbers from the survey are presented here only to suggest that abstract labor time can be quantified in relation to specific project types, and in order to highlight relative differences between such types.
5. In a 2010 study, the International Union of Architects (UIA) reports that fee scales exist in fifty-three countries and are mandatory in less than one third of them. The final database is available, but with several imprecisions, at: http://www.uia.archi/en/exercer/exercer-dans-le-monde/commission-uia#.VAv8KxBfZaY (accessed 4 September, 2014).
6. See: http://www.sia.ch/fileadmin/content/download/sia-norm/vertraege/e1002_2003_e.pdf (accessed 15 June, 2014).
7. According to the Fees Bureau of the British professional research company Mirza & Nacey, for example, the difference in architects' professional fees for the same amount of building value between the most expensive locale (London) and the least

expensive region (Northern Ireland) in 2013 Britain was double for £1m projects, and 1.6 times for £5m projects, http://www.feescalculator.co.uk/AF_Regions.aspx (accessed 18 August, 2014).

Ironically, comparative building cost indexes allow greater building scope for the same amount of money—and thus higher demands on professional labor—in Northern Ireland than in London.

8. Sebastian James' school audit for the British Government, *Review of Educational Capital* (2011), highlights the significant differences in building expenditure per square meter between schools in different European countries as well as across Britain (26–7), https://www.education.gov.uk/consultations/downloadableDocs/James%20 Reviewpdf.pdf (accessed 18 August, 2014). The final review of the *Building the Education Revolution Implementation Taskforce* in Australia (BERIT, 2011, no longer available digitally) also reports major cost variations per square meter between school buildings of similar type across regional jurisdictions with a different economic base. In Italy, it has long been customary to award competitive construction tenders on the basis of bidders' ability to lower (often beyond 50 percent but on average around 35 percent) the cost base published in the call for tenders. Subsequent professional fees, already very low, have no longer anything to do with the actual scope of the contract.

9. According to Mirza & Nacey, the architects' fee index in Britain has fluctuated twelve points between 1998 and 2013 (2000 = 100), http://www.feescalculator.co.uk/AF_Index.aspx (accessed 18 August, 2014).

10. In the March/April 1993 issue of *Architecture Australia*, an investigation into billing procedures ("The Fees Crisis—New Data") revealed that office operating costs for a project were on average equal to or higher than the fees charged to work on it. In 1998, a report to the Victorian Department of Education—*Consultant Fees for Building Works*, prepared by the Sainsbery Reed Group and Hayball Leonard Stent Pty Ltd, August 1998, detailed the losses incurred by architectural consultants to produce the documentation required by the public client. (In August 2014, the Victorian Government's Department of Education and Early Childhood Development (DEECD) decided to reintroduce fixed fee scales for architectural services.)

11. See: George Zillante, "Into the Abyss," Opinion, 4 August, 2014, http://www.aca.org.au/article/into-the-abyss (accessed 18 August, 2014); "Architects Should Charge More for Small Projects, ACA Survey Initial Findings Show," 17 August, 2012, http://acarchitects.co.uk/aca-fee-scales-survey/ (accessed 10 July, 2014). The ACA survey was triggered by a series of articles in *The Architect's Journal* in 2010 that reported the "suicidal undercutting" practices by British firms.

12. This statement finds concrete articulation in the experiences reported by the Melbourne architect Anthony Di Mase in his opinion piece, "Architectural Fees: What, How and Where To …" published on the Association of Consulting Architects' website in September 2014, http://www.aca.org.au/article/architectural-fees-what-how-and-where-to-294 (accessed 4 September, 2014).

13. The work of the offices of Bawa and Plesner in Sri Lanka in the 1960s, Gion Caminada in Switzerland, Koning Eizenberg in the United States, or Donovan Hill in Australia today, shows the breadth and richness of the results obtainable through such way of practicing.
14. Custom residential design fee percentages in Melbourne and Sydney are between 4 percent and 18 percent of construction costs; these, in turn, have been recorded to be between $2,000 and $5,700 per square meter, thus showing up close to threefold increases. (When considered against OECD PPP (Organization for Economic Cooperation and Development, Purchasing Power Parity) exchange rates, the equivalent remuneration range in the United States would be between $5 and $63 per square foot.)
15. In construction management, for example, the passage from overall schematics to individual bid packages transforms any design revision into a construction contract variation, where the marginal cost of the change is extended to the entire supply chain of the element being revised as well as those of its interfaces across the project.
16. It is essentially for these reasons that the suggested remuneration document produced by the Architectural Institute of British Columbia (AIBC) in Canada recommends that fees be adjusted by 20 percent when construction is carried out by separate contracts, or by an additional one percent of the construction cost when the building is procured either in project or construction management. See: AIBC, *Tariff of Fees for Architectural Services,* Fourth Edition, Revision 3, February 2009, http://www.aibc.ca/wp-content/uploads/2013/11/tariff_feb091.pdf (accessed 15 July, 2014).
17. Small buildings provide a balanced and resilient architectural labor environment because the construction process allows for proper design resolution before tendering as well as marginal modifications to building parts up to and beyond its completion.
18. It would be difficult, for example, to argue that the differences in construction technology between Le Corbusier's Chapel of Notre Dame at Ronchamp (skeletal frame) (1954) and Church of St Pierre at Firminy (mass construction) (begun 1971, completed 2001) are more important than their commonalities in the users' perceptions of the internal space. Likewise, the quality of Alvar Aalto's Church of the Assumption of Mary at Riola (1978) is not impacted by the use of the prefabricated concrete frames that support its envelope.
19. In: Karl Marx, *Capital*, Volume 1, Part III, Chapter 7, Section 1, "The Labor Process or the Production of Use-Values" (1867).

Chapter 7

Form and labor: Toward a history of abstraction in architecture

Pier Vittorio Aureli

1.

In his essay, "Abstraction and Culture," the American painter Peter Halley lamented the persistent belief that abstraction is a stylistic device or invention, borne out of the artist's formal concern.[1] He was disappointed that abstraction unfortunately continues to be seen as a free play of form that is completely self-referential *vis-à-vis* social and political issues. "In thinking about this most rarefied of visual languages," Halley writes,

> it seems we intellectually retreat into the cloister of high culture; we deny that abstraction is a reflection of larger historical and cultural forces. We deny that the phenomenon of abstraction only gains meaning to the extent to which it does reflect larger forces and is embedded with their history.[2]

This understanding of abstraction as a retreat from the world is dominant within the discipline of architecture, where it is associated with modernist formal simplicity and the reduction of architecture to a platonic object. The term "abstraction" evokes an aesthetic of formal restraint, a reduction to essentials.

Recent popular phrases such as "back to basics" and "hardcore architecture" seem to resurrect abstract form against the exuberance of complex form-making that has characterized the last twenty years of mainstream architecture,[3] and abstraction is again appropriated as an aesthetic goal and as a way to affirm architecture's autonomy with regard to what architecture is supposed to contain or confront. I would like to challenge this idea of abstraction in architecture and revisit the social and political dimension of this phenomenon within architectural form. In what follows I'll argue that the rise of abstraction within architectural form is a direct consequence of the fundamental role that labor has played within industrial civilization.

2.

In order to redirect the understanding of abstraction away from style, it is useful to understand it as a process. *To abstract* comes from the Latin verb *trahere*, meaning to pull something essential out of the totality of which it is a part. Abstraction in architecture has been interpreted as the reduction to and proliferation of simple forms. But history tells us otherwise. Le Corbusier's reduction of architecture to simple forms—one thinks of the platonic objects with which he reduced the complexity of the city into a language of basic geometries—was both an aesthetic goal and an attempt to finetune form for industrial processes of production. His Maison Dom-ino model for housing—a structural skeleton composed of horizontal slabs and *pilotis* where façade and internal partitions would be filled in incidentally—shows, in Adolf Max Vogt's words, two apparently opposing conditions for architecture: the perfectly pure and the raw real.[4] While the perfectly pure is the structure's iconic simplicity, the raw real is its construction system through which the technology of industrial architecture is applied. Architecture, we see here, is inexorably linked to industrial processes of production.

"Abstraction" as not-style also suggests form devoid of symbolism. A generic structure made of elements such as walls, columns, beams, slabs, windows, doors, stairs, ramps, toilets, etcetera whose function is to distribute occupancy within the building is purely *functional*. Modern architecture in this narrative is freed from unnecessary form and reduced to its function, i.e., to its *use-value*. Paradoxically, Robert Venturi's and Denise Scott Brown's theory of the "decorated shed" implied a functionalist, abstracted modern object—the shed—when the rhetorical, symbolic façade is torn away.[5] But this "functional" abstraction wears its industrial heritage not by being merely useful; it shows it by its generic, frictionless quality that lets occupation and labor happen seemingly invisibly, by its total lack of representational presence, and by the *asymbolic forms* that induce specific uses and specific modes of distribution.[6]

Here, the essence of modern architecture fully emerges as an assemblage of elements whose goal is no longer to represent power, but to *effect* power by framing, enabling, eliciting, making accessible, or excluding. When Walter Benjamin commented that architecture within modernity is viewed in a state of distraction,[7] he did not want to diminish the importance of architecture; on the contrary, he wanted to stress the fact that precisely by influencing subjects in a state of distraction, architecture becomes a powerful means of forming subjectivity. The architectural plan, one of the fundamental abstractions of architecture present since the rise of modernity, enacts this frictionless function. Apart from its technical reliability, the plan allows the architect to control and distribute the different parts and functions of the building. The plan thus reveals the *economy* of the building: its role as an apparatus whose goal is the correct management of uses and functions.[8] The activity of housekeeping is a spatial practice often described in ancient texts as the housewife's ability to know the location of every object needed to maintain family life within the house. The form of the house manifests the most tangible "economy" of life translated into a *typical* spatial arrangement more than it does its spatial symbolism. The frictionless trumps the representational.[9]

The "asymbolic" nature of abstraction lies also in the cognitive apparatus through, and in which, architecture operates. Architecture as a discipline emerged within the realm of commodity exchange, itself inherently abstract. When a commodity is sold and bought, it must adhere to a system of equivalence, one privileging exchange over use value. As Alfred Sohn-Rethel noted in his seminal book, *Intellectual and Manual Labor*,[10] this process required abstraction, since what is abstracted from the commodity is economic value.[11] It is for this reason that in the fourteenth century, the practice of exchange imposed a radically different way to experience the world through the lens of *abstract knowledge*. For Sohn-Rethel, the rise of abstract knowledge is the cause for the shift from artisanal to industrial labor. While artisanal workers mastered their production through practical know-how and by the expertise of their hands, the industrial worker relies on means of production wherein technology and calculus—abstractions—become crucial.

Commodity exchange foregrounded a new form of life in which abstraction was the basis of experiencing the world. On the one hand, this meant a new notion of the rational in which a set of conventions was based less on content than on abstract forms of equivalence. If before the fifteenth century there was no difference between ideation and the construction of an artifact, with the foundation of architecture as a discipline, practicing architecture meant to *project*. Already Vitruvius distinguished between *fabrica* and *rationcinatio*.[12] While "fabrica" refers to the practice of building, "ratiocination" refers to *reasoning*, which is precisely the *conception* of the building before it is realized. With the centrality of reasoning—wherein geometry, calculus, economy, and the management of resources play an important role—abstraction becomes concrete within architectural form. Form is no longer the outcome of individual craft, but the result of a socialized knowledge made of abstract conventions—such as the use of orthogonal projections within architectural drawings—and systems of measure. It is in this context that we have to place the abstraction of architectural form.

On the other hand, abstraction also became embedded within daily routines, social conventions, and ways of looking at the quotidian world.[13] Concepts such as value, wealth, exchange, or labor, which until Marx were considered simple logical categories of thought, are concrete abstractions because they are deeply rooted in the concrete workings of capitalistic society. As Marx wrote: "As a rule, the most general abstractions arise only in the midst of the richest possible concrete development, where one thing appears as common to many, to all."[14] In an advanced capitalist society, *reasoning*—that is the re-composition of a multiplicity of things and events within a coherent "scientific" system of thought—is not a simple depiction of reality but what makes reality work.

However the abstract essence of labor lies not only in the process through which labor becomes a commodity, but also in the very nature of human labor itself. This understanding of abstraction can be found in the way Marx in his *Economic and Philosophical Manuscripts of 1844* defines man as a species-being (*Gattungswesen*), as an animal devoid of specialized instincts and who has to constantly produce its own environment.[15] Here we see the generic and abstract source of labor, which Marx in *Capital* theorizes as *labor power*. According to Marx, labor power is "the aggregate of those mental and physical capabilities existing in the physical form, the living personality, of a human being."[16] As such labor is an indeterminate basin of unforeseen capabilities which man *objectifies* into his own production. In capturing and organizing labor power, capital tears from man not just his own production, but the generic source of labor: man's species-being. In order to put in motion this process, capital has to mobilize the power of abstraction as a social process to such a degree that the latter inevitably became a form of life. Within this condition, the form of architecture had to approximate the generic and indeterminate form of labor power, and to perform this task, it has had to build the necessary infrastructure to reproduce life: from housing to workplaces, from recreation to infrastructures to circulation. Again, in order to contain the generic essence of labor, architecture (and the city itself in its physical form) relied less on its symbolic and representational power and more on composing the frames within which life occurs.

In what follows I would like to provide a series of examples that traces a history of how architecture has reached such degrees of abstraction. This rather fragmentary excursus provides, I believe, the best vantage point from which to analyze the relationship between architectural form and labor.

3.

Arguably one of the earliest manifestations of abstraction in architecture is the institution that for a long time represented "transcendental" power in the Western world: the monastery. Within Christianity, monasteries were built not only as places for prayer and contemplation, but also as *apparati* aiming to regulate life in all its physical and mental aspects. Monastic life was an incessant *opus dei*.[17] Within it, *life as such* became the content of architecture. Within the monastic building, each moment of the monk's daily life is translated into a typical space: dormitory (sleeping), refectory (eating), library (studying), workshops (working), chapel (praying). It is at once a schedule and the embodiment of a form of life. In this, labor was of fundamental import since self-sustenance and the production of goods were essential to survival. Hence, Saint Benedict's rule for his monastic order: *ora et labora* (pray and work). As highly efficient compounds where both individual and communitarian life followed detailed temporal and spatial regulations, monastic buildings—made of simple and generic forms whose only goal was to provide a rhythm for life—are far less symbolic than previous religious architecture, and the organization of discrete, specific incidents is abstracted into more generalizable and repeatable patterns.

It is within Benedictine and later Cistercian monastic architecture that the most abstract dimension of architecture—the plan—acquires a primary role in the formation of architectural space. Indeed, the first known drawing of architecture is the ideal plan of a monastery preserved in the library of Saint Gallen, Switzerland.[18] Drawn on five parchments sewn together, the plan shows a complete monastic complex made of approximately forty buildings arranged in a grid, allowing maximum efficiency in organizing disparate programs: churches, houses, stables, kitchens, workshops, brewery, infirmary, storage, and a special house for bloodletting. The result is a plan where the management of life becomes more pressing then the liturgical dimension of the building.

Beyond indexing programmatic economy, the organization of medieval monasteries shows as well how the *diagrammatic* abstraction of architecture became the form of architecture itself. "Diagrammatic" is here understood, in the mode of Michel Foucault, Gilles Deleuze, and Félix Guattari, as a machine that *directly* produces effects of power and not merely as a means of the synthetic representation of concept and form.[19] The plans of Saint Gallen—in which the thick walls of the monastery are abstracted as thin lines, thereby shifting attention from the physical structure to functional and spatial organization—are, in this way, not representations but diagrams: instances in which power is not simply legible but *effective*.

Within economic modernity, the ascetic life that took place in the monastery became a fundamental model for industrial civilization. By carefully choreographing daily routines and thus ensuring the monks' productive lives, the monastery expanded the spatial condition of *animal laborans* from domestic to totalizing space. Within the monastery, labor was recognized as an essential aspect of life (unlike in antiquity when it was considered an unworthy sphere of life delegated to slaves), thus allowing it to become a model for institutions such as the hospital, the factory, and the school.

4.

The domestic itself—the archetype of productive space—is the social scene of labor management. If labor is the reproduction and the maintenance of life, its reach is clearly seen in the house. While the noun "house" emphasizes the symbolic dimension of the domestic realm, the term "housing" focuses on the function of the house—the process of containing subjects by subtly defining their way of life. In this sense, Le Corbusier gave the most precise definition of housing when he said that the house is a *machine à habiter*.[20] This definition allows us to understand housing not only as shelter—the space of the "everyday"—but also as a multifarious apparatus which coalesces social, economic, juridical, and cultural issues.

In the fifteenth century the practice of rental housing started to become diffuse within the city. Houses were built not only to shelter the family or the clan, but also to be rented to people outside the boundaries of kinship. In the mid-sixteenth century, Sebastiano Serlio devoted the sixth of his *Seven Books on Architecture* to an unprecedented subject: housing for all social classes.[21] Understood as the first architectural theory to mark anything other than a church, a public building, or a palazzo for a rich family as worthy of design, it represents the success of the bourgeoisie, whose wealth was made in commerce and manufacturing, in wrestling property rights from the aristocracy, whose economic power was largely based on land ownership. For this reason, Serlio's models had a fundamental influence on the development of standardized solutions for domestic architecture.

Serlio's book not only includes house models for the rich bourgeoisie, but also for what he defines as the "poor"—that is, poor peasants, poor merchants, and poor artisans. Serlio makes clear that the lowest social level is the beggar whose habitat is a self-made hut, but he excludes the beggar from architectural consideration because they, like the clergy—an important and powerful segment of society at that time—were considered "unproductive," and thus outside of the economic functioning of the city.[22] For Serlio, the poor peasant thus represents the lowest socially-productive stratum and his house is understood as the location of his production.[23]

Serlio's house for the poor peasant is a simple, two-room space: one room is for living and the other is the stable for the oxen. If the peasant can afford it, he can build a small portico in front of the house. If he is a bit wealthier, he can build an oven and a cellar (*cantina*) at the two ends of the portico. For the middle-ranking and rich peasant, the same model is expanded to include more spaces. Although Serlio does not provide a comprehensive example of city making, his careful and unprecedented engineering of domestic space implicitly acknowledges that the project of the city starts from the domestic unit, from the possibility of enacting the productivity of the house as both a space of production and reproduction.

The radicalness of Serlio's architecture for housing was not only in its incorporation of the "poor," but its asymbolic nature. The architecture that emerges from these models—defined by the repetition of generic windows, doors, and pitched roofs in the house; and the house itself repeated in the rowhouse—has to be measured against the fact that until the eighteenth century, these elements were symbols whose relevance was superior to their "function." Within earlier Renaissance architecture a column was not only a means of support, but also the representation of the human body, the embodiment of the perfection of nature, and the image of God. Leon Battista Alberti went so far as to understand the column as an ornament whose function was to civilize bare structure and add to it a moral meaning.[24] When confronted with labor in its most generic form of production and reproduction of life, this rhetorical dimension of architecture was lost, and, it can be argued, architectural form reaches its most generic essence: the framing of life through a series of spatial compounds.

5.

Since the nineteenth century, human labor has found its most explicit spatial embodiment in the architecture of the factory. Although as we have seen it is a mistake to confine labor to the "workplace," the factory represents the form within which the abstraction of industrial labor becomes fully explicit. While we have already alluded to the abstract nature of labor as described by Marx, his implicit attachment of this concept to American advances in factory labor are indicated in this passage:

> On the other side, this abstraction of labour as such is not merely the mental product of a concrete totality of labours. Indifference towards specific labours

corresponds to a form of society in which individuals can with ease transfer from one labour to another, and where the specific kind is a matter of chance for them, hence of indifference. Not only the category, labour, but labour in reality has here become the means of creating wealth in general, and has ceased to be organically linked with particular individuals in any specific form. Such a state of affairs is at its most developed in the most modern form of existence of bourgeois society—in the United States. Here, then, for the first time, the point of departure of modern economics, namely the abstraction of the category "labour," "labour as such," labour pure and simple, becomes true in practice.[25]

For Marx, labor as such, or what he called *labor sans phrase*, was the product of a specific historical passage: advance industrial capitalism. It is precisely this abstraction—an abstraction that is both method and concrete ethos—that the factory materializes in zero-degree form: its architecture.

The most radical example of this factory architecture was Albert Kahn's design for the Ford Motor Company Plant in Highland Park, Michigan built in 1909.[26] In this complex, Kahn reduced architecture to its barest form possible: a structure made of reinforced concrete and consisting of columns supporting horizontal slabs. The goal of this architecture was to create an unobstructed space where production could be organized smoothly under one roof. The Highland Park Plant became the first factory to host the assembly line, the method of production where human labor was reduced to its most abstract form: a sequential organization of workers, tools, machines, and workstations within which the workers' motion is reduced to one simple operation. It is labor without quality.

The Highland Park Plant represents the most radical archetype of the *daylight* factory, a space whose level of flexibility, uniform daylighting, and fireproof safety was unprecedented. And yet as Francesco Marullo has demonstrated, the daylight factory was hardly the product of rational thought only.[27] The relentless scientific abstraction of this space, where every minimal detail was bespoke towards the highest management of space, was the result of workers' struggles against the alienating conditions of industrial labor. The more workers rebelled against work, the more capitalists were forced to improve the efficiency of workers' exploitation. For this reason within the daylight factory amelioration of working conditions and further exploitation of workers were the two faces of the same coin. Above all, the open floor of the daylight factory creates an even, spatial condition in which men, machines, and goods all occupy the same horizontal datum. In the history of capitalism, the daylight factory translated into architectural terms a fundamental principle of a money economy:

the equivalence of all things determined by the abstraction of exchange value. Inside this unobstructed space, it was possible to reduce humans and raw materials to measurable parameters in order to prevent congestion and, especially, worker insubordination.

The application of reinforced concrete in the daylight factory was a prelude to a general transformation of the city into an extended factory, in which all of the premises of the city are integrated with the same spatial logic. Indeed, the architecture of the "free plan" became the structural system of choice for different institutions, from offices, to universities, to exhibition spaces. Just as the productive logic of the factory expanded to the whole of society, the logic of the "free plan" became the underlying principle of contemporary spatiality. The daylight factory renders this condition in the most essential terms by introducing a space that is no longer made of architecturally recognizable figures, but is the direct outcome of norms, standards, and quantities, the goal of which is the optimization of the production and circulation of people and goods.

6.

With the advent of mass education, universities were designed as factories whose goal was to produce not goods but subjects. The quasi-industrial nature of universities was made explicit by buildings such as the Maclaurin Buildings at Massachusetts Institute of Technology (MIT), designed by William W. Bosworth in the early 1910s. Bosworth conceived this group of buildings as an assembly line complex that would permit communication between schools and departments while keeping them efficiently organized as defined compounds. Not by chance he built the complex using the same technology of reinforced concrete that was used for factories. The plan of the building itself was conceived as a typical factory plan, reflecting Bosworth's interest in Taylorist techniques of management.[28] The neoclassicist grandeur of the elevation of the MIT complex merely mitigated the relentless necessity of managerial efficiency of generic and flexible space.

Nor was this unique to MIT. After World War II, with the dramatic increase of the student population, especially in Europe, universities were built as large-scale complexes using the same spatial logic as industrial buildings and the same factory construction techniques. One of the most notorious examples of this development was the new university campus of Nanterre near Paris, the birthplace of the May 1968 students' revolt. Asked to explain why these revolts started there, philosopher Henri Lefebvre, then a professor at Nanterre, invited the interviewer to have a look at the campus from the window of his faculty office.[29] Built outside Paris and next to one of the poorest slums surrounding the city, the industrial architecture of the campus resembled a production plant. When confronted with such an alienating environment, Lefebvre commented, students became aware of their status as workers and revolted like the manufacture laborers at the nearby Renault factory. If during May 1968 students allied themselves with factory workers, it was because they perceived university training as preparation to enter the job market and become docile wage earners.

The university, unlike the factory, produces not commodities but knowledge. Within the traditional university this knowledge aims to empower elites and to form good, obedient citizens. Since the 1980s and the rise of "immaterial production," however, knowledge has increasingly become an economic asset.[30] Higher education is no longer an ivory tower reserved for the ruling elite and dealing with esoteric knowledge but has become a mass phenomenon directly linked to economic production.[31] Today, when knowledge and information are bought and sold as commodities, universities are centers of production. The vehicles for this exchange, however, are not the academics and their departments but the students themselves—subjects controlled through the manipulation of their desires, feelings, affections, and perspectives. Unlike material production, in which commodities are objects detachable from the subjects who produce them, knowledge production precludes detaching the commodity from life itself. Bios, dynamics, and experience are both means and ends; rather than absorbing specific forms of knowledge, university students learn how to live, network, and compete. In this way the university becomes an edufactory empowered by the mass production of subjects ready to be implanted into the increasingly precarious conditions of work.[32]

A radical example of this space is one of the most prominent universities in the field of applied science—the Rolex Learning Center at the École Polytechnique Fédérale de Lausanne (EPFL) designed by SANAA and opened in 2010. This facility was built to provide a meeting place for the departmentally segregated university population. The president of the EPFL describes the building as a place where traditional boundaries between disciplines are broken down. Indeed, the center is conceived as one indoor public space subtly articulated by slopes, terraces, and patios inhabited by a continuous flow of programs such as library, café, places for study and informal gatherings.[33] While the slopes and the patios with no walls and minimal vertical articulation provide a minimum of separation, the Rolex Learning Center is a flowing space where there is no difference between programs, between studying and socializing, or between working and relaxing. By promoting "drift," improvisation, and the possibility of meeting and networking, the "free space" of the lounge promotes both the student and the researcher as capitalist entrepreneurs rather than passive receivers of knowledge.

7. Conclusion

The "free space" as exemplified by the Rolex Learning Center reflects the state of precariousness that affects not just the contemporary university but new organizational "campuses"—Google, Apple, Facebook, etcetera—that form the dislocated researcher whose self-promotion is the result of the lack of economic support and social security.[34] The abstract spaces of these campuses promote seemingly "progressive" tendencies—openness and self-organization—but in fact enact capitalism's total exploitation. While the rigid abstraction of the monastery and the factory *confronted* subjects with explicit forms of discipline and coercion, the soft abstraction of these spaces exploits subjects by withholding any difference between modes of life, and defines research not as a public good but as a personal investment.

And yet it is precisely the explicitness with which this process is made into a tangible spatial experience that offers a vantage point for a critical position *within and against* this mode of production. From the monastery to the factory, from the office space to the university, labor has always been based on social cooperation. Productive labor always implies, at its core, a public sphere. Contrary to Hannah Arendt's strict separation between the public sphere and the sphere of labor, within industrial civilization, labor is the place where we act (as Arendt would say of public space) under the eyes of others.[35] It would be a mistake to view the space of labor as merely shaping docile subjects. Precisely because of its collective nature, the space of production has always been both a space of exploitation and a space for solidarity and struggle. Capital constantly updates its forms of exploitation precisely because it has always confronted potentially rebellious subalterns. In his seminal book, *Operai e Capitale* (*Workers and Capital*), Mario Tronti wrote that "labor struggles are an irreplaceable instrument of self-consciousness for capital: without these struggles, capital would not be able to recognize its adversaries and thus it would not acknowledge itself."[36] In this sense the rise of abstraction within architecture should not only be seen fatalistically as capital's sovereignty over human life, but also as the most tangible traces of living labor and its political centrality within industrial civilization.

Notes

1. Peter Halley, "Abstraction and Culture" in *Selected Essays, 1981–2001* (New York, Paris, Turin: Edgewise, 2013), 163–71.
2. Ibid., 163.
3. See: Nathalie Frankowsky and Cruz Garcia, *Pure Hardcore Icons: A Manifesto on Pure Form in Architecture* (London: Artifice, 2013).
4. Adolf Max Vogt, *Le Corbusier, the Noble Savage: Toward an Archaeology of Modernism*, trans. Radka Donnell (Cambridge, MA: The MIT Press, 1998), 24.
5. Robert Venturi, Denise Scott Brown, and Steven Izenour, *Learning From Las Vegas* (Cambridge, MA: The MIT Press, 1972).
6. What I'm defining as asymbolic form paraphrases the way in which Félix Guattari and Maurizio Lazzarato have defined *asignifying semiotics* in opposition to *signifying semiotics* within their analysis of capital's processes of subjectivation and enslavement. For these thinkers, signifying semiotics addresses the process of subjectivation where symbolic representation plays a fundamental role. Signifying semiotics works through the establishment of narratives and cultural representations such as the worker, the student, and the entrepeneur. Asignifying semiotics refers to all those procedures and functions, such as economic indexes, diagrams, computer language, accounting, which escape narratives and representations and act more as *machinic enslavement*. For Guattari and Lazzarato, the subject of machinic enslavement through the power of asignifying semiotics is a partially-conscious subject. An example of this would be the driver of a car who cannot be fully conscious about all the routines he or she has to rely upon in order to comply with the procedure of driving. See: Félix Guattari, *Molecular Revolution*, trans. Rosemary Sheed (London: Penguin, 1984), 164–5; Maurizio Lazzarato, *Signs and Machines: Capitalism and the Production of Subjectivity* (Los Angeles: Semiotext(e), 2014), 39–42.
7. Walter Benjamin, *The Work of Art in the Age of Mechanical Reproduction*, trans. J. A. Underwood (London: Penguin, 2008).
8. Here the relationship between plan and economy is crucial. The Greek word for economy is *oikonomia*, which comes from *oikos* (house) and *nemein* (management). In its original form (and until the eighteenth century) economy was understood as the management of the household. It is for this reason that Hannah Arendt located the sphere of labor, understood as the biological reproduction of life, within the space of the house. Hannah Arendt, *The Human Condition* (Chicago: University of Chicago Press, 1999 [1958]), 79–135.
9. Perhaps the most radical representation of the plan as an abstraction of form in relationship to labor is a drawing made by Archizoom Associati as an illustration of their project *No Stop City*. The drawing depicts a city plan in the form of an abstract field of dots and Xs. The geometry that orders the disposition of the dots and Xs is provocatively simple: the orthogonal spacing of the typewriter itself. The dots and Xs represent the architecture of a city. Or better still, they represent the basic condition

required for a city to exist: the minimum infrastructure for living, according to which the city reproduces itself. Read in this way, Xs are columns occurring every 50 meters. The remaining infrastructure fits within the grid of plug-ins occurring every 5 meters. According to this logic, Archizoom defined other elements in a nonfigurative architectural language: a wall occurs every 10 meters, a bed every 20 meters, an elevator every 25 meters, etcetera. The overall layout illustrated an urban condition governed by the minimum welfare necessary to guarantee the reproduction of those living and working in this urban field. The drawing stripped the city of any architectural attribute, such as figures, and mercilessly rendered it in all its infrastructural and biopolitical objectivity. Archizoom sarcastically defined this type of city as, "a bathroom every 50 square meters." This drawing therefore forces us to reconsider the idea of abstraction as something different from the stylish modernist or minimalist architecture with which it has often been associated.

10. Alfred Sohn-Rethel, *Intellectual and Manual Labor: A Critique of Epistemology* (London: Macmillan Press, 1978).
11. Ibid., 36.
12. Vitruvius, *Ten Books on Architecture*, eds Ingrid D. Rowland and Thomas Noble Howe (Cambridge: Cambridge University Press, 1999), 21.
13. One of the most powerful manifestations of abstraction becoming the *form* of the world was the diffusion of perspective as a means of representation. Invented by Arabs as a science of sight, in the Western world perspective became a tool to represent space. However it would be a mistake to think of perspective as a tool to create the illusion of space on a two-dimensional surface. The mathematical nature of perspective implied the possibility to reduce space to a measurable entity and to discipline human sight according to a general law of vision. This law manifested itself in an urban space that would be increasingly regularized according to geometric parameters: abstraction then became concrete in the form of the city and its architecture. Think of the importance of regularity and modularity of form, the rationalization of design processes, the rise of typology and standards as ways to both govern the city's development and to transmit architectural knowledge.
14. Karl Marx, *Grundrisse: Foundations of the Critique of Political Economy*, Part 3: "The Method of Political Economy" (New York: Penguin Classics 1993), 105.
15. Karl Marx, *Economic Manuscripts of 1857–58*, trans. Martin Milligan, Chapter XXIV (London: Dove, 2007). (This is different from *Economic and Philosophical Manuscripts of 1844* which has been referred to in other chapters as "Grundrisse.")
16. Karl Marx, *Capital: Volume 1,* trans. Ben Fowkes (London: Penguin Books, 1976), 270.
17. On the history of monastic architecture in the West see: Wolfgang Braunfels, *Monasteries of Western Europe: The Architecture of the Orders* (Princeton, NJ: Princeton University Press, 1972). For a radical interpretation of monasticism as the making of a form of life see: Giorgio Agamben, *Altissima Povertà. Regole monastiche e forma di vita* (Vincenza: Neri Pozza, 2011); I've expanded this topic in my book: *Less is Enough: On Asceticism and Architecture* (Moscow: Strelka Press, 2013).

18. On this drawing see: Walter Horn and Ernest Born, *Plan of St. Gall: Study of the Architecture and Economy of, and Life in, a Paradigmatic Carolingian Monastery* (Los Angeles: University of California Press, 1980).
19. See: Michel Foucault, *Discipline and Punish: The Birth of the Prison* (New York: Vintage Books, 1977); see also: Gilles Deleuze, *Foucault*, trans. Sean Hand (London: Continuum, 2006).
20. Le Corbusier, *Toward an Architecture*, trans. John Goodman (Los Angeles: Getty Research Institute, 2007), 35.
21. Myra Nan Rosenfeld, ed., *Serlio on Domestic Architecture* (New York: Dover, 1996). See also Sebastiano Serlio, *Sebastiano Serlio on Architecture, Volume 2*, trans. Vaughan Hart and Peter Hicks (New Haven, CT: Yale University Press, 2001).
22. Sebastiano Serlio, *Sebastiano Serlio on Architecture, Volume 2*, 45.
23. In this idea we see the emergence of what for Max Weber would be a fundamental ethical principle of capitalism: the abnegation of work and production as the fundamental basis of the population's wellbeing. Weber identified this ethos as inner-worldly asceticism, different from the hermit's or the monk's renunciation of mundane reality in order to augment spiritual contemplation, and fully concentrated in the abnegation of work. Serlio translated the same ethos into a domestic architecture reduced to its bare minimum.
24. Leon Battista Alberti, *On the Art of Building in Ten Books*, trans. Joseph Rykwert, Neil Leach, and Robert Tavernor (Cambridge, MA: The MIT Press, 1988), 154.
25. Ibid., 104.
26. On Albert Kahn's work for Ford see: George Nelson, *The Industrial Architecture of Albert Kahn Inc.* (New York: Architectural Book Publishing Company, 1939); see also Federico Bucci, *Albert Kahn: Architect of Ford* (New York: Princeton Architectural Press, 2002).
27. See Francesco Marullo, "Architecture and Revolution: The Typical Plan as Index of Generic," in *The City as a Project*, ed. Pier Vittorio Aureli (Berlin: Ruby Press, 2014), 216–60.
28. On this issue see: Mark Jarzonbek, *Designing MIT: Bosworth's New Tech* (Boston: Northeastern, 2008).
29. Łukasz Stanek, *Henri Lefebvre on Space: Architecture, Urban Research, and the Production of Theory* (Minneapolis: University of Minnesota Press, 2011), 186.
30. On the rise of immaterial production and its consequences there is a vast literature. See: the seminal Maurizio Lazzarato, "Immaterial Labor," in *Radical Thought in Italy: A Potential Politics*, eds. Paolo Virno and Michael Hardt (Minneapolis: University of Minnesota Press, 1996), 133–47.
31. This phenomenon is best represented by the so-called Treaty on Higher Education signed in 1999 in the city of Bologna and known since then as the "Bologna Treaty." For a general overview of this 'Treaty', see: Alberto Amaral, Guy Neave, Christine Musselin, and Peter Maaseen, eds., *European Integration and the Governance of Higher Education and Research* (London: Springer, 2009). For a critical analysis,

see: The Edufactory Collective, *Towards a Global Autonomous University* (New York: Autonomedia, 2009).
32. The architecture that seems to embody this condition is the atrium or, better, the *lounge*, as this typology is emerging in many university campuses around the world.
33. Francesco della Casa, *The Rolex Learning Center* (Barcelona: Actar, 2010).
34. See: Maurizio Lazzarato, *The Indebted Man: An Essay on the Neoliberal Condition*, trans. Joshua David Jordan (Los Angeles: Semiotext(e), 2012).
35. A concept most notably discussed by Hannah Arendt in *The Human Condition*.
36. Mario Tronti, *Operai e Capitale* (Turin: Einaudi, 1966), 289.

Part III

Design(ers)/Build(ers)

Chapter 8

Writing work: Changing practices of architectural specification

Katie Lloyd Thomas and Tilo Amhoff

Wednesday May 2nd
General Murray
   Writing Descriptions of Work & figuring plans of Ore Place. (Neill)
General Murray
   Copying Plans of Ore Hall. (Donnell)

Tuesday June 5th
Lord Mulgrave
   Drawing Plans of Mulgrave Hall. (Donnell)
Edward Pratt Esq.
   Writing descriptions of the additions and alterations at Ryston. (Neill)
Mr Gooch
   Moneying bills of sundrys at faseting hall. (Neill)
Mr Beckford
   Drawing Chimney Pieces & Niche at Fonthill. (Sanders)
                     John Soane, *Order Book, No. 2*, 31 March to 6 July 1787[1]

John Soane's *Order Book No.2* records the work that he and the employees in his small office carried out on a daily basis. Most of the entries for the period 31 March to 6 July 1787 (cited above) describe the work of designing and preparing drawings, but other administrative tasks are also recorded: measuring work, making out bills, settling accounts, as well as "writing descriptions," meaning the preparation of architectural specifications. Today, the contractual and administrative tasks performed by architects are a formal part of their education and architectural bookshops are full of guides to best practice. It has not always been so. These manuals only began to appear in the UK in the early nineteenth century, in parallel with the professionalization of architecture and the establishment of the Royal Institute of British Architects (RIBA) in 1834. Architectural history and theory has focused almost exclusively on the work of drawing and design, but tracing the development of those administrative tasks so carefully set out by Soane's office reveals a series of transformations that increasingly place the production of written documents at the center of the architect's work. What might it mean to include these "office products" and the work of producing them in our accounts of architectural practice, design, history, and theory? How do these documents change in their form, content, and use of language? What do these changes mean for the work of the architect, the architect's relation to the work of others involved in the building process, and for design?

This chapter focuses on one aspect of this "writing work," the production of the architectural specification. These textual descriptions have a longer and more primary relationship to building than drawings do because of their key role in determining and fixing expenditure.[2] The increasing length and complexity of these documents during the late eighteenth century is already evidence that they were playing a more significant part in the architect's work. For example, the "Articles of Agreement for a Town House for Sir William Heathcote at St James Square, London" (1734–6) were just the length of a single sheet of parchment, while the "Specification for Newgate Gaol and the Sessions House at the Old Bailey" (1769) comprised eight pamphlets for each building, the longest of which was a full eight pages. The writing of these architectural documents is ever more central today. For example, the "Specification for H...y Building" (2006) for an office building in London runs to 401 pages. In the first of the published manuals to give guidance on this type of writing work, *Specifications for Practical Architecture* (1841), the author Alfred Bartholomew described the architect's production of writing as "labor," and went on to claim that, "no other branch of the architectural or building art, is so much neglected, as the giving a correct comprehensive and clear description, of any intended Architectural work."[3]

In Soane's daybook, his clerk Thomas Neill uses the term "Writing Descriptions of Work" (Wednesday, May 2, 1787), to record his work of preparing a specification. The double meaning of Neill's phrase is particularly apt to our approach. First, the scope of the architect's activities may well be prescribed in individual clauses within the specification itself. Such clauses, often found in the Preliminaries sections of the specification, directly delimit the architect's work, as well that of other parties such as surveyors, contractors, and builders. The nature of the architect's roles and obligations and the extent to which they are defined varies in the documents we examine. As such, the documents supply clear evidence of changes in the nature of the architect's work. Second, the manner in which specifications describe that work changes greatly. For example, specifications from the early eighteenth century focus largely on the dimensions of the building and say nothing about the methods of construction to be used in building, but specifications from the nineteenth century are full of detail about these processes that would be invisible if we looked only at drawings. The architect's writing work necessarily requires that they are knowledgeable of the areas they have to write about in the specification, and therefore reveals something of the changing nature of their work.

By reading closely the changing nature of these written documents, where and how shifts arise in "Writing Descriptions of Work" can be identified. Acknowledging that, as Michael Ball has insisted, histories of building practice are very localized, and that these documents need to be understood in the contexts in which they arise and in turn affect, we limit our study to documents prepared in and around the London area.[4] Few studies have examined the changing format of architectural specifications, and those that do tend to see as decisive the shift from guild-based building, where contracts were let out to master builders of particular trades (usually carpenters or bricklayers), to the full emergence of contracting in gross in the 1830s, wherein a general contractor (not necessarily a builder and often sub-contracting) organized the building work for maximum profit.[5] During this period new specifications were needed to set out building work in detail. They were meant to guard against contractors cutting corners for profit and had to secure the quality of work by prescribing it in full. The documents' legal authority replaced the older system of trust and social obligation. Such an overview accounts for changes in the writing of the specification in the broadest sense, particularly as their format stabilized during the nineteenth century, showing few substantive changes beyond increased detail and the inclusion of new methods of construction, until the 1960s when new forms of specifications were introduced. However, the evidence of documents written during the transitional period of the late eighteenth and early nineteenth century, before contracting in gross became widespread, reveals a more complex picture and requires more nuanced explanations. Specifications from the late eighteenth century are particularly instructive because they are produced in a great range of contractual situations, and in turn give rise to a rich variety of formats. For example, one part of Soane's specification for the Tendring Hall (1783–9) shares characteristics with nineteenth-century documents, although there was no general contractor in this project and Soane acted as both architect and contractor. Only a few years earlier, the "Particulars for a Bakehouse, Dwelling and Lofts in Parish of St Anne, Middlesex" (1770), for the gingerbread maker John Steinmetz, comprised a single sheet in the manner of the medieval indenture and was written by the surveyor. No architect was involved in the project.[6] Documents from this period, therefore, aid in understanding the multiple factors that continue to influence the practice of specification writing.

Howard Davis includes the bakehouse specification in his perceptive discussion of building culture in the Georgian period, but only to make the general claim that specifications increased in precision and continued to do so.[7] However, important changes can be identified in what specifications were precise about (whether dimensions, or the process of building, for example) and in the modes of language and description that they used to convey precision. If architects were simply required to describe the dimensions of the building (as in the early eighteenth century indentures), or to describe "work in place" (as was the intention behind the new National Building Specification (NBS) launched in 1973), they engaged with the building as an object. This is a very different kind of precision to that of setting out processes of building in detail, as began in the late eighteenth century and persisted until the 1960s, which requires familiarity with the construction process and the kind of labor involved. It is different again to the quantitative materials-science-based description of buildings and their parts through performance criteria, as in the specifications that support design and build contracts today. In the description of building processes, from its emergence as a practice in late eighteenth century architectural specifications, until the zenith of this form of description in the 1960s, the labor of builders and of architects remained visible, despite the transformation of building to capitalist production.

The development of a new standardized specification by the RIBA during the 1960s aimed to describe "work in place," and to omit descriptions of building processes wherever possible. More recently, specifications have been devised that aim to be "open" and litigation-proof by avoiding specifying particular materials and processes to be used. Methods of construction, the design of specific details, and the materials to be used are left to the contractor, allowing them to find the most expedient solutions for maximum profit, and quality is secured by specifying performance criteria. As in the early nineteenth century, profit motivations and distrust of contractors drive the mode of specification, but the format these documents take and how they achieve these ends has been radically altered. For architects, the newer forms of document engender an ever greater distance from the process of building. Their work is primarily concerned with the design of form, while building labor is rendered invisible.

Contrasting recent specifications with those produced between the 1760s and the 1960s highlights the relative absence in contemporary documents of labor and processes of building. As we see it, contracting in gross and building's incorporation into capitalism brought about a shift away from what Karl Marx calls "direct social relations between individuals at work" toward "material relations between persons and social relations between things" that were now enacted through the specification.[8] Specifications, and the contractual documents of which they were part, took over what had previously been lived, personal negotiations between architects and builders on site. But because these documents retained descriptions of building and labor processes (of both builders and architects), it is still possible to retrieve from these texts some aspects of building as a social process. Moreover, the architects who wrote these documents were in fact becoming *more* familiar with the work of building, even if the architect's work was largely taking place in the office and away from the building site. However, in the specifications typical of today's advanced capitalism, "building" as process is almost entirely eradicated.

"Writing descriptions of work": The roles and authority of the architect

Although the "writing work" of architects was formalized in the 1830s and 1840s with the emergence of contracting in gross, documents from the latter part of the eighteenth century reveal that the architect's work already included an increasing number of administrative tasks, such as the preparation of lengthy specifications, and directions within them show the architect's changing involvement with the supervision of construction on site. The wide range of formats of specification in use at this time can each be identified with different forms of contractual organization. The move to writing work was a result of new practices of pricing building "in advance" rather than the traditional practice of pricing by measure, which in turn altered the way buildings are described and known by architects.

The "Articles of Agreement for a Town House for Sir William Heathcote at St James Square, London" (1734–6), designed by the architect Henry Flitcroft (who had himself been a carpenter) and built by the master carpenter Benjamin Timbrell, is a one-page document in the form of a medieval indenture (see Figure 8.1). The description of the building was written out by a notary in duplicate, and each text was signed by builder and client, and witnessed by the architect, before being cut in two with a wavy line that forever keyed the two parts to each other. At St James Square, the architect's task was mainly to describe the form and extent of the building, and to produce the drawings. We can assume the construction of one London townhouse was much the same as the next and there was little need to describe the work in detail in advance. Therefore, the architect's "writing work" could be minimal. The indenture only specifies one area of his responsibility on site: "Ornaments and carving (of the three chimney pieces in the 'two best rooms') of fifty pound value in all to be done as the said Mr Flitcroft shall direct."[9] It was still the carpenter who was to carry out the building of the house and to direct the building work of the other trades. This contract would have been paid, as it had been traditionally, by measure, and the quality and manner in which the work was to be completed was largely a matter of trust between the parties involved.

Already in 1769 much lengthier preparation would have been required for the "Specifications for Newgate Gaol and the Sessions House at the Old Bailey, London" printed in their separate pamphlets, one for each trade. Sub-contracting to each of these trades was administered by the architect,

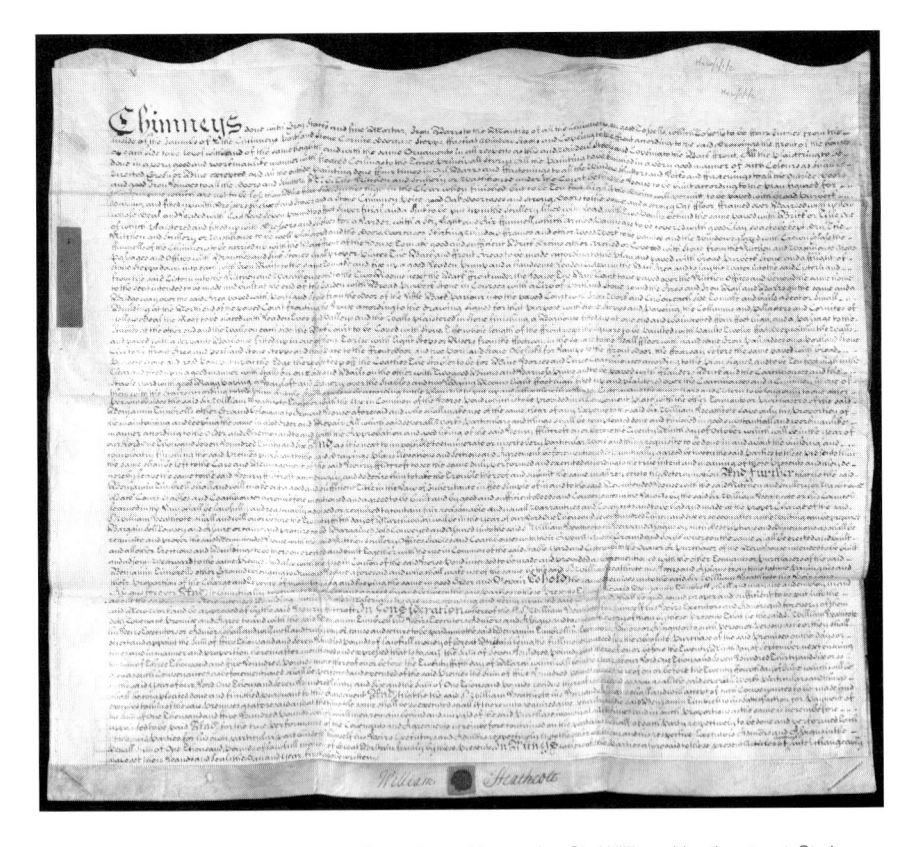

Figure 8.1 "Articles of Agreement for a Town House for Sir William Heathcote at St James Square, London," (1734–6). Architect: Henry Flitcroft.
Source: Courtesy of the Royal Institute of British Architects Library Drawings and Archives Collections.

George Dance the Younger, on behalf of the Newgate Gaol Committee. Appended to the descriptions of their work are some further clauses setting out the scope of the architect's responsibility under whose direction the "Whole of the Works are to be executed in the best Manner possible," and according to his "minute Precision" and "utmost Degree of Exactness" to the "Letter of the Particulars."[10] It was also the architect's role to settle disputes between the different trades:

> NB.
>
> The Architect is to settle and adjust all Differences and Disputes between any two or more Workmen, relating to their executing their Works in Concert, or otherwise, and his Decision shall be final and binding to all Parties, both in the above Instance and every other which shall occur during the whole Course of carrying on this Building.[11]

This is an unusually early example of this newer type of specification, but the project was publicly funded and therefore demanded more stringent accounting and contractual procedures and thus the writing of full detailed specifications in advance. Even before the emergence of the capitalist general contractor, new state involvement in construction was already changing the building industry, and demanding of architects new responsibilities and skills in administration, writing, and direction of work on site.

Like Dance at Newgate Gaol, Soane administered the contract for Tendring Hall (1784) and employed sub-contractors himself. Interestingly though, "The particulars and estimates of the several works" for the project are split in two parts (see Figure 8.2). The specification for the "finishing" followed the traditional format, as finishing was discussed while work was in progress until completion and paid by measure. This had been the practice in speculative building, where master builders built the "shell" for purchase by customers to finish to their own taste.[12] The "shell" of the building—planned and estimated in advance of construction—required a different specification format. This document has similarities to the Newgate Gaol specifications, which also supported pricing in advance, and it is a precursor of nineteenth-century specifications that were associated with the introduction of contracting in gross. This new form of contracting was part of a public reform that followed arrears in the accounts of several offices and aimed to control the expenditure of public money. Contracting in gross introduced competitive tendering, and the general contractor aimed to secure profit by employing or contracting others to reduce costs below the fixed sum, often leading to a decline in quality. Specifications, and a growing number of other legal documents, were a means to ensure quality, understood as the exact execution of the architect's intentions. The production of specifications subsequently became an increasingly significant part of the architect's practice.

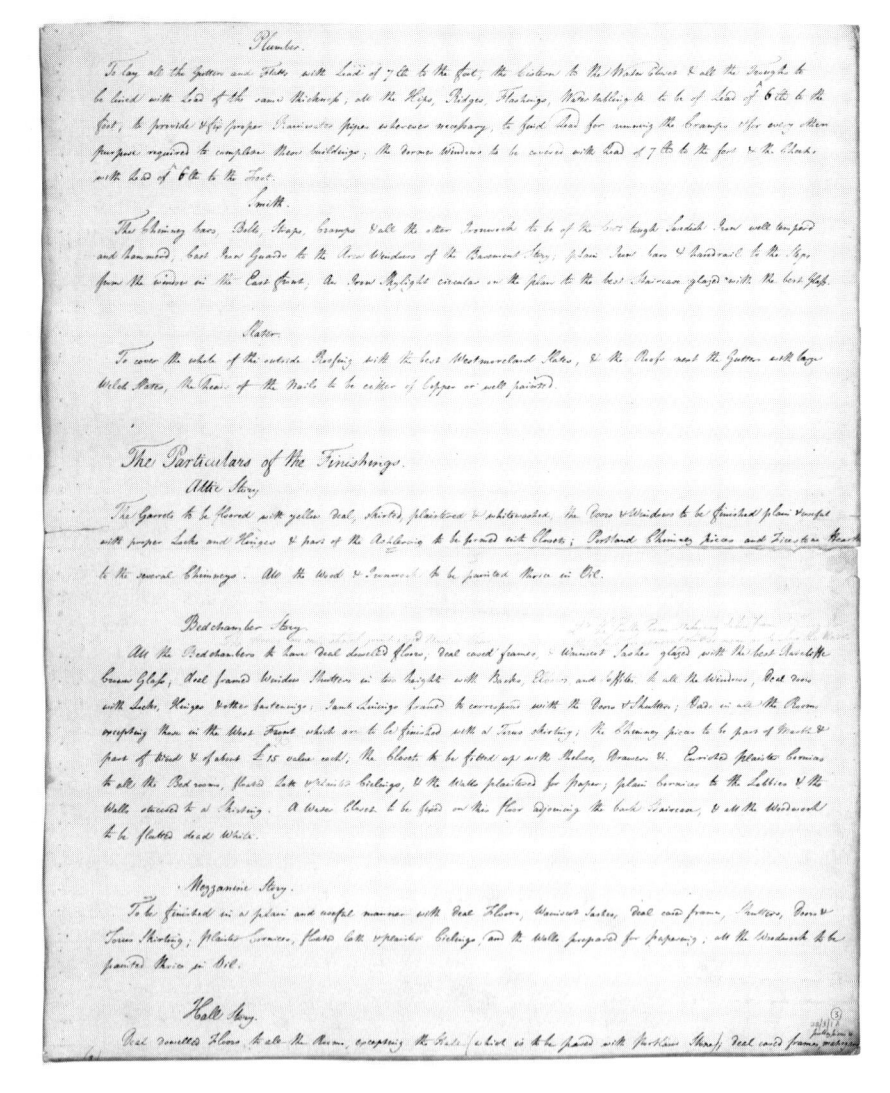

Figure 8.2 "The particulars and estimates of the several works," Tendring Hall, (1784). Architect: John Soane.
Source: Courtesy of the Trustees of Sir John Soane's Museum. Photo: Ardon Bar-Hama.

Moreover, the authority of these material objects and their legal wording replaced the direct verbal exchanges of architects and builders on site, as evidenced by the change of wording of a key phrase in the specifications that determined the supervision of construction. In documents prior to contracting in gross, the common phrase "as shall be directed" indicated there would be further future direction about the building process *outside* the specifications and drawings. With contracting in gross, new phrases such as "except where *herein* otherwise directed" and "except as *hereinafter* mentioned" were used.[13] These phrases refer back *inside* the documents, foreclosing the possibility of unspecified future direction. Decisions, directions, and negotiations are already prescribed and defined within the writing itself.

Nineteenth-century architectural handbooks and practical guides all advised the use of clauses that reinstated the authority of the specification. For example, Bartholomew includes the following exemplar clause produced by his own office:

> Mode.   1010. The whole of the brickwork, *except where herein otherwise directed*, is to be done in manner of English bond, and is to be completely laid in and to be entirely flushed up at every course with mortar; and the whole of the foundation-work is to be grouted with liquid mortar at every course (or at every second or third course, if deemed sufficient, and in thicker walls the work may be grouted all the way up.)[14]

This change in phrase from "as shall be directed" to "except where herein otherwise directed" indicates both the central role of legal documents in the material relations of construction, and the shift in building towards the execution of the prescribed documents. If, on the one hand, these new circumstances produced a real change in the architect's work towards writing and administration, on the other hand, the architect needed a deeper grasp of work processes on site in order to specify and administer them.

Out of this, a certain authority and expertise became necessary to the work of architects, especially in relation to the work of their builders who might now be unknown to them. It also demonstrates the growing importance of "writing work" as the architect's means to compensate for no longer having the assurance that had been afforded by dealing with known and trusted builders. Hence for Donaldson, the author of one of the handbooks of specifications (1859), "much of the characteristic practice of the architect, and his tone of mind are evidenced by the manner in which he writes his descriptions."[15] It can even be argued that in this new context it was documents, rather than architects, that were to direct the building process.

"Writing descriptions of work": Trades-based specification and the description of process

The new forms of specification that emerged with pricing in advance may have changed architects' work and given them and the documents they produced greater authority in the building process, but they also involved new kinds of trades-oriented description that transformed their knowledge and understanding of building. The two kinds of specification—for payment by measure and for a named sum in advance—at Soane's Tendring Hall (1784) each follow a very different structure. The specification for the "finishing" is organized in order of the stories of the building from top to bottom ("Attic Story," "Bedchamber Story," "Mezzanine Story," "Hall Story," "Great Staircase," "Basement Story"), whereas the particulars for building the new house and office describe the "shell" of the house according to trades and in sequence of work (digger, bricklayer, carpenter, mason, plumber, smith, slater).[16] This trades-based organization continued to be the norm throughout the nineteenth and twentieth centuries, and is the recommended structure in the index to the first edition of a new annual journal, *Specification*, launched in 1898 to give architects guidance on writing specifications (see Figure 8.4). "In this arrangement," the journal's editor explained, "the trowel-using trades are kept together as are also the hammer-using trades, the metal trades and the finishing trades."[17] And each trade was celebrated in the wonderfully anachronistic title blocks showing them at work (see Figure 8.3).

Figure 8.3 Joiner title block, *Specification* (1898).

Source: Courtesy of EMAP.

TABLE OF CONTENTS.

Editorial Announcements:
To Readers—Literary Contributions—Illustrations—To Correspondents .. 2

Introduction:
Points to ensure a well-written Specification—Note for Subscribers 5—10

DIVISION I. Construction.

General Conditions:
General Notes—Specification Clauses—The London Building Act 13—17

Excavator:
General Notes—Foundations—Piles—Specification Clauses—The London Building Act—Glossary 19—23

Well-Sinker:
Shallow Wells—Deep Wells—Glossary 25—29

:cretor:
General Notes—Materials—Application to various Positions—Specification Clauses—The London Building Act—Glossary 31—35

Bricklayer:
Bricks—Details and Purposes—Piers—Furnace Chimney Shafts—Workmanship—Specification Clauses—The London Building Act—Glossary 37—47

Drainlayer:
House Drainage—Town or District Sewerage—Specification Clauses—The London Building Act—Glossary 49—53

Terra Cotta Worker:
Designing—Materials—Manufacturing Notes—Building—Specification Clauses—The London Building Act—Glossary 55—59

Mason:
General Notes—Selection—Setting Masonry—Specification Clauses—The London Building Act—Glossary 61—69

Pavior:
Plain Paving—Decorated Paving—Specification Clauses—The London Building Act—Glossary 71—73

Carpenter:
General Notes—Floors—Girders—Roofs—Partitions, Linings, and Fencing—Hall Timber Work—Selection and Detection—Spectator's Stands—Specification Clauses—The London Building Act—Glossary 75—87

Joiner:
Materials—Floors—Doors—Windows—Specification Clauses—The London Building Act—Glossary 89—99

Ironmonger:
Doors—Door Checks—Windows—Specification Clauses—The London Building Act—Glossary 101—105

Slater:
Slate Rocks—Roofing—Specification Clauses—The London Building Act—Glossary 107—111

Tiler:
Roofing Tiles—Tables—Miscellaneous Roofings—Specification Clauses—The London Building Act—Glossary 113—117

Thatcher:
General Notes—Materials—Workmanship—Specification Clauses—The London Building Act—Glossary 119—121

Structural Engineer:
General Notes—Structural Castings—Wrought Iron—Steel—Iron and Steel Sheets—All-iron Roofing—Cast Iron Columns and Stanchions—Iron and Steel Joists or Girders—Compound Joists or Girders—Painting Iron and Steel Work—Specification Clauses—The London Building Act—Glossary 123—141

Fireproof Construction:
General Notes—Materials—Fireproof Construction—Specification Clauses—The London Building Act 143—149

Heating Engineer:
General Notes—Systems—Specification Clauses—The London Building Act 151—155

Horticultural Engineer:
Conservatories—Glasshouses for Special Purposes—Miscellaneous Houses: Heating, Cooling, and Ventilating—The London Building Act—Glossary 157—161

Hydraulic Engineer:
Power—Pumps and Engines—Lifts—Specification Clauses—The London Building Act—Glossary 163—167

Mechanical Engineer:
General Notes—Buildings—Foundations—Boilers—Specification Clauses—The London Building Act—Glossary 169—175

Ventilating Engineer:
General Notes—Natural Ventilation—Specification Clauses—The London Building Act—Glossary 177—181

Founder:
General Notes—Light Constructional Cast-iron Work—Grates, Chimney Pieces, Stoves, etc. Specification Clauses—The London Building Act—Glossary 183—187

Smith:
General Notes—Small Structural Smithery—Specification Clauses—The London Building Act—Glossary 189—193

Art Metal Worker:
Ornamental Ironwork—Ornamental Copper—Specification Clauses 195—197

Zincworker and Coppersmith:
Zincworker—Coppersmith—Specification Clauses—The London Building Act—Glossary 199—203

Electrician:
Lighting—Specification Clauses—The London Building Act—Glossary 205—213

Bellhanger:
Mechanical Bells—Pneumatic Bells—Electric Bells—Specification Clauses—The London Building Act—Glossary 215—219

Gasfitter:
Illumination—Service—Specification Clauses—The London Building Act—Glossary 221—225

Plumber:
General Notes—External Plumber—Specification Clauses—The London Building Act—Glossary 227—235

Plasterer:
Limes—Cements—Plasters—Internal Work—External Work—Specification Clauses—The London Building Act—Glossary 237—243

Glazier:
Glass—Glazing with Putty—Specification Clauses—The London Building Act—Glossary 245—249

Painter and Decorator:
General Notes—Painting—Varnishing—Gilding—Distempering—Specification Clauses—The London Building Act—Glossary 251—257

Paperhanger:
General Notes—Old Work—Specification Clauses—The London Building Act—Glossary 259—263

Blind Maker:
Inside Blinds—Outside Blinds—Specification Clauses—Glossary 265—267

Furnisher:
Private Building—Public Buildings—The London Building Act—Glossary 269—273

Gardener:
Entrance Gates, Lodge, and Approach—Garden Plan—Flower Garden—Specification Clauses—Glossary 275—279

Road Maker:
Roads and Streets—Footpaths—Specification Clauses—The London Building Act—Glossary 281—285

DIVISION II. Professional Practice.

Surveyor:
Dilapidations—Ancient Lights—Mensuration Rules—Tables—Scales of Fees—Glossary 289—295

Hygienic Engineer:
Water Supply—Sewerage—Specification Clauses—The London Building Act—Glossary 297—303

Legal:
Some leading Principles of the Law of Contracts in England and Ireland—Announcements 305—307

Miscellaneous:
Customs 309

DIVISION III. Buildings in Progress.

The Surveyors' Institution 312
Colchester Town Hall 313
North Bridge Street, Edinburgh 314
Belfast City Hall 315
Paddockhurst, Sussex 316
The Guildhall, Cambridge 317
Town Hall and Law Courts, Cardiff 318, 319
House for Mr. Julian Sturgis 320

For Advertisers' Directory see Page 8.

Figure 8.4 Contents page, *Specification* (1898).

Source: Courtesy of EMAP.

Organization by stories, however, is shared with specifications of the traditional type as in the "Articles of Agreement" for St James Square (1734–6). Descriptions of each floor start from the lowest point of the house and move upwards to the garrets and outbuildings (a plan of: "the lower storey," "hall and parlour floor," "chamber floor," "attick storey," "garrets or upper storey," "kitchen and scullery or washhouse"). Moreover, each section is almost entirely concerned with the dimensions of rooms and structural beams, and the information the document conveys has more in common with a drawn section of the house:

> No.3 Plan of the Chamber floor
>
> The same to be thirteen foot six inches high in the clear when finished the teaked flooring framed of sound and good fir timber Beams fourteen inches by twelve the ceiling joysts a little below the Girder to preserve the Ceilings from cracking the upper joyst not less then neine inches by two and an half to be floored with clean deal dowelled except the landing of the two staircases.[18]

Both Davis and Summerson note the rather general nature of the indenture's description of the works. Materials are only sometimes named, and there is no mention of methods or of quality to be achieved. This form of description was adequate as a contractual agreement for payment by measure, but also required little engagement from the architect with the sequences of work involved in building. Here, building is seen as an object.

The practical advantage of the newer division by trades is made clear by the pamphlets of the specifications for Newgate Gaol and the Sessions House (1769). Each single pamphlet varied in length and covered the work of one of the various trades ("Bricklayer," "Carpenter," "Glazier," "Mason," "Painter," "Plaisterer," "Plumber," "Joiner," "Smith/Ironmonger") to whom the contract was let out.[19] The description of the carpenter's work ran to eight pages, while the "Description of the Painter's Work" comprised just one clause on the title page:

Writing work: Changing practices of architectural specification

> Description of the Painter's Work
>
> To paint all the outside Wood and Iron-Works, in every Part of this Building, *four Times in Oil*, and to paint all the inside Wood and Iron Works, in every Part of this Building, *three Times in Oil*, of such plain Colours as shall be directed.[20]

As for all the trades, and in contrast to the St James Square specification, this clause includes some instructions for methods of work. These "process-based clauses" became lengthier and more frequent towards the end of the eighteenth century, and were widespread by the nineteenth century. They were particularly suitable for describing materials made up on site, such as mortars and concrete, as in the following early example from Thomas Hardwick's handwritten "Description of the several works to be done in erecting a new chapel and wing buildings in St James Burial Ground, Tottenham Court Road" (1791–2):

Brickwork	The joints of all the brickwork of the vaults to be struck and jointed
Foundations	The mortar used in the said work to be compounded of good and well burnt lime made from chalk or stone and mixed with clean sharp grit sand attested to be taken from the river Thames, between Fulham and London Bridge. The mortar to be made up in as small quantities as the nature of the business will admit and to be thoroughly beaten with stampers. All the lime shall be Sieve'd very fine and well chafed slaked under cover and mixed in such proportions as the surveyor shall approve.[21]
Top Of Plinth	

This clause demonstrates more than increasing precision. The architect is here engaged with a wider range of parameters than in eighteenth-century specifications—from the stretch of the Thames where sand shall be drawn to instructing the work of the surveyor—and he acknowledges the experience and judgment of the builder who mixes the mortar. Importantly, this form of description allows materials and buildings to be understood as the result of processes of work, rather than just as raw materials or commodities on the market, since techniques of labor are specified and made visible.

For the architect, the requirement to set out the work of the trades in the specification must have engendered a real familiarity with building, but it is also the case that the architect takes hold of an area of knowledge and experience that once belonged to the artisan and the guilds. In his marvelous *History of Techniques*, Bertrand Gille traces the origin of written descriptions of techniques such as these to medieval craft treatises like Theophilus' *On Divers Arts*, and others covering such domains as locksmithing, pottery, and metallography, where the craftsperson committed to writing "an accumulation of concordant observation in a given domain based on experience and memory."[22] For Gille, the "birth of a technical literature" allowed the transmission of technical know-how through means other than demonstration and gesture.[23] The process-based clause transfers authority and expertise from the builder to the architect, while at the same time the act of writing implies for the architect a certain intimacy with the processes of building and renders visible the work of others. For the Victorian architects, it was a central part of their practice. Brian Hanson has observed that theoretical concerns with craft by architects such as August Welby Pugin and writers such as John Ruskin coincided with the emergence of contracting in gross.[24] At the point at which the separation between builders and architects intensifies architects develop an intellectual interest in the processes of building. Because architects were newly required to describe building processes in full, there was, in addition, a familiarity with those processes developed through their writing work which may also have influenced their burgeoning theoretical interest in the craft of architecture.

The trades-based organization of the specification continued until the 1970s, and process-based clauses became ever more detailed, with some of the most compendious specifications produced in-house by the London County Council in the 1960s. Their "Specification for the Elfrida Rathbone School" (1961) consists of 161 closely typed pages describing in extraordinary, prose-like detail every aspect of the building process, from washing out buckets to the preparation of material samples for approval. The section for the "Concretor" runs to fifteen pages, despite the fact that the school was built almost entirely in brick. Interestingly, and in addition to the description of the physical process of construction, the process-based clauses in these documents also make numerous references to the work of the parties involved in building (as to a lesser extent in the example of the clause for mortar at St James's Burial Ground). In the clauses for casting concrete there are references to the contractor, the builder, and the architect as well as to building standards and to procedures of measurement and control. For example, in the Elfrida Rathbone School specification, the checking of bags of cement upon arrival on site is prescribed:

> Cement C2.
>
> Bags of cement which arrive on site must have their weight checked, each quality of cement is to be tested on site, and the contractor must keep enough cement on site to satisfy the architect and send him manufacturer's advice note after each delivery.[25]

Even the workman's lunch break is incorporated into a clause concerning the care to be taken with cleaning out the mixer:

> Mixing C10
>
> On the cessation of work, including short stoppages for meals, or on any change of type of cement used in the mix, the mixers and all handling plant shall be washed out with clean water.[26]

Certainly these clauses demonstrate greater "precision" of the documents. But at another level, the trade and process-based specifications that dominated the building industry for 200 years were "descriptions of work." They forced architects to be familiar with the building process, to spell out the labor of building workers, and to maintain some understanding of "building" as labor process. Furthermore, in these "building specifications," the work of architects, contractors, and surveyors, and the work of laborers, are to some extent set out side-by-side in writing. Here building is rendered as a social process between different workers.

From "means" to "ends" in specifications since the 1960s

In the 1960s, as concerns grew within the profession that architects would lose control of the production of the specification, "building specifications," with their organization around trades and their detailed descriptions of work on site would gradually be superseded. In 1963, a "specifications panel" was formed as part of the RIBA technical committee, and there was intense debate between members, contributors, and in the architectural press on a subject usually at the margins of architectural practice. On the one hand, the traditional form of the specification with its "repetitiveness between the various documents, the danger of discrepancies, and an archaic form of wording and presentation," was no longer efficient.[27] On the other, with the rising use of building systems and components in construction, all too often it was manufacturers who specified their own products and supplied texts for the specification documents.[28]

Although specifications had previously been written by different parties—a clerk employed by the day in Soane's practice, a specification writer working within a standardized framework at the London County Council, and often by architects themselves—they were always produced in-house. By the 1960s, parts of the specification were being written by manufacturers, amongst others, and the fear among architects was that this would only increase.[29] According to panel member Allen Ray-Jones, the answer was not to rail against the new "industrial building" methods but to find ways to at least control the manner in which these components were put together through retaining the practice of their specification.[30] As another panel member put it, "The Architect must be the initiator of the specification. He alone must determine the materials, workmanship and components to go into the building."[31] The panel concluded that to retain their authority, architects needed to produce more concise, streamlined documents, and their inquiry led finally to the preparation of a new standardized "master" specification to be developed by the RIBA and used throughout the profession. This new National Building Specification (NBS) was launched in 1973.

Notably, the long-held techniques of describing methods of construction in detail were also to be superseded. According to Colin McGregor, a member of the NBS feasibility team, a guiding principle was that "the specification describes 'work in place,' that means the finished result rather than the process of achieving it."[32] The new NBS was intended to move away from describing the *processes* of building that had been so central since the late eighteenth century, towards an emphasis on the building as *object*. As Tony Allot, another member

Writing work: Changing practices of architectural specification

of the NBS development team, explained in 1971, "NBS policy is based on the belief that specification should state requirements in terms of ends rather than means, but that there are practical limits in most cases."[33] Although the new document would include much more detail than the single-page specifications that disappeared in the Georgian period, it shared with them the emphasis on "work in place."

The emphasis on "ends" was manifested in the new NBS in two ways. First, the work sections were organized by product.[34] For example, what had been the "Concretor" section in previous trade-based specifications became "B" (Concreting Formwork Reinforcement Concrete finishes), "Painter" became "V" (Painting Film coatings). Each section was titled with a letter and arranged alphabetically, suggesting a more abstract, unchanging logic to the organization of construction in contrast to the previous division by trades, although the order of the product-based sections still followed roughly the order of work on site. (See Figure 8.5.) The introduction to the NBS made its intended rupture with the old order clear: "Each work section deals with one main type of product in a defined range of applications. No attempt has been made to identify these kinds of work with 'trades.'"[35] In 1997, the more computer-compatible system UNICLASS (United Classification for the Construction Industry) was introduced,

Figure 8.5 Cover, *National Building Specification* (1973).

Courtesy of RIBA Enterprises.

and its letter titles and product classifications still structure UK specification. Even as performance specification becomes more widely used, the standard structure of the specification still retains the object-oriented organization derived from the first NBS.

Second, the focus on describing ends rather than means drastically reduced the number of clauses describing methods of work. This approach was intended to avoid architects giving instructions that were redundant or mistaken. It also allowed contractors to find expedient methods that suited them and relied in part on quality of work being specified in building standards and regulations, determined outside the architect's remit. But in practice, the NBS continued to use a variety of forms of description. Even in today's NBS, process-based clauses appear alongside those naming products and materials to be used. NBS documents also include the newer type of clause, performance specification, that describes "work in place" through the performance criteria to be achieved by building components and systems selected by the contractor. As in the Georgian period, when different types of building project and contractual organization required a range of forms of specification, the variety of types of clause in the NBS responds to the demands of very different practices of building, from small-scale and innovative projects requiring bespoke descriptions of work, to larger commercial projects making use of standardized systems that can be performance-specified. Within the NBS framework, "writing work" can still take place in-house and include directions for builders to seek the architect's approval. In the digital version of the NBS drop-down menus of pre-set materials and products are provided. Product placement in the menus can be paid for by manufacturers. Nevertheless, the pre-set selections and texts can be overridden, and more importantly detailed description of unfamiliar processes and techniques remains possible.

In newer forms of performance-based or "open" specification produced by consultants such as Schumann Smith, and in-house by some larger architectural practices, the eradication of process-oriented specification has been more complete.[36] If the NBS endeavored to describe "work in place," it did so by naming particular materials, components, and systems. This "closed" specification still left architects liable for their selections of materials, components, and systems, and limited contractors' choice. In the "open" specifications used for large-scale building projects and for design and build contracts, clauses are carefully worded to remain as free as possible of prescriptions for one method of work over another, and also of the names of specific materials and products.[37] Wherever possible, performance specification is used, and the "means" of building are excluded, just as the NBS team member Allot envisaged. Here, the description of the "ends," through quantities and units of performance measurement, results not in the description of the building as object, but as a yet more nebulous, even immaterial, abstraction.

The specification produced by Schumann Smith for a London office building in 2006, for example, designed by a well-known UK practice, was intended as far as possible to make use of open specification. The document is still organized in the A-Z categories of UNICLASS, but two types of specification are defined: "prescriptive," where the architect names methods or products and is therefore responsible for the solution, and "descriptive," where the architect only "indicates the *visual intent* with which the contractor must comply when undertaking the detailed design."[38] In this case it is the contractor who "retains full responsibility for completing the detailed design and the execution of the works and for meeting the specified performance criteria."[39] What is left to the architect is the design, comprising only the specification (already emptied out of detailed design) and the design drawings. The design drawings are defined in the preliminaries of the specification as follows:

A.1004   Definitions
    f)   "Design Drawings": Drawings issued by the Employer's Retained Architect, representing the Design for Tender purposes, showing the visual and design intent, scope, layout, principal dimensions, arrangement of services and structure, technical, function, visual and aesthetic requirements.[40]

Here the architect's primary role is to show "visual and design intent." As long as the contractor's detailed designs conform to the performance criteria and to the architect's "visual and aesthetic requirements," how and with what they are achieved is not the business of the architect. Their "writing work," or that of the consultants they employ, involves the correct specification of performance criteria, usually already determined in standards and regulations, and by referral back to their drawings. There is a strange chimerical quality to this "writing work" in so far as it only brings architects closer to the *limits* of their involvement with building.

Building as "ideal form"

In contrast to the trades-based specifications produced from the late eighteenth century until the 1960s, neither the lengthy "open" specifications produced today nor the briefer documents associated with the work of the architect in the early eighteenth century and before, yield much in the way of "Descriptions of Work." The relative absence of building processes and instructions concerning the architect's remit may be common to both types, but it arises out of very different contractual and economic contexts. Where individual trades decided the details of construction on site, and payment was by measure, the work of building could be based on personal relations, trust, and speech—there was no need for such work to be written out in full in the specification. With the rise of the general contractor in the early days of capitalist building production, building came to involve professional relations, legal obligations, and writing, where a minute description of the project had to be set out in the specification in advance. Material documents mediated, and even stood in for, the relation of the architect to work carried out on site. At that time, the requirement to describe building processes in detail in order to compensate for loss of trust made *building* as well as the built object a central part of the architect's work. Today, in conditions of advanced capitalism, amidst a heightened atmosphere of mistrust between contractors and architects, and an increase in claims and litigation, the same requirement to secure quality via the specifications conversely *empties* such documents of descriptions of work.

In their essay "A Historical Context for Theories Underpinning the Production of the Built Environment," Linda Clarke and Jörn Janssen stress the necessity for (historical materialist) analyses and theories of the built environment that are capable of understanding that "production is itself a social, not a physical process."[41] While the trades-based specifications that emerged with pricing in advance in the eighteenth century were instruments in the transformation of building production (particularly with the rise of contracting in gross), and in the constitution of the work of architects, builders, and others, the nature of their descriptions maintained some *presence* of the processes of building production. Consideration and knowledge of such processes were necessarily part of the architect's work. There was a presence of building and labor in the documents even before the historian's theorization that Clarke and Janssen demand.

What is striking in contemporary specifications is the very *absence* of these processes, and the efforts of the industry to obscure them yet further. Clarke and Janssen go on to explain:

Once buildings, the built product, are looked at only as objects of market exchange and distribution, the social relations that they incorporate are no longer apparent. This is because, through exchange, buildings in some sense become *ideal forms*, their value appearing to be embedded in them rather than referring to the human labor involved in their production.[42]

What may be most telling about reading specifications for their descriptions of work is seeing in which contexts those descriptions disappear. The performance-led open specifications produced by specification consultancies such as Schumann Smith go further towards the description of building as "ideal form," and making social relations invisible, than NBS specifications that aimed to replace "means" with "ends." With respect to the work of architects, the writing work of specifying building processes and materials is increasingly outside their remit. "Design" or "visual intent" is reinstated as the architect's primary task. To take the architect's writing work seriously in our analyses raises some questions for design. For example, is the prevalence of "form-finding" in contemporary architecture less the result of new digital tools, geometries, art theory, or philosophy, and more the result of how the architect's role is prescribed in the changing contractual context of an increasingly market-driven building industry? To examine architects' writing work also raises questions around human labor in architectural production. For almost two centuries the processes of work, the labor of builders and architects, were written into specifications, whereas today's open specifications represent buildings primarily as "ideal forms", obscuring social relations and the value of human labor involved in producing them. In today's context of advanced capitalism building as labor process and the social relations between the parties involved are as veiled for researchers reading the documents, as for the architects who write the architectural specifications.

Notes

1. John Soane, "Order Book, No. 2" (31 March to 6 July, 1787), Sir John Soane's Museum, London, authors' emphasis.
2. For historical examples dating back to classical Greece and Egypt, see: John Gelder, *Specifying Architecture: A Guide to Professional Practice* (Milsons Point: Construction Information Systems Australia, 2001).
3. Alfred Bartholomew, *Specifications for Practical Architecture, Preceded by an Essay on the Decline of Excellence in the Structure and in the Science of Modern English Building; with the Proposal of Remedies for those Defects* (London: John Williams and Co., 1841), 1.

4. In order to explain the development of the construction industry, it is necessary to examine the social relations that have evolved in individual countries rather than attempt to plot a path towards the emergence of a large-scale market. This is one of the peculiarities of the construction industry. Even between advanced capitalist countries there are wide variations in the social forces influencing the industry's development.

   Michael Ball, *Rebuilding Construction* (London: Routledge, 1988), 37.
5. For accounts of this shift, see: John Summerson, *Georgian London* (London: Pleiades Books, 1945); Linda Clarke, *Building Capitalism. Historical Change and the Labour Process in the Production of the Built Environment* (London: Routledge, 1992); Akira Satoh, *Building in Britain: The Origins of a Modern Industry* (Aldershot: Ashgate, 1995).
6. "Particulars for a Bakehouse, Dwelling and Lofts in Parish of St Anne, Middlesex," (1770), RIBA Archives WiR/1.
7. See particularly: Howard Davis, *The Culture of Building* (Oxford: Oxford University Press, 2006), 186, 193.
8. Karl Marx, *Capital*, trans. Samuel Moore and Edward Aveling (Oxford, New York: Oxford University Press, 1999 [1887]), 84.
9. "Articles of Agreement for a Town House for Sir William Heathcote at St James Square, London" (1734–6), RIBA Archives, HeW/1/1/2.
10. "Specification for Newgate Gaol and the Sessions House at the Old Bailey, London" (1769), RIBA Library, Early Works No.790.
11. Ibid.
12. As late as the mid-nineteenth century, it was still common practice to divide building work under two general headings: "carcase" and "finishing." See: Thomas Leverton Donaldson, *Handbook of Specifications: or, Practical Guide to the Architect, Engineer, Surveyor, and Builder, in Drawing Up Specifications and Contracts for Works and Constructions* (London: Atchley and Co., 1859).
13. See: Bartholomew, *Specifications for Practical Architecture*, 987–1011; Thomas Larkin Walker, *An Essay on Architectural Practice* (London: R. A. Sprigg, 1841), i-ii.
14. Bartholomew, *Specifications for Practical Architecture*, 990, authors' emphasis.
15. Donaldson, *Handbook of Specifications*, xii.
16. "The Particulars and Estimates of the Several Works for Tendring Hall" (1784), Sir John Soane's Museum, London, SM 28/3/1a/1-6.
17. *Specification*, 1898, 1.
18. "Articles of Agreement for a Town House for Sir William Heathcote at St James Square" (1734–6), RIBA Archives, HeW/1/1/2.
19. "Specification for Newgate Gaol and the Sessions House at the Old Bailey, London" (1769), RIBA Library, Early Works No.790.
20. Ibid.
21. "Description of the Several Works to be Done in Erecting a New Chapel and Wing Buildings in St James Burial Ground, Tottenham Court Road" (1791–2), RIBA Archives, AC/HAR/Add/2.

22. Bertrand Gille, ed., *History of Techniques Volume 2, Part 3, Techniques and Sciences*, trans. J. Brainon and K. Butler et al. (New York: Gordon + Bream Scientific Publishers, 1986), 1147.
23. Ibid.
24. Brian Hanson, *Architects and the "Building World" from Chambers to Ruskin: Constructing Authority* (Cambridge: Cambridge University Press, 2003).
25. "Specification for the Works at the Elfrida Rathbone School for the Educationally Subnormal, Camberwell" (1961), RIBA Archives, LCC/AD/1.
26. Ibid.
27. "Michelmore's Report," 1963, RIBA Library, Specifications Panel Papers Box 1.
28. "Allen Ray-Jones Report," 1963, RIBA Library, Specifications Panel Papers Box 1.
29. As adviser Maurice Golding wrote in his 1963 notes to Anthony Laing, Chair of the Specifications Panel, 9 July, 1964, "The architect has to some considerable extent delegated the specifying and choosing of materials and sub-contractors ... The quantity surveyor and other interested parties including the contractor often avail themselves of the opportunity to influence what materials and whose services should be used." RIBA Library, Specifications Panel Papers Box 1.
30. "Allen Ray-Jones Report," 1964, RIBA Library, Specifications Panel Papers Box 1.
31. "Mr George Report," 1963, RIBA Library, Specifications Panel Papers Box 1.
32. Colin McGregor, email correspondence with co-author Katie Lloyd Thomas, 3 June, 2006.
33. Tony Allot, "NBS; A Progress Report," *RIBA Journal* (February 1971): 82.
34. The structure of the first NBS was based on a Swedish classification system, "SfB." See: L.M. Giertz, *SfB and Its Development 1950–80* (Dublin: CIB/SfB International Bureau, 1982), 3.
35. *National Building Specification* (London: RIBA Publications Ltd., 1973).
36. Since this research was carried out in 2006 (with the caveat that full details of the specifications consulted would not be published for legal reasons), the specifications consultancy Schumann Smith has been bought out.
37. Some anomalous process-based clauses still appear in the "Specification for the H...y Building (2006)," for example, describing the cleaning of bird-droppings from stone.
38. "Specification for the H...y Building (2006)." The authors were asked by Schumann Smith to anonymize this specification in any publications.
39. Ibid.
40. Ibid.
41. Linda Clarke and Jörn Janssen, "A historical context for theories underpinning the production of the built environment," *Building Research & Information* 36.6 (2008): 660.
42. Ibid., 662, authors' emphasis.

Chapter 9

Working globally: The human networks of transnational architectural projects

Mabel O. Wilson, Jordan Carver, and Kadambari Baxi[1]

When the *Fédération Internationale de Football Association* (FIFA) named its host city for the 2022 World Cup—the small Gulf nation of Qatar, which had outbid ambitious proposals from the United States, Japan, South Korea, and Australia—the highly anticipated announcement underscored the stratospheric costs (and debt) that these global sporting events place on host countries.[2] All of the World Cup matches are to be played in or near Doha, Qatar's capital and major city, where the scorching desert sun regularly tops 100 degrees Fahrenheit. Recently, Doha has undergone exponential urban growth fueled by a windfall of revenues from oil and natural gas. This urbanization has been instigated by the Qatari monarchy in part to absorb capital surpluses that help diversify the nation's post-oil economy of education, culture, and leisure.[3] (See Figure 9.1.) While Doha has several existing sports facilities and has hosted smaller international sporting events, the demands of hosting the World Cup have necessitated not only investment in the construction of football stadia, but also the construction of hotels, transportation systems, and the various other infrastructures required to support an international event of this magnitude.

Like the Olympics, the quadrennial FIFA World Cup functions as much as a global entertainment spectacle as it does as an international sporting event. The backdrops against which the matches are played are dramatically designed stadia and iconic high-tech facilities often launched into public view via international architectural design competitions and the intense media focus surrounding the development of large-scale sporting events. These large-scale efforts highlight the networked and globalized nature of contemporary architectural practice. Aided by the globalization of the finance market and the media industry, the expanded spheres of design and construction have lured architects to create uniquely designed and highly prized projects that draw tourist dollars and investment capital to cities—the so-called Bilbao effect.[4] The building sites for these mega-projects—like the Beijing Olympic "Bird's Nest" (2008) designed by Swiss firm Herzog and de Meuron in consultation with the Chinese artist Ai Weiwei—bring together architects, planners, and engineers with contractors, developers, financial institutions, and thousands of construction workers who erect the showcase structures desired by governments, publics, and architects

Figure 9.1 Aerial view, Doha, Qatar.

Source: Photo by Jordan Carver.

alike. Like their neighbors in Abu Dhabi and Dubai, Qatar's various state-sponsored ministries and investment arms have embarked upon a shopping frenzy for international architectural and engineering firms to craft its global brand of a twenty-first century steel and glass oasis in the desert. The nation is already home to completed buildings or large–scale, in-process projects by a roster of international firms that include OMA, Ateliers Jean Nouvel, Legoretta + Legoretta, Arata Isozaki, I.M. Pei, Santiago Calatrava, Foster + Partners, Woods Bagot, David Adjaye Associates, HOK, Arup Associates, and AECOM to name a few (see Figure 9.2). At the same time these globalized networks of production have also distanced architects from the building sites where their buildings are under construction, deferring the intricacies of construction knowledge to a system of contractors and subcontractors who manage the sequencing of labor (and materials) to and on the site.

One controversy that exemplifies this perceived disconnection between architects and construction workers was set-off by remarks from the London-based architect Zaha Hadid. When questioned by the *Guardian* newspaper in March 2014 about ongoing human rights violations associated with the construction of FIFA projects in Qatar, where her firm has been commissioned to design the

Figure 9.2 Education City Central Library, Doha, Qatar, designed by OMA.
Source: Photo by Jordan Carver.

premier al-Wakrah stadium, Dame Hadid stated, "I have nothing to do with the workers."[5] Asked to comment on the more than 800 migrant deaths connected to World Cup projects already under way, Hadid—the Pritzker Prize-winning architect, whose office has designed and built hundreds of projects for transnational corporations, cultural institutions, and governments in Europe, Asia, and North and South America—stated that it was the governments commissioning these buildings who were in the best position to address the problem. As she put it: "I cannot do anything about it because I have no power to do anything about it. I think it's a problem anywhere in the world."[6]

Hadid's remarks about Qatar's deadly migrant labor problem attracted the attention, much of it critical, of the architectural community and media. Her statements were interpreted as being tone-deaf to the dire conditions facing the workers. But public commentary also straddled what was identified as a strict professional divide between the diverse scope of services architects provide, including those that fall under the rubric of professional ethics, and what services they are contractually obligated to perform given the legal constraints of liability. Many commenters noted that there is no contractual relationship between architect and contractor because each establishes separate contracts with the owner. Architects and contractors work at the behest of the owner's direction and best interests. In this legal scenario, Hadid, as the architect in this case, is not directly responsible for the construction of the project, since that responsibility falls under the contractor/subcontractor's purview. There exists, in other words, a deliberate separation of powers mediated through the contractual obligations of those parties involved in the building process. Yet this separation of authority and accountability belies and negates fundamental practices in architecture that transmit knowledge about the construction process to the building trades and deliver implicit and explicit instructions to the various teams of workers who assemble her buildings on site. If architects build their reputations based on their intricately detailed building designs, then is there a way that this process might also force a recognition of the value of those workers who construct buildings and the conditions under which they work?

An architect may claim to be powerless, but the question remains: How are architects connected to the workers who erect their buildings? How can architects understand that the problems endured by migrant construction workers—poor worker housing, lack of access to social spaces and civic life in their off-time, and the treacherous route of recruitment—are inherently spatial, and because of this would benefit from design expertise? Why is it a challenge for contemporary architects to comprehend their connection to labor?

Modernity, globality, and the construction industry

In the mid-1920s, architect Walter Gropius, assessing the Bauhaus's position on the relationship of older craft practices to emerging industrial techniques, posited that these differences in building practices had less to do with the types of tools and specified skills deployed in craft or industry and more to do with their respective divisions of labor, which he believed were moving closer together and could be politically unified. Gropius observed that, "the crafts of the past have changed, and the future crafts will be merged in a new productive unity in which they will carry out the experimental work for industrial production."[7] Industrialization, fed by the expansion of capitalism and modernization, would greatly transform how modern architects practiced and compel them to consider not only how building materials were produced, but also the how industrialized construction influenced methods for erecting buildings. Fellow German architect Ludwig Mies Van der Rohe, in opposition to this, championed industry over craft and believed that if materials were manufactured and buildings assembled through industrial methods then all of the building trades would be forced to adapt to new techniques, radically changing how tradesmen constructed buildings. The son of a master mason reprimanded any nostalgia for the old ways of building by cautioning: "(W)hoever regrets that the house of the future can no longer be constructed by building craftsmen should bear in mind that the motor-car is no longer built by the wheelwright."[8] The *Congrès International d'Architecture Moderne* (CIAM) La Sarraz Declaration, issued in 1928, declared that "rationalization and standardization" would "act directly on working methods in both modern architecture (conception) and in the building industry (realization)."[9] Tradesmen would become workers, fully integrated into industrialized manufacturing systems. While Modernists envisioned, in their heroic manifestos and speculative projects, an architecture suitable for a fully industrialized and mechanized civilization international in reach, their early projects were, nevertheless, mostly situated within a European context of local, traditional building practices. For Modernists, an industrial division of labor in construction proved more a concept than a practice.

Since this time, construction *has* become an industry—one no longer defined by a local set of centralized relationships between architects and building trades but by logistics and material supply chains whereby labor, goods, and knowledge are sourced according to a logic of globalized material production. Global capitalism has expanded the scope and scale of the building industry to form an expansive supply chain, a vast network of manufacturers, suppliers, and builders whose operations are aided by digital technologies and facilitated by transportation systems infiltrating most regions of the world. It employs an array of actors linked via legal and professional relationships—architects, construction managers, engineers, contractors, consultants, and construction workers. This has led to the atomization and dispersion of fields related to the design and construction of any built project, and the proliferation of contractual legal ties binding them together. These actors work off and on site to erect the educational, leisure, residential, cultural, commercial, industrial, and governmental projects in major urban hubs. In these scenarios, the design firm might be based in New York City, work with an architectural and engineering services firm based in Germany, and develop designs for a client headquartered in Sydney who has secured financing for a new mall in New Zealand built by construction workers from the Philippines. In addition to being thousands of miles apart and within their own respective nations, economies, socio-cultural milieus, and class statuses, the links between architects, contractors, clients, and construction workers have become mediated by a host of legal proscriptions and financial arrangements. The outcome of this distancing is a decoupling of design from both the labor and the regulations governing architectural and building practices. Moreover, as design and construction processes become more global and building codes and design standards follow suit, the regulations that govern the construction workforce, the construction site, and safety standards are left to local municipalities to enforce or ignore.

The workers

Since the 1970s, the liberalization of economies has propelled the movement of capital and labor to new markets around the world. These globalized connections of production have spawned economic lifelines, as families and home nations depend upon the remittances sent back by legions of migratory workers.[10] As the number of workers seeking employment in other parts of the world has increased exponentially, so has their exploitation and abuse through predatory recruitment networks and unsavory employers seeking to maximize profit by reducing wages and expanding work hours. The construction industry has taken advantage of these labor trends by contracting seasonal and short-term workforces from abroad—a labor procurement practice ideal for the one-time-only, site-specific nature of building projects.[11] (See Figure 9.3.) Vulnerable migrant construction workers often face unscrupulous conduct by recruitment firms, subcontractors, and local authorities—each jockeying to extract a bigger cut of the workers' salaries.

150   The Architect as Worker

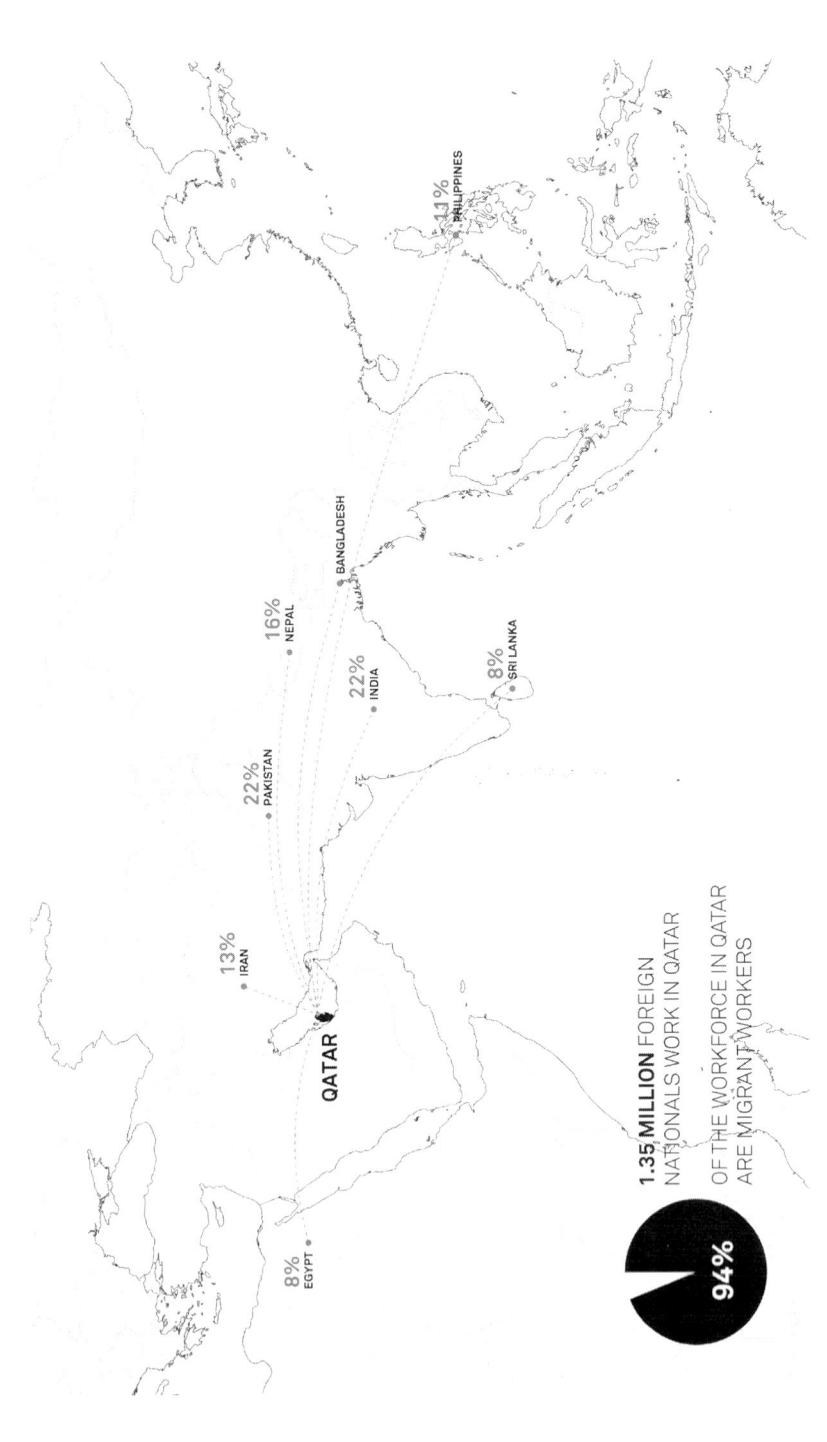

Figure 9.3 Foreign national workers in Qatar. Content for map from Amnesty International *Dark Side of Migration*.

Source: Map by Tiffany Rattray.

Persistent problems with the recruitment process include exorbitant fees exacted from workers to secure a position abroad, as well as fraudulent representation of the type of work and level of compensation. On poorly managed jobsites, migrant workers can be repeatedly exposed to dangerous working conditions. Construction companies and subcontractors seeking to limit expenditures will house thousands of men in poorly maintained, substandard accommodations that lack basic amenities for food preparation and delivery, proper hygiene, and reliable climate control in regions with extreme temperatures. Amnesty International reported a case in Qatar, for example, where workers were required to sleep in shifts due to scarce accommodation.[12] With "worker camps" often built outside the city limits, the migrant worker—shut out of the public spaces that architects and urban theorists claim are vital to a robust urban life—are isolated from the civic and social spheres of local residents. Since migrant workers are not citizens of the nations in which they work, they have very few rights and avenues of recourse to protest their poor treatment.[13]

One incident in Qatar illustrating the breadth of migrant construction worker abuse has been documented by the human rights organization Amnesty International in *The Dark Side of Migration* (2013). In a section that investigates the travails of several Indian, Nepalese, and Sri Lankan construction workers, the report exposes how large-scale building projects link vast networks of professional, skilled, and unskilled workforces around the world. Krantz Engineering, a Qatar-based firm who hired the men in question, had been subcontracted in 2010 to provide mechanical and electrical engineering services for the construction of Ras Laffan Emergency and Safety College (RLESC), located about 100 kilometers north of Doha.[14] The clients, state-owned Qatar Petroleum and Qatar's Ministry of the Interior, were in the midst of building a large campus that would provide regional courses in firefighting, safety, and emergency response—much needed skills on a desert peninsula dotted with Qatar Petroleum's sprawling refineries, energy exporting ports, and off-shore oil rigs.

Amnesty's report narrates how in mid-2012 Krantz encountered cash flow problems, forcing the firm to fall months behind in paying their employees' salaries. As a consequence of delayed compensation, workers could not send monies back to their families to pay rent, mortgages, recruitment fees, and other debts; nor did the men have money for food or other basic needs.[15] Attempts made by the workers to plead their cases to Qatari officials and respective embassies were to no avail. Amnesty's report alleges that Krantz, who had confiscated the workers' passports—a common tactic used by employers to prevent flight—was also unwilling to prepare and submit official paperwork for the men to return home, including those who were willing to leave Qatar without receiving their back pay. Amnesty documented in detail how the dire situation wrought emotional and financial distress on the workers as well as their families, many of whom were indebted to recruitment companies back home.[16] When half of the seventy stranded workers were finally able to leave Qatar, Amnesty reports that "they had to sign papers stating falsely that they had received their salaries and they had no claim against the company."[17] Amnesty contacted the primary client, Qatar Petroleum, about the fate of the Krantz workers, their poor treatment, and lost pay. Official responses deflected responsibility to the main contractor and to the subcontractor Krantz for what had happened to the men. Amnesty promptly issued a reminder that the United Nations' Guiding Principles on Business and Human Rights require that "businesses should seek to prevent, address and mitigate human rights abuses related to their operations—even if they have not contributed to them."[18]

The architects and the contractors

The job site at RLESC brought together a host of other construction industry actors (see Figure 9.4). To design the Academic Building at RLESC, Tetra Tech Architects and Engineers, an architecture/engineering firm with offices in the northeastern United States and a subsidiary of Pasadena-based Tetra Tech, was hired. In large AE firms like Tetra Tech, architecture is a small division incorporated into large project teams of allied consultants. Tetra Tech assigned over one hundred employees from their worldwide roster of 350 offices to provide architectural, structural, mechanical, and other engineering services for the design of the Academic Building.[19] Along with SEG, Black Cat Engineering, based in Qatar, served as the other primary contractor. Additional engineering and construction firms headquartered in parts of the United States, Europe, the Middle East, and Asia provided various services and expertise for the construction. Aided by Building Information Modeling (BIM) software, which allows architects, engineers, and managers to coordinate design decisions in real-time even though they may be thousands of miles apart, these firms worked collaboratively to prepare the construction documents that the various subcontracted workforces, like those hired by Krantz, executed on site. Digital technology in this segment of the construction sector connects participants in their respective workplaces and expediently delivers their services to the job site.

Within this complex network of firms and companies—many of which are subsidiaries of giant transnational corporations specializing in mining, logistics, energy extraction, infrastructural development, engineering and

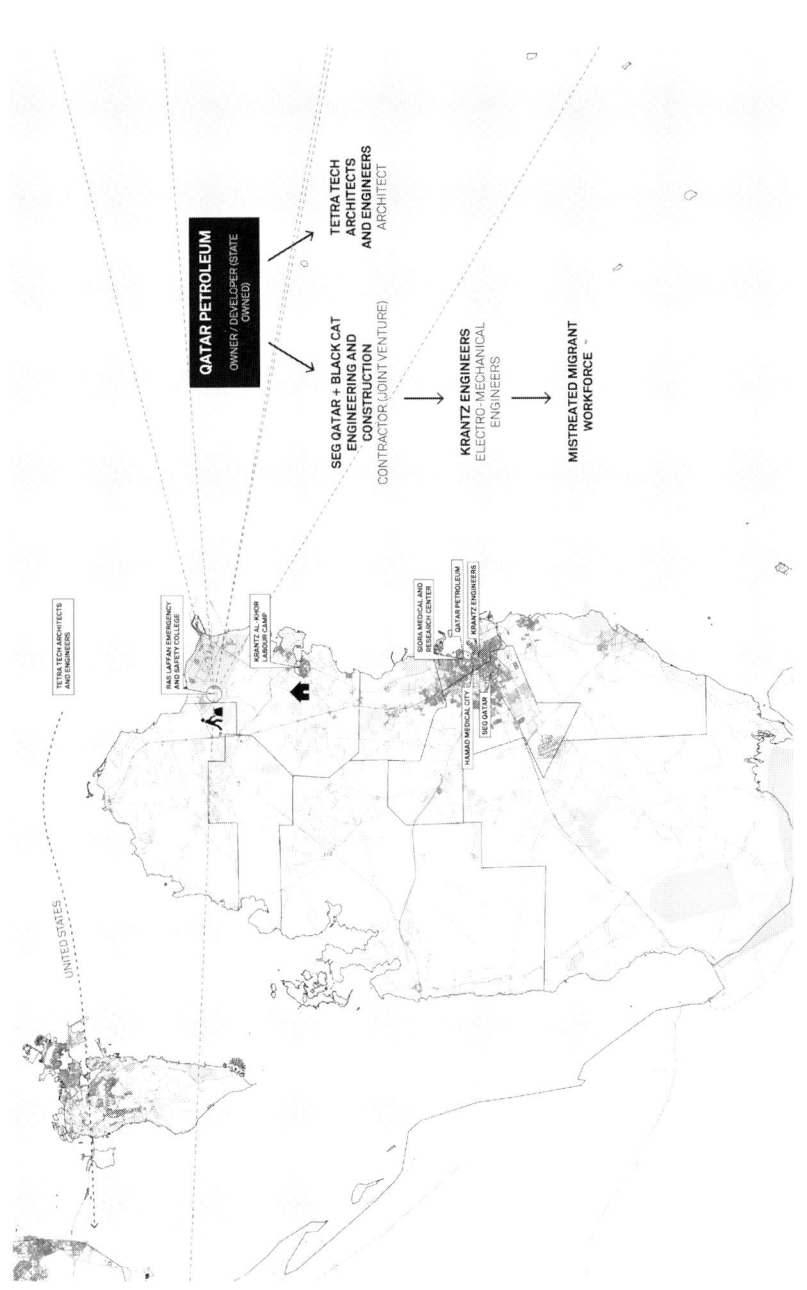

Working globally: The human networks of transnational architectural projects   153

Figure 9.4 Case study Ras Laffan Emergency and Safety College. Content for map from Amnesty International *Dark Side of Migration*.
Source: Map by Tiffany Rattray.

architecture—the contractual obligations and chain of accountability can prove daunting to discern if not impossible to access, as the workers employed by Krantz Engineering discovered. Professionals, such as the architects, engineers, and managers who operate in one sector of this global supply chain of labor, may not encounter the same problems as unskilled workers because their education and class privilege necessitate adequate compensation and suitable working conditions. However, professional positions in architecture are not immune to the influence of cheaper labor markets. The increase in subcontracting in architecture firms, observes sociologist Andrew Ross, has "meant that routine design operations—drafting, rendering, modeling—are increasingly assigned to cheaper labor in offshore locations."[20] In some echelons of architectural practice, unpaid labor in the form of internships also exerts downward pressure on wages.[21] Contractual agreements and the subcontracting process along with physical distances and socio-cultural differences divide architects from construction workers in a labyrinthine division of labor. On the one hand, large global projects benefit from the transnational connectivity of multinational companies and the accessibility to communication technologies that link participants. Yet on the other hand, the complexity of these networks also creates hierarchies and distinctions that separate actors within the system. As a result, timely resolution for the myriad of problems faced by migrant construction workers when they do occur can be elusive inside this black hole of accountability.

The above case of the Krantz workers at RLESC demonstrates how large-scale building sites function as dynamic territories. In his analysis of networks of finance, media, ideology, technology, and migration, cultural theorist Arjun Appadurai affixes the suffix "-scape" to these terms to "indicate that these are not objectively given relations that look the same from every angle of vision but, rather, that they are deeply perspectival constructs …" Traveling within an "ethnoscape" as a tourist, migrant, or architect, or circulating data and construction information via a "technoscape" can be, according to Appadurai, "inflected by the historical, linguistic, and political situatedness of different sorts of actors …"[22] From the perspective of an American architect working in an office in Rotterdam, for example, a connection via daily virtual BIM modeling sessions at her computer with an Indian engineer in Doha may be forged even as it fosters a disconnection from the migratory Nepalese construction worker hired to execute her detail one year later on the site of Doha's new national library.

"Building design can be conceived as composed of a host of different tasks," writes architect Paolo Tombesi, "spread across official project inception and management, professional design, manufacturing and building production operations."[23] But the construction documents that come out of this mix are not neutral networks in which tasks operate independently of human intention. Rather, participants at all skill levels act within the construction process to create results that come about through "linkages established between distinct components, the nature and ordering of these linkages, the choices behind their selection and the relationship of power among the actors making these determinations." Thus, power relations between all actors are implicit within the building construction process as knowledge moves from architects' conceptualization of a detail through the drawing, to the construction managers, to supervisors, and to workers in the field who execute the assembly and draw upon their own expertise in performing any given task. Tombesi suggests "there is no such thing as 'a building design', but rather a bundle of design intentions/briefs that are active and interacting within a socially dynamic framework."[24] It was this socially dynamic framework that allowed ecological sustainability into the system of design and construction as environmental information could be shared amongst actors.[25] Labor sustainability can and should be a part of this exchange as well.

For Hadid to announce, "I have nothing to do with the workers," stands in stark contradiction to how today's globalized design and construction process operates via networks of labor whose participants have unequal access to power and whose movements are influenced by a myriad of political, cultural, and economic factors. The ethical obligation toward construction workers resides within the design process itself and with the architects through their platforms of professional communication and public engagement.

Coda

As this chapter goes into production, architect Frank Gehry has publically announced that he and human rights lawyer Scott Horton have been working with various parties involved in erecting his design for the Guggenheim Museum in Abu Dhabi. Since 2009, Gehry and Horton have been negotiating to ensure the fair treatment of the migrant construction workers who will build the new museum.[26] In spite of this, it seems clear that many (most?) architects remain uncertain how to bring pressure to bear to improve working conditions for construction workers.

This chapter is the outcome of the advocacy of work of WBYA? (Who Builds Your Architecture?) whose members are Kadambari Baxi, Jordan Carver, Laura Diamond Dixit, Tiffany Rattray, Beth Stryker, and Mabel O. Wilson. For further information see: http://whobuilds.org.

Notes

1. Some of the names identifying architects, architecture firms, and businesses from related industries cited in this essay have been removed due to publisher concerns over litigation. For a full account of the incidents referenced here please refer to the documents cited in the endnotes. In particular, the authors recommend the Dark Side of Migration published by Amnesty International and the ongoing investigation reporting from the *Guardian* newspaper that cover detailed human rights abuses on construction sites in Doha, Qatar. This editing explicitly demonstrates the difficulty in exposing the inequalities inherent in the global construction supply chain and the challenge raising questions about ethical practices within the architecture profession.
2. The 2014 final match between Germany and Argentina registered three billion Facebook "interactions" and 672 Twitter messages. Television viewership in the United States set records for World Cup viewing. See: David Bauder, "The World Cup Final was Most Watched Soccer Game in U.S. History," *Associated Press*, 14 July, 2014, http://www.huffingtonpost.com/2014/07/14/world-cup-final-viewers-record_n_5585861.html (accessed 15 July, 2014).
3. Geographer David Harvey has argued that investments of surplus capital have been funneled into building booms in major cities like Dubai, Moscow, and Johannesburg. See: David Harvey, *Rebel Cities: From the Right to the City to the Urban Revolution* (London: Verso, 2013), 12.
4. Named after the model of urban-regeneration by the construction of the Guggenheim Museum in Bilbao, Spain, designed by architect Frank Gehry, that turned a deindustrialized city into a tourist destination and site for urban redevelopment. See: Kurt Forster, *Frank O. Gehry: Museo Guggenheim Bilbao* (Stuttgart: Edition Axel Menges, 1998). However, critics have argued that cultural projects like major "world-class" museums have become the agent for debt-financed redevelopment that does little to assist disenfranchised populations in cities like Bilbao. See: Allan Sekula, "Between the Net and the Deep Blue Sea: Rethinking the Traffic in Photographs," *October* 102 (Autumn, 2002), 3–34, and Andrea Fraser, "Isn't This a Wonderful Place?: A Tour of a Tour of the Guggenheim Bilbao," *Museum Highlights: The Writings of Andrea Fraser* (Cambridge: The MIT Press, 2007), 233–54.
5. James Riach, "Zaha Hadid Defends Qatar World Cup Role Following Migrant Worker Deaths," *Guardian*, 25 February, 2014, http://www.theguardian.com/world/2014/feb/25/zaha-hadid-qatar-world-cup-migrant-worker-deaths (accessed 26 February, 2014).
6. Ibid.
7. Walter Gropius, "Principles of Bauhaus Production [Dessau]," *Programs and Manifestoes on 20th Century Architecture*, ed. Ulrich Conrads and trans. Michael Bullock (Cambridge, MA: The MIT Press, 1970), 96.
8. Ludwig Mies Van der Rohe, "Industrialized Building," *Programs and Manifestoes on 20th Century Architecture*, ed. Ulrich Conrads and trans. Michael Bullock (Cambridge, MA: The MIT Press, 1970), 82.

9. "CIAM La Serraz Declaration," *Programs and Manifestoes on 20th Century Architecture*, ed. Ulrich Conrads and trans. Michael Bullock (Cambridge, MA: The MIT Press, 1970), 110.
10. In the mid-1990s, social policy analyst Jill Wells observed that "excess supply of labor in the construction market had the potential to drive down wages and conditions of work for migrant construction workers." See: Jill Wells, "Labour Migration and International Migration," *Habitat International* 20.2 (1996): 295–306.
11. For an in-depth study of neoliberalism, urban development, and the exploitation of migrant construction workers, see: Michelle Buckley, "Locating Neoliberalism in Dubai: Migrant Workers and Class Struggle in the Autocratic City," *Antipode* 45.2 (2013): 256–74.
12. Amnesty International, *The Dark Side of Migration: Spotlight on Qatar's Construction Sector Ahead of the World Cup* (London: Amnesty International Publications, 2013), 47–48.
13. The *Guardian* has published extensive reports on the problems of construction labor exploitation in the Middle East. This reportage relied in part on reports by human rights organizations such as Amnesty International, Human Rights Watch, and the International Trade Union Confederation (ITUC). See: Amnesty International, *The Dark Side of Migration*; Human Rights Watch, *'Island of Happiness' Exploitation of Migrant Workers on Saadiyat Island, Abu Dhabi* (New York: Human Rights Watch, 2009); Human Rights Watch, *'Island of Happiness' Revisited* (New York: Human Rights Watch, 2012).
14. See: Amnesty International, *The Dark Side of Migration,* 17. Run by the nationalized Qatar Petroleum, Ras Laffan Industrial City functions as a major hub for the production of liquefied natural gas. The lucrative oil and natural gas profits have provided the citizenry of Qatar with the highest standard of living in the world. Qatar's approximately 278,000 citizens depend on an additional 1.5 million expatriates to provide the labor necessary to run the country.
15. The Krantz workers were owed three months' back pay when they staged a protest by refusing to go to the job site. In a punitive measure against the work stoppage, Krantz levied additional fines that were to be deducted from their back pay. Amnesty International, *Dark Side of Migration,* 17–19.
16. Krantz had not provided appropriate resident passes and therefore the workers faced additional fines from Qatari authorities. Krantz did not have the financial resources to pay for services; this included electricity and therefore there was no air conditioning in the Krantz camps. During this same period in Spring 2013 food supplies were also periodically disrupted. Amnesty International, *Dark Side of Migration,* 21–4.
17. Amnesty International, *Dark Side of Migration,* 23.
18. Amnesty International, *Dark Side of Migration,* 27–8.
19. See Margaret Frank, "QCD Construction Nearing Completion! Tetra Tech," *Architects and Engineers' Blog,* 17 August, 2012, http://tetratechae.wordpress.com/2012/08/17/qcd-construction-nearing-completion (accessed 6 January, 2015).

20. Andrew Ross, "Forward," in *Building (in) the Future: Recasting Labor in Architecture*, eds. Peggy Deamer and Phillip G. Bernstein (New Haven, CT: Yale School of Architecture, 2012), 11.
21. Arjun Appadurai, "Disjuncture and Difference in Global Cultural Economy," *Modernity at Large: Cultural Dimensions of Globalization* (Minneapolis: University of Minnesota Press, 2003), 33.
22. Ibid.
23. Paolo Tombesi, "What Do We Mean by Building Design?," *Digital Workflows in Architecture: Design-Assembly-Industry*, ed. Scott Marble (Basel: Birkhauser, 2012), 188.
24. Ibid.
25. Sustainable development has been incorporated at all levels from the producers of materials to the architects who specify materials, from the contractors and construction workers who install materials to the clients who fund and maintain the building. Advanced technology in climate control is being developed, for example, for the Qatar stadiums to maintain a comfortable environment for spectators while also being energy efficient in its cooling process. However, this same attentiveness is not being given to the workers who toil in the same heat while constructing the stadiums.
26. According to *Architectural Record* Gehry hired attorney Horton shortly after reading the Human Rights Watch report *The Island of Happiness* (2009). See Anna Fixsen, "What is Frank Gehry Doing about Labor Conditions in Abu Dhabi?," *Architectural Record*, 25 September, 2014, http://archrecord.construction.com/news/2014/09/140922-Frank-Gehry-Works-to-Improve-Worker-Conditions-on-Abu-Dhabi-Site.asp (accessed 18 October, 2014).

Part IV

The construction of the commons

Chapter 10

Labor, architecture, and the new feudalism: Urban space as experience

Norman M. Klein

Over the past sixty years, since the passage of the Taft-Hartley Act in 1947, the power of unions has steadily eroded in the United States. At first, union membership kept growing, peaking in 1953 at over one third of all private-sector jobs. However, by 1983, under the early ravages of globalism, union membership had dropped by half. Meanwhile, the Reagan Administration gave the green light to anti-unionism, "carefully (fostering) the notion that collective bargaining is a relic."

It has taken thirty years for that Reagan-era policy to fully take root. While polls show anti-union sentiment fluctuates, concerning the future of collective bargaining there is little public disagreement. To most Americans, if the union was a species, its habitat would be disappearing. The last-ever union shop steward would be featured on the cover of *National Geographic* as another bio-political casualty.[1]

With the decay of unions comes a change in natural law, in what labor rights are publically accepted as natural. It is as if the political Enlightenment ended circa 1973, and has been widely lamented ever since, in hundreds of commentaries.[2] Since 2005, for example, thousands of blogs and tweets have featured variations on the word "neo-feudalism". Nevertheless, despite the sheer tonnage of source material, if I center the evidence for growing social inequality on the term "feudalism," a very clear pattern easily emerges, like a collective pathology. This pattern has led me to a research model that fits most of the extant evidence. I will introduce this model briefly, then apply it to trends affecting the urban condition: to our new production of space.

Feudalisms

Over the past forty years, a new kind of feudalism has surfaced, one in synch with neo-liberal policies. It is, first, emergent, even though this emergence seems counter-intuitive; feudalism presumably died six hundred years ago, a saga from the Dark Ages. Second, it is urban and industrial, concerning cities and industrial plutocrats, barons of industry more than a King Arthur. Third, it is not European, even though most histories of feudalism are centered on the European Middle Ages. And most of all, it is pluralistic, as referenced in the term *feudalité* in the eighteenth century, referring to medieval laws still on the books, favoring land tenure and aristocratic privilege.

Many of these feudal laws were needed for the British colonization of America.[3] As many as two thirds of migrants to America in the seventeenth century had to sell their labor as indentured servants, working on average for four years to pay off the cost of their transit. These, and other undemocratic truths about the New World, were legally sponsored through medieval tenant laws, updated slightly after 1607, but not by much. In many respects, the colonies of the New World represented a redux of feudal pluralism dominated by the mercantilist, "corporate bodies" of the day—the British West India and East India Companies, who acted like sovereign lords of shipping lanes, coastal warehouses, and wilderness territories. Bourgeois revolutions were designed to remove this unfair vassalage, but it nevertheless survived in the United States into the Gilded Age, when a uniquely urban, industrial feudalism was put into place. For over a century, there was resistance to and regulation of this feudal capitalist infection, but over the past forty years, it has more than returned.[4] Indeed, America may not have had a medieval period, with feudal manors—and it was surely a place to be a freer agent (land was cheap, feudal labor laws faded)—however, the legal apparatus set in place by 1750 has often come back to haunt us. It has legally justified laws discriminating against immigrants, blacks, unions, and women.

The flexible and pluralistic nature of feudalism's emergence and duration is key—in Japan for seven hundred years, in India, Brazil, Russia, Egypt—and in unexpected centuries—in eighteenth century Cairo, in China circa 500 BCE, and in nineteenth-century China, along with spheres of influence conceded to the great European powers.[5] Consider the work of historian Marc Bloch, the esteemed member of the French Annales School, who wrote a two-volume history of feudalism in the 1930s, much of it while he was a soldier in the French Army during World War II. The second volume is partly a response to the broad cultural impact of Nazism; also to the Great Depression; and finally, to the collapse of France in 1940.[6] Bloch saw feudalism as intrinsic to any culture, as a standard response to political fragmentation arriving in stages. This is what he saw in Europe in the 1930s, starting with the shared nightmare of watching the political economy steadily go to hell.[7] Bloch's response was similar to that of many historians in the '30s and '40s, notably Johann Huizinga, who titled his uncanny history of pre-Renaissance Flanders as, *The Waning of the Middle Ages*—as dissolve more than collapse; not as the death of feudalism.[8]

Historian Lauren Beaton calls aspects of the mishmash experienced by these multiple cultures "legal pluralism."[9] Such "legal pluralism" and "medieval leftover" were apparent to me as a boy in Brooklyn. As the son of a kosher butcher, I grew up in a very medieval world—like a Breughel painting with meat—an immigrant household, surrounded by Hungarian peasant attitudes. My studies pointed out how closely my childhood resembled feudal continuities in *Mittel Europa* during the seventeenth century, one of which was Brooklyn itself. As of 1620, one of the freest places to do business in the mercantilist world was New York City, because it was governed at the edge of nowhere by the Dutch East India Company. I learned how the Jewish ghettoes in Venice helped Italian bankers, and how Greek and Armenian traders in the Ottoman Empire relied on Turkish feudal laws, as did Jews across Arab North Africa.

In writing about the Great Migration by southern blacks to the north—in the twentieth century—Isabel Wilkerson writes: "A feudal caste system grew out of the unmet promises made after the Civil War."[10] Feudalism has often re-emerged as another kind of apartheid: in the Jim Crow South, when indentured labor and the policy of separate-but-equal were installed. Beyond this, every immigrant group who arrives in the United States, particularly in its early years, has the sense of being thrown into a medieval economy. Immigrants feel indentured to their neighborhood, beholden to the swindler who runs interference for them in the normal American world.[11]

The key to understanding feudalistic pluralism lies in its built-in imperfections: its fragile infrastructure and barely controlled anarchy.[12] It emerges during an interregnum, when an empire falls, when an invasion destroys the state, even when a country is colonized by its own economy, like the American story since 1980. As Tocqueville explained, feudalism is "confusion divided by a thousand hands, and broken apart in a thousand ways."[13] It is a fractured system based on "infinite delay."[14]

In such a world, delays become normal. Each deregulated pause helps to feed another financial derivative, another overlapping authority. In eighteenth-century mercantilism, corporations were often defined as if they had diplomatic immunity—they called them "corporate bodies." They were, in other words, a friendly group of comrades who were legally an individual of the highest rank.[15]

Unlike the first stages of feudalism, when warriors were given fiefdoms within a system of military blackmail during a time of troubles, in the new version of feudalism, we push directly on to a second stage, when blackmail turns into sheer venality. The first stage lasted seven hundred years: parasitical behavior enshrined into law throughout the *ancien régime* continuing as late as 1750. Despite two revolutions, the aristocratic ascendancy persisted in England, even while capital shifted totally from land to trade. In France, the nobility remained nearly untouchable, by divine right, even with nobles *de la robe*, the children of businessmen who had bought patents of nobility a century before. The feudal dead hand was stronger in France than in England, but was standard all over Europe—and in Latin America, India, the Arab world, and Japan. We pray that the current stage does not last as long.

As long as authority is horizontalized and overlapping, the oligarchic tendency that resembles feudalism will inevitably reappear. It is hard-wired into every nation, in different ways, in different regions. The telltale clues are the depletion of the nation state, the return of corporate individualism in labor contracts, and relentless entropy; different from the fury of a fascist movement that relies on a wholly vertical, state-run government to crush any horizontal imposition.

In the United States, unquestionably, the term "industrial feudalism" became commonplace from the 1880s to World War I in response to that era's labor conditions and the rise of industrial plutocrats. It returned as a pop reference on the internet after the year 2000. Today, it is profoundly linked to the secrecy of global and digital industries, and to widening gaps in class structure.[16]

Voids

Feudalism is pluralized because it generates voids—holes in sovereignty. While feudal systems lingered, these voids incubated capitalism, socialism, communism, anarchism, mercantilism, industrialism, fascism, totalitarianism—and many historians are convinced, also globalism—and then, as the final irony, a new species of feudalism yet again.[17]

Perhaps the greatest medieval achievement, within a void, was the feudal city-state, an entity that has a great deal to teach us now. They were engines in the emerging trade economy, in banking, within Renaissance and Baroque culture. And they were part of the survival of feudalism in its pluralistic way. French kings (the Capetians) were, in fact, originally dukes of the Isle de Paris, and very weak. In order to wrest control from dukes and princes, the Crown needed cash, not land. The Capetians often formed alliances with townspeople who gradually modeled their cities in parallel with manorialism. The basic principle was *axis mundi*, the ladder to God, where each person knows his place; this applied to free trade within cities.

Of course, the growth of capital, so essential to nourishing the feudal chaos, meant that cities were allowed special laws. They required a more open sociality, but were oligarchy nonetheless. Cities fought hard to maintain their legal separation.

The medieval city-state had its own sovereignty, often its own army, and certainly its own alliances. By the twelfth century, Venice had become the dominant military and economic power on the European side of the eastern Mediterranean—more powerful than the Holy Roman emperors who preceded it. Venice became the template for mercantilism; very much an imperialist system of trade, but thoroughly at odds with the Crown. By the fifteenth century, Venice had begun to decline, but northern coastal cities like Lübeck, within the Hanseatic League, flourished, forming their own navies and sovereign alliances.[18]

Again, these—in their guild structure, in their churches, in their wars of all against all—are feudal cities—even Bruges in Flanders, even Antwerp in Holland. Starting with these wealthy city-states demanding better contracts with their monarchs, another mode of urban pluralism eventually developed. By the seventeenth century, by way of European competition over the Indian Ocean and the Atlantic, mercantilism appeared, having been given a special legal relationship to the Crown in order to compete with Indian and Chinese shipping. This was a new corporate mutation: these companies—the most powerful embodiments being the English and the Dutch East India Companies—were considered individual sovereigns protected by an updated feudal law, but generally free of the monarch, free to act.

By 1630, there existed a vast feudal network of European cities and foreign concessions in Asia, Africa, and the New World. The Hanseatic League, already in decline, was centered on the north German coast and extended its reach through Flanders all the way to London. The Amsterdammer cities were the League's growing rival using many of the same water routes. Amsterdammer ports (built by the Dutch) included Gothenburg in Sweden, and continued as far east as Russia (why Peter the Great went to Holland as a young man, to imagine his own great coastal city, Petersburg). The most interesting and surprising of the Amsterdammer cities was Fort Amsterdam across the Atlantic, with only about two hundred settlers. Something of a free port—very much a void—where pirates, Jews, Anabaptists, and even black freemen could settle, this tiny enclave eventually became New York. Russell Shorto, in his *The Island at the Center of the World: The Epic Story of Dutch Manhattan and the Forgotten Colony that Shaped America* (2004), claims that New York was the seed of American democracy, more so than Massachusetts.

Here is another irony: a great many of the feudal, mercantilist trading cities of the sixteenth through the eighteenth centuries are doing extremely well in today's new economy. They include London, New York, Amsterdam, Copenhagen, and Macao; and the great mercantilist ports of nineteenth century China that were set up by European powers to dominate China's vast territory—but in the old-fashioned feudalistic way, more as a concession (typical of the Portuguese in the sixteenth century) than a colony. The two most important of these Chinese port towns, Hong Kong and Shanghai, are now the engines of the Chinese miracle. However, consider their vast size today. A clue lies in their having stretched incomprehensively ever larger. Hong Kong/Shenzen has over 100 million residents; the Shanghai region has 50 million or more. These are urban regions, almost sovereign federal states with immense economic reach, not just cities. They are medieval Venice redux, or an Asian Hanseatic League with unique legal relationships to a unique species of nation state—China today.

Pluralism will vary profoundly from era to era. But in every country, there is a feudal/oligarchic tradition lying dormant.[19] Every sovereign state (even "revolutionary" democracies) contains a surviving feudal remnant, often embedded in old feudal-era laws—usually about land tenure and labor—from a subliminal place in their history. This is true of fascist and military governments, which cannot sustain their own sheer cliffs of totalitarian governance. These sublimated traditions (often) grew originally from strange deals cooked up between the monarch, the warlords, and the towns. In the past, the sovereign (struggling against the feudal warlords) would make uneasy alliances with his natural enemies (like the bourgeoisie); because, as a standard fact in feudal societies, taxes were never collected fully. The sovereign would need trading towns to pitch in, and form an enclave of some kind—against the feudal barons.

The feudal remnants of old contracts are malleable; they can be easily reconfigured. In England, the changing labor contracts by law from the Middle Ages survived into the sixteenth century and afterward. Thus, capital—the landowner, the capital if you will—always had a first position. In short, collective bargaining was never really built thoroughly into the system at all, even well into the twentieth century. In fact, remnants of indentured quit law remained to legally justify the indenture of blacks in Jim Crow America. Debates over such laws are now being re-initiated by the Supreme Court in rulings about corporations treated as people, etc., eerily like feudal corporate theory in the *ancien régime*. The moniker "too big to fail" is essentially another way of saying that you claim feudal privilege—moral authority based on blackmail.

Feudalistic Metropolis

"Globalism" is a bit of misnomer. Its impact has been to reinforce the regional, metropolitan eras turning into sovereign regions (like medieval city-states). If the trend continues, instead of internationalism we will find regional pluralism—niches, voids, data clouds—buried in tax havens; more firewalls.

The Feudalistic Metropolis: a social-network model of labor within the built environment, overlapping oligarchic cityscapes. Within these regions, urban towns are emerging, especially across the developed world. These are not the same as gated communities, suburbs, urban villages, or gentrified neighborhoods. They are often towns that were annexed by great cities in the late nineteenth century. They often center on narrow, curving older streets; not on boulevards—streets with shoulders, but inside the urban hub. I live in an area called Highland Park—an urban town in northeast Los Angeles. It annexed itself to Los Angeles in 1895, and has a narrow business street circa 1920.

At the same time, Western cities are pluralizing into hubs of about 500 thousand people, or a million at most. Banking centers are beginning to aggregate near urban districts, as in east London towns like London Fields (with a small park filled only with plants known to England in the year 1400).

These urban towns often feature shops with handmade objects for sale—in keeping with the trend for the haptic, the tactile, for a farmers' market version of the everyday. Various sustainable lifestyles, like bike riding, are easier, but these urban towns are very close to slums, as a rule. They presumably offer city life below the radar, away from boulevards, and part of the inner city.

Many renewal projects today reconfigure modernist infrastructure that has gone into ruin, including the abandoned factories in Shenzen. As gaps in the class structure widen even further, the migration of poor Latinos to suburban villages and old farming towns will continue. The economic turmoil in the United States will bring enormous surprises to rural towns and x-urbias. This interregnum will take perhaps twenty years. By then, the digital economy will have thoroughly embedded itself into the rhythms of the brick and mortar world. Whether the American constitutional democracy will survive—as it has been—is doubtful. We need three young Thomas Jeffersons somewhere. A new political Enlightenment will have to be invented all over again, as if 1760 had not happened at all.

In our era, the future ages faster than the present. At first, we became tourists in our own cities. Now we are tourists in our own bodies. Somewhere, out of the past eight hundred years, there must be answers that we have neglected.

Notes

1. I can see the same trend very clearly in the academic world—"the fall of the faculty," as it is called—manifested in tenure fights, shrinking pensions, adjunct sublations, and part-time salaries. When I started my career as a college teacher, labor guarantees were considered inviolable, a hard-fought right. Today, very few of my students expect any such protection as part of their own social contract.
2. I am currently writing my next book, entitled "History of the Present: The Dismantling of the American Psyche." You can imagine how much supporting evidence I found for its hypothesis, quite easily. My office is literally overflowing with boxes; the historiography is vast. Each year, a new buzz-word emerges for the "Great Stagnation" in America. In 2014, the keyword was "inequality"—a word that's thoroughly accurate and, I might add, self-evident. But the implications of inequality studies are much less clear, as I will explain.
3. Christopher Tomlins, *Colonizing America, 1580–1865* (Cambridge: Cambridge University Press, 2010). See also: Tomlins, *Freedom Bound: Law, Labor and Civic Identity* (Cambridge: Cambridge University Press, 2010), 304: "lordly elites in (colonial) New England"; "Entailing Aristocracy in Colonial Virginia;" "ancient feudal restraints."
4. Among many sources, Karen Orren on the neoliberal collapse of the federal government: "traditional social alignments seem to be overlaid by new, subjectively defined groupings … Old commitments are thwarted by new institutions, new institutions by old commitments, new institutions by old institutions, new commitments by old institutions, in a pattern that is as discontinuous with the future as with the past." Karen Orren, *Belated Feudalism: Labor, Law and the Liberal Development in the United States* (Cambridge: Cambridge University Press, 1991), 3.
5. There was a fascination with feudalism across the globe after World War II, especially in American scholarship, initiated by Rushton Coulborn, ed., *Feudalism in History* (Princeton, NJ: Princeton University Press, 1956), and by essays like, John Whitney Hall, "Feudalism in Japan—A Reassessment," *Comparative Studies in Society and History* 1 (October 1962): 15–51.
6. Marc Bloch, *Feudal Society, Volume II: Social Class and Political Organization*, trans. L. A. Manyon (London: Routledge and Kegan Paul Ltd, 2005 [1961]), 18:

    > We should not think of this (feudal) mode of existence as having invariably a rural setting. Italy, Provence and Languedoc still bore the age-old imprint of the Mediterranean civilizations whose structure had been systematized by Rome. In those regions, each small community was traditionally grouped round a town or large village which was at one and the same time an administrative centre, a

market, and a place of refuge; and consequently the normal place of residence of the powerful. These people continued as much as ever to inhabit the old urban centres; and they took part in all their revolutions. In the thirteenth century, this civic character was regarded as one of the distinctive traits of the southern nobility.

7. I could easily amend the story from there. Instead of progress, there is a culture dominated by blackmail. One's life turns into a picaresque, a comedy in a slide area.
8. Johan Huizinga, *The Waning of the Middle Ages* (New York: St. Martin's Press, 1949 [Anchor edition, 1954]), 248, on fifteenth-century feudal culture in Burgundy:

    "The overcrowding of the mind with figures and forms systematically arranged … the tendency to not leave anything… without ornament. The flamboyant style of architecture is like the postlude of an organist who cannot conclude. It decomposes all the formal elements endlessly; it interlaces all the details … A *horror vacui* reigns, always a symptom of artistic decline."

9. Beaton's most recent study on legal pluralism is an anthology co-edited with Richard J. Ross: Lauren Beaton and Richard J. Ross, eds, *Legal Pluralism and Empires, 1500–1850* (New York: New York University Press, 2013).
10. Isabel Wilkerson, *The Warmth of Other Suns: The Epic Story of America's Great Migration* (New York: Random House, 2010), 9.
11. My parents never recovered from that feeling, a psychic shock. But my uncles did; they made an easier transition—except for the truly crazy one who abandoned his family to become a kosher butcher in Las Vegas. (That was a miserable flop, of course. He wound up sweeping the casinos at night, while Alzheimer's set in.)
12. Jospeh Strayer and Rushton Coulborn made this classic statement on why this confusion incubates other forms so easily: "There is indeed a dramatic irony in the fact that the better feudalism works the more rapidly it generates a political structure which is no longer completely feudal." Stayer and Coulborn, "The Idea of Feudalism," Conference on Feudalism, Princeton University, 31 October to 1 November, 1950, edited by Rushton Coulborn as the influential anthology, *Feudalism in History* (Princeton, NJ: Princeton University Press, 1956).
13. Alexis de Tocqueville, *Democracy in America*, *Volume* 1, trans. Henry Reeve (London: Saunders and Ottley, 1835), 118.
14. Ibid.
15. Beaton and Ross, eds, *Legal Pluralisms and Europe, 1500–1800*. See also: Karen Orren, *Belated Feudalism: Labor, the Law and Liberal Development in the United States* (Cambridge: Cambridge University Press, 1991); Vladimir Shlpentokh and Joshua Woods, *Feudal America: Elements of the Middle Ages in Contemporary Society* (University Park: The Pennsylvania State University Press, 2011).
16. We sense a fracturing of our federal government. Feudal wars are everywhere. Kinships by blood never seem to endure; mutual trust is always rejected. Vassals easily turn on their sovereign lord. Indeed, to paraphrase Hobbes, the war of all

against all is natural. As we know, *Leviathan* (1651) was Hobbes' attempt to shorten the gruesome English Civil War, the bloody interregnum.
17. I have been writing around the edges of this process for decades now, never quite getting to the core of its simplicity. I have used various terms that pointed in that direction (mostly in the late 1990s), like "electronic feudalism," or the scripted spaces of themed architecture as the "Electronic Baroque." I was even interviewed once about Las Vegas as a Baroque city. I discussed how gated communities were the return of medieval walled cities. And now, for the past seven years, I have been excavating carefully, as the morphology of the global has given way to a new localism. It is a tattered patchwork all right but the corpse does make a stunning impression, across media—most obviously in post-neo-retro movies, from 1980s cyberpunk onward.
18. Hendrik Spruyt, *The Sovereign States and Its Competitors* (Princeton, NJ: Princeton University Press, 1994), 68: Despite agreements between Hansa towns, "the confederated nature of the Hansa led to continuous freeriding and defection. There were always incentives to disavow the edicts of the diet."
19. In the past decade, among critics and scholars of globalism, there is increased interest in the feudal process, for example, Saskia Sassen, *Territory, Authority, Rights: From Medieval to Global Assemblages* (Princeton, NJ: Princeton University Press, 2006), 32:

> Each mode of politico-economic organization embodies specific features when it comes to territory, authority and rights. In Europe, the Middle Ages was a period of complex interactions among particular forms of territorial fixity, the absence of exclusive territorial authority, the existence of multiple crisscrossing jurisdictions, and the embedding of rights in classes of people rather than in territorially exclusive units.

Chapter 11

The hunger games: Architects in danger
Alicia Carrió

To Eduardo Serrano, with gratitude

Introduction

An assumed futuristic setting; oppressive; a clear metaphor of reality carried to its extreme, like a scenario imagined by George Orwell, Ray Bradbury, or J. G. Ballard. Director Gary Ross's 2013 movie adaptation of the book trilogy *The Hunger Games,* by Suzanne Collins, describes a society with clear references to our current crisis: the one percent dominates the remaining 99 percent, as demanded by Spanish and American protests of recent years, including the different struggles of the Arab Spring: "We are the 99 percent!" chanted the people.

The world of *The Hunger Games* is one where the top one percent of society— through tricks and grim competitiveness disguised as global public entertainment—allows the most disadvantaged to survive through incredible sacrifice and humiliation. The gigantic television screens, wherein contestants show off their skills, beauty, and exclusive clothes, and are cheered by screaming crowds—it is a perfect satire of today's trash TV and society in general.

Dystopic societies like these are not fiction; capitalism functions to preserve the one percent. But the crises are different from those generated in marginal countries where the system isn't self-written but injects itself, prevailing over societies where traditions and modes of production are "pre-modern."

This action, which is made in the name of progress, has devastating consequences for the societies on which it is imposed as it produces, through the plundering of natural and human resources, an imbalance in the order of subsistence, and generates added value in exchange for chaos, loss of life, and fragility: poverty for many and wealth for an elite.

Will the financial excesses of recent years—which undercut fundamental rights by legitimizing the existence of vulture funds, real-estate bubbles, heartless evictions, privatization in health, education, and pensions—take us to realities as extreme as those we see in *The Hunger Games* movie? It is hard to answer "No."

A brief review of the configuration of professions as we know them today

As Herbert Spencer explains, the professions had their origins in the power base that both feudal lords and organizations linked to the Church had over their subjects and followers. As these groups became economically independent, acquiring an inheritance or codifying their artisans' craft or agricultural knowledge, they became special structures with their own ethics and moralities.[1] These early forms of the transfer of knowledge have developed and determined new transmission structures.

In general terms we can say that the professions, such as we know them today, come from a long evolution where capitalism played a fundamental role, managing to mediate between artisans, small farmers, and day laborers.[2] This evolution—not a peaceful one—begins between the fifteenth and sixteenth centuries, coinciding with European colonialist expansion; land privatization is implemented under the cover of wars and religious reform. But the concentration of knowledge into professions finds its foundational core in the mid-eighteenth century, when knowledge accumulated by artisans and laborers is investigated in a systematic way in order to be apprehended and, subsequently, mechanized for the Industrial Revolution. This removes the intervening role of specialized collaborators, a financial burden that allows for subsequent capitalist development, to the detriment of workers' and craftsmen's creativity and autonomy. It is in the course of these battles, waged between the power of industrialization and the slave, servant, or employee—depending on the time period—that the systematization of knowledge begins to appear.

As the objectification of these skills and knowledge sets occured, the possibility of reproduction and accumulation excluded their original holders and introduced another type of agent who mediates the chain of production. Those considered today as *professionals* benefitted from this process and, investigating, fragmenting, and decoding this knowledge, made it their own. This process finds social and academic consideration in the universities, gradually organized to become mechanisms for the standardized production of experts who made available a "naturalization" of knowledge.

When intermediation occurs in the course of capitalist accumulation, each party introduces the rules that legitimize them, taking control of the processes of fragmentation, coding, regulations, and protocols (relying on an increased incidence of experts, specialists, and intermediaries without whose legalized intervention the system would not hold up) that produce a lack of autonomy and allow enormous resources to escape from the hands of the "customer, consumer, patient."[3]

Ivan Illich, in his well-known essay "Disabling Professions," makes an interesting tour through this process:

> Unlike yesterday's liberal professions that provided the ethical backing for high-status hawkers, the new dominant professions claim control over human needs, *tout court*. They turn the modern state into a holding corporation of enterprises which facilitates the operation of their self-certified own competences: equal needs are laid on the citizen/client, only to be fulfilled in a zero-sum game.[4]

The crisis we experienced in this last economic cycle yields the end of the autonomous professions. In the specific case of architecture, although it applies to other professions, our work until very recently was primarily the work of intermediating between:

1 the specific knowledge and construction of habitat;
2 the particular developer's requirements and the general interest supervised by the State;
3 the needs of the people to inhabit spaces suitable for their development.

These three instances of agency between practitioners and their specific activities are being replaced by corporations. Using the same encoding rules that ordered professional practices, architects are now professionals at the discretion of corporations, and are thus controlled and limited in the free exercise of their services. This mechanism of appropriation is closely linked to job insecurity affecting society as a whole.

The architect is no longer the only mediator between those in need of expertise and the society that claims her knowledge, secured by a social structure that legitimized both expert and client; that structure operated under the supervision of a State which, through various institutions, organized all the processes of her practice. Expert knowledge has become part of what is known as a "means of production," acquiring an added complexity resulting from the accelerated advance of technological know-how, computer science, and the role of both in the production processes.

Today, under fierce neo-liberal appropriation, the structure that became "natural" disintegrates, destroying at the same time, among many other things, the functioning of professions such as we have known them. The social field, through the digital revolution, has already produced qualitative changes for the professional, enabling interconnections that express a deep desire for social convergence where generosity, free exchange, and autonomy recover the concept of a common good. We need to use this and all other means to direct the profession toward a common good, a more perfect society.

Quoting Brian Holmes from his lecture, "Three Crises: 30s-70s-Today:"

> To live with dignity through the coming years, and to fulfill our responsibilities to the future, we need to propose and realize a radical break that is neither apocalyptic nor messianic, but instead, pragmatically utopian. Nothing less will do it. For the organic intellectuals who carry out this work—that is, for people who turn the common capacity of language to an intense and passionate curiosity—that might suggest a reinvention of what Marxists used to call *praxis*. In other words, the merger of complex thinking into concrete activity. Such is the aim of a disciplined and experimental discourse that seeks to engage with the material-ideational-affective forms of society as a whole. In short, the research program that I am proposing here is about the transformational effects of intellectual engagement in social movements.[5]

A case study: "La Casa Invisible"

In the field of the architectural, because requirements have changed, unexplored paths open. The slogan "HOMES WITHOUT PEOPLE AND PEOPLE WITHOUT HOMES" was one of many called out during Spanish protests that occurred during what is known as the 15-M Movement.

Due to the Spanish housing bubble, there is currently a huge amount of empty housing stock, often owned by private banks whose portfolios were rescued with taxpayer money. The uselessness of these operations encourages us to try to find those cracks within each profession that could become useful again for positive change. We already know that there has been huge waste; we have built more than what society can absorb. We have repeatedly heard that colluding private corporations control the largest portion of the State's budget, and that this portion has suffered comparatively minor cuts relative to other areas of the budget because of the close ties between these corporations and the management of public infrastructure.

There are victims of this waste: the one percent make money, the 99 percent pay for their excesses. The lack of dignified work demands exploring creative alternatives. There is a large amount of unused infrastructure, much of it composed of buildings that deserve rehabilitation in order to strengthen an architectural heritage worth preserving. A new conception of the territory is essential to address an architectural practice more in line with current circumstances. Migrating to developing countries is viewed by professionals as another alternative to start or reignite their truncated careers. These possibilities are developed by different groups with greater or lesser success, but can hardly escape the laws of the market which produce unwanted effects throughout. Nor do they meet or satisfy the underlying question: how to approach architecture so as to provide services that assist in the creation of a viable social fabric.

We don't have the answer … we don't have *one* answer; instead we have a multitude of collective groups working through their desires and needs, intertwined by common conditions.

"La Casa Invisible:" An experiment in citizen management and self-organization

We create the house and the house creates us.

(Greek saying)

In March of 2007, a significant number of activists from the social movements of Málaga and its environs, together with artists from different activities, students and academics from disciplines such as architecture, geography, urban planning, sociology, economics, communications, and ecology, occupied a building owned by the City Council.

They had expertise in social rights and cultural claims, immigrant pledges, and the loss of public space to private interests and thus could mediate by economic interests. The aim was to claim both a space for those citizens "without voice" and to highlight the lack of policies that take into account the bonds of a neighborhood in an area where the process of gentrification is moving from the usual quarters of life-long residents who see with astonishment how the historic downtown area is pasture for speculation. What was at one time a quiet life of squares and markets, public spaces where day-to-day life was peaceful and placid, has become a territory for large retail brands, international franchises, banks, and tourist equipment headquarters: nothing new, if we consider that these processes have been developed in European historical cities for decades displacing residents to peripheral areas, with the loss of social fabric and consequently a way of life hardly replicable in the new dormitory towns.

The chosen building is a beautiful mansion dating back to the 1870s, built with technologies of the time and presenting a specific typology, with facades on two streets within the intricate maze of narrow, pedestrian streets. They consist of two blocks of three floors surrounding a beautiful courtyard with native vegetation, a sprouting fountain, and a special decadent air, reminiscent of what was the historic center at a time when the rhythms of life were different and there was time for contemplation.

It should be said that negotiations were conducted with the City Council, which in principle agreed to transfer the building for a certain period of time on condition that the Group conform to agreed upon deadlines. Now the situation has acquired a status of "stand by," leaving us in a kind of legal limbo, since the authorities have refused, without explanation, to continue with the assignment. "La Casa Invisible" proposes various activities, with a program that is organized on annual cycles and accommodates all the initiatives that promote culture and research, workshops, a concert hall, and a long etcetera. "La Casa Invisible" functions without subsidies, in a horizontal process, where decisions are taken in an assembly style.

It is important to note that the fabric of the building, not having been maintained over a long period of time, was in a poor state and therefore in need of renovation. To remedy this situation the system adopted was this: maximum knowledge-minimal intervention.

The project benefited from the constant advice and help of experts in building heritage, in addition to the direct involvement of students at the School of Architecture of Málaga, an unprecedented exercise that produced a detailed survey of the existing building and a proposal that met the needs of the center.

The work has been carried out by the users of the center under the guidance of architects who specialize in sustainable building and rigorously respect the system of construction of the original building: in this way, the logic has remained intact without causing contradictions between varied construction methods that could produce unwanted interferences in a scheme that has survived more than a century thanks to the quality of the original construction.

Fundamental differences between a conventional process and the intervention carried out at "La Casa Invisible:"[6]

The hunger games: Architects in danger

1 Between subjects and agents

Conventional	"La Casa Invisible"
Task of experts, influenced only by the developers.	Community task with wealth of experience and exchange.
Dissociation between laymen and experts.	Exchange of knowledge and skills.
Subject to the regime of copyright intellectual production.	Enabling "the Commons": not public, not private, enabling the conditions of reproduction for those who need it.
Owners/Developers: one way communication to passive users.	Users: active citizens interact with technicians who can redirect their knowledge.
Closed process without benefit in terms of social fabric.	Process of interaction that creates sociability.

2 Project process

Conventional	"La Casa Invisible"
Development of a single document. Full building license.	Particular development of documents for each working stage. Detailed building license.
Means and objectives are on different levels of performance.	The project is an end in itself: the method is developed at the same time as the content.
Because of the complexity of the project the usual decision is to empty its contents, leaving only the façade (result: theme park).	The process of inhabiting the space produces a dialogue with the users that interact "live" with the place.

3 Economics of the process

Conventional	"La Casa Invisible"
Concentrated expenditure. Large expenditures.	Expenditure is divided into small interventions prioritizing according to relevant phases.
Primary objective: economic profitability.	Primary objective: control in the intervention

4 The work

Conventional	"La Casa Invisible"
The drafting and approval of the project is a closed phase that over-determines the work.	The project and works are conditioned and developed together.
The traditional performance precludes inhabiting the building until the completion of the works.	The carrying out of the work in stages on small parts of the building, with manual means, allows use of the building in areas which are not intervened.

So far, the inhabitants of the community seek an active use of the assets that belong to all of them: an experience-experiment achieving the transformation of the environment using non-traditional methods with a decisive component of citizen involvement. This is the spirit with which a space of interaction has been forged between all of us highlighting the importance of those activities involving users in the process of identification and solutions of their needs.

I firmly believe that these partnerships should be the roadmap to the future for a profession that has been seen as a succession of nonsense from the constructive to the territorial, with architects as mere intermediaries, members of an undeserved privileged caste: star dust.

These mechanisms of a strong participatory action—that begins with the people developing their requirements within the budget and working with their local authorities—is a practice already used in some municipalities in Spain and Latin America. These experiences, the result of the study of the teachings by the Brazilian educator Paulo Freire, among others, have been widely shaped by researchers in social pedagogy determined to take participatory methods to the inhabitants, enabling them to exercise their active citizenship.

The complex problem of social housing should be faced with the same spirit. Collectives formed by young architects—debating, working, and analyzing the quality of life—can and should be integrated into the citizen's expression in order to meet common objectives. These experiments—that could utilize traditional construction methods and centuries of environmental knowledge—can both revitalize the economy and link the communities to a newly formulated "counselor architect" who organizes a sustainable, real, and deeply democratic world.

Concluding speculation

In order to give context to what should be the practice of architecture today, we can recall the work of two thinkers. In the 1950s Gilles Ivain defined our practice in his "Formulary for a New Urbanism":

> Architecture is the simplest means of *articulating* time and space, of *modulating* reality and engendering dreams. It is a matter not only of plastic articulation and modulation expressing an ephemeral beauty, but of a modulation producing influences in accordance with the eternal spectrum of human desires and the progress in realizing them ...
>
> It will be a means of *knowledge* and a *means of action.*
>
> On the bases of this mobile civilization, architecture will, at least initially, be a means of experimenting with a thousand ways of modifying life, with a view to an ultimate mythic synthesis.[7]

Martin Heidegger was also prescient, asking himself what it is *to dwell*. Dwelling, he insisted, is inextricably related to *building*: an autopoiesis.[8] According to Heidegger, we build to the extent that we dwell; we build in a permanent process of interaction with the dwelling that is at the same time our personal growth process, manifesting longings, desires, and ways of being in the world.

Both thinkers offer a new way to understand the place of architecture through the value of the experimental, and hint at a future way of dwelling in the world and enjoying its creations: *a revolution of everyday life.* Why must we accept that the social structure which links us to the realization of our habitat is only the responsibility of professionals, politicians, and experts who are induced to build by interests so distant from our own?

Notes

1. See: Herbert Spencer, *The Principles of Sociology*, Volume 3, Part VII, "Professional Institutions" (New York: D. Appleton, 1896).
2. One cannot forget the place of women in the transfer of ancient knowledge in general placed at the service of what we today call care, including the knowledge of the properties of herbs for medicinal use. See: Silvia Federici, *Caliban and the Witch: Women, the Body and Primitive Accumulation* (New York: Autonomedia, 2004).
3. Consider the fundamental role that patents play in the economic process, denying autonomy to those professional pioneers whose work is patented. Large corporations promote the use of patents in order to capture this professional workforce and turn them, effectively, into merchandise.

4. Ivan Illich, "Disabling Professions," in Ivan Illich, Irving Kenneth Zola, John McKnight, Jonathan Caplan, and Harley Shaiken *Disabling Professions* (London: Marion Boyars, 1977), 16.
5. Brian Holmes, "Three Crises: 30s-70s-Today," in *Disrupting Business: Art and Activism in Times of Financial Crisis*, eds. Tatiana Bazzichelli and Geoff Cox (New York: Autonomedia, 2013), 221.
6. Scheme developed by the Rizoma Fundación, a critical collective formed by architects and geographers, among other professions. They have been producing critical thinking since 1990 in Malaga City and environs, and have intellectually supported our project since the beginning.
7. Gilles Ivain, "Formulary for a New Urbanism," *Internationale Situationniste* 1 (October 1953), trans. Ken Knabb, *Situationist International Online*, http://www.cddc.vt.edu/sionline/presitu/formulary.html?utm_source=buffer&utm_campaign=buffer&utm_content=buffer0ad86&utm_medium=twitter (accessed September 2014). Note from translator: In October 1953 the Lettrist International adopted this report by Gilles Ivain on urbanism …The present text was drawn up from two successive drafts containing minor differences in formulation, preserved in the LI archive, which have become documents 103 and 108 of the Situationist Archives.
8. Autopoiesis refers to a system capable of reproducing and maintaining itself. This term was introduced by Chilean Biologists Humberto Maturana and Francisco Varela to define the self-maintaining chemistry of living cells. An application of the concept to sociology can be found in Systems Theory by Niklas Luhmann. See: Humberto Maturana and Francisco Varela. Autopoiesis and Cognition: the Realization of the Living, Boston Studies in the Philosophy of Science, Volume 42 (Dordecht: D. Reidel Publishing Co., [1972] 1980); and Niklas Luhmann, Essays on Self-Reference (New York: Columbia University Press, 1990).

Chapter 12

Foucault's "environmental" power: Architecture and neoliberal subjectivization

Manuel Shvartzberg

Introduction

How are we to understand labor in architecture, today? In this chapter I will explore this relationship by analyzing how processes of neoliberal "economization" constitute a particular type of subjectivity. "Economization" refers to performatives that qualify social and technical practices as "economic," rather than seeing "the economy" as an *a priori* stable category.[1] My thesis—building on Michel Foucault's prescient intellectual history and analysis of neoliberalism as a new mode of capitalism and government[2]—is that a particular form of political rationality, distinct from both liberal political and economic rationality, has taken hold through the wide dissemination of neoliberal regulatory and epistemological frameworks. In other words, we have become neoliberal *by design*, through the pervasiveness of its modes of economization. The neoliberal ideas and paradigms explored by Foucault have effectively taken root and become our own socio-ontological or onto-epistemological apparatus. It is not a question of posing a one-to-one relation between neoliberal architecture and neoliberal subjects, but of showing how the rationality and the metrics—the epistemologies; social and technical systems of symbolization—that configure both are intimately entangled and effectively produce each other. Among these metrics, the popular notion of "creativity" is particularly interesting because it has become a generalized imperative of neoliberalized societies: creativity (and its proxies, "innovation" and "disruption") are seen today as an essential component of any "competitive" worker. Creativity is a fundamental metric within what neoliberals call "human capital"—a concept that, as we shall see, lies at the core of neoliberal subjectivization.

From liberal "discipline" to neoliberal "environment"

In his landmark lectures at the Collège de France in 1978 and 1979, later compiled in *The Birth of Biopolitics*, Foucault extended his research on "governmentality" to neoliberalism,[3] outlining a key difference between liberal and neoliberal rationality that is also mirrored in the conceptual differences between liberal and neoliberal subjects. Liberalism, says Foucault, is a kind of "governmental naturalism"[4]: the governmental principle of liberalism is to govern according to the market, because the market is understood as a site of truth—the natural truth implicit in the relation of exchange between autonomous individuals whose interests cannot be anticipated or known, and which therefore only the market can compute. Liberalism thus poses the principle of *laissez-faire* as the most expedient mechanism for governing—finding the right measure between governing "too much" and "too little" according to what "naturally" works in the market.

According to the thinkers of neoliberalism discussed by Foucault, however, the market is not at all a natural mechanism, but an *ideal model* for society. With roots in Germany's traumatic experience of the Weimar Republic in the 1920s and the subsequent totalitarian Nazi regime, neoliberal thinkers conceptualize market society as a way of keeping the excesses of governmental authority at bay. They seek refuge in the idea that the social processes instituted by markets—rewarding utility and punishing slack—could stem the authoritarian "slippery slope" of planned national economies and bloated state sovereignty.[5] However, to ensure that the market becomes the instituting social logic, neoliberals argue, one cannot rely on liberal notions of the "invisible hand"—relations of economic competition must be artificially produced and induced, not just accepted as they are. The fundamental shift of neoliberalism is therefore to "govern *for* the market, rather than *because* of the market"[6]—which is very much a break or a qualitative intensification of liberal thought, with a constructivist rather than a naturalist notion of social policy.[7]

Neoliberalism thus entails a paradox in political economy: in order to actualize competitive economic behavior, government must employ all types of policies, except precisely those that traditionally may be considered economic (price control, employment policies, public investment, etcetera). The by-passing of economic policies means that this governmental rationality programmatically restricts its field of action to *socio-technical* operations: rather than trying to shape economic processes themselves, the prime aim of government becomes the design of certain facts—"technical, scientific, legal, geographic"—that are conducive to particular socio-economic behaviors, while structurally eliding other processes.[8] In such a regime of power, Foucault argues, the ultimate horizon and "object of governmental action is what the Germans call '*die soziale Umwelt*': the social environment."[9]

This word, "environment," however, is not used by Foucault metaphorically. The neoliberals' approach is to *literally* engage material processes and spaces—an infrastructural and architectural framework—rather than just abstract economic, juridical, or ideological prescriptions. Throughout the latter part of *The Birth of Biopolitics*, Foucault thus returns again and again to the word "environment," making it the central operator of a fundamental shift from his previous model of power: from liberal "disciplinary" power, the correlate of liberal governmentality, neoliberalism shifts to "environmental" power:

> [W]hat appears on the horizon of this kind of analysis is not at all the ideal or project of an exhaustively disciplinary society in which the legal network hemming in individuals is taken over and extended internally by, let's say, normative mechanisms. Nor is it a society in which a mechanism of general normalization and the exclusion of those who cannot be normalized is needed. On the horizon of this analysis we see instead the image, idea, or theme-program of a society in which there is an optimization of systems of difference, in which the field is left open to fluctuating processes, in which minority individuals and practices are tolerated, in which action is brought to bear on the rules of the game rather than on the players, and finally in which there is an environmental type of intervention instead of the internal subjugation of individuals. … Not a standardizing, identificatory, hierarchical individualization, but an *environmentality* open to unknowns and transversal phenomena.[10]

From "labor" to "human capital": Environmental *economo-subjectivization*

Foucault does not dwell much more than this on the specifically formal or material aspects of this new form of power that he consistently labels "environmental," but he does clearly articulate the mechanics of how the neoliberal subject is instituted. Through environmental controls, governmental practice becomes the open secret of social management according to certain idealized economic "rules of the game"; a game that defines the subject and the population as essentially entrepreneurial. The intention is for the market to become the form of society; to encourage the mechanism of economic competition by and between subjects.[11] But how exactly can this process of subjectivization be instituted through "environmental power"? The answer, Foucault's analysis suggests, lies in the neoliberals' re-conceptualization of "labor," and indeed, the whole of life, into "human capital."

Neoliberals pursue a critique of classical economists' definition of labor, arguing that it has been treated as an empty category devoid of any qualitative content or meaning.[12] Deliberately disregarding the actual material realities historically faced by laborers (as captured, for instance, by Marx's critique of the logic of capitalism as commodifying and alienating labor power), the neoliberals launch a qualitative discourse of labor as something *other* than exploitation, hours of time worked, or productivity. It is a shift or re-qualification of labor from the large and abstract neoclassical models of land, work-time, and historical capital processes to an understanding of labor as the potential accumulation of capital by and for the laborer herself; a type of accumulation here labeled "human capital." The subject is not seen as externally exploited, but becomes an "entrepreneur of himself."[13] All qualities, innate (i.e. the subject's genetic make-up) or acquired (education, training, etcetera), are thus functions of human capital—they can be "invested in" or regulated by the subject in order to make its "enterprise" more productive, profitable, and credit-worthy. According to this view, all people have some form of human capital that can be optimized, regardless of their social class or status. The laborer's particular abilities, strengths, skills, special and general knowledge are seen as a "machine" owned by (and inseparable from) the laborer herself; a set of conditions, practices, and knowledges turned into "capital" that she can invest in, put to work, and gain a return from by means of a wage or an income.

This shift in the understanding of labor as "human capital" brings any possible human activity or condition into the field of economics, and therefore re-defines the discipline itself, turning "human behavior"—in all its general and particular forms, including the logics and rationalities ascribed to behaviors—as central to economic discourse.[14] "Human capital" provides a metrology by which the subject—as a set of behaviors and material conditions—can become homologized with an environment that is adaptive and responsive to these narrowly-defined metrics. Foucault points to behavioral economics as a science born at the same time as neoliberalism was being theorized and that aims, precisely, at extending the grid of economic qualification to behaviors that previously may have been considered non-economic, such as family life, education, or criminality, without due regard to whether such behavior is "rational" or not.[15] No matter the reasons for its behavior, environmental governmentality will understand the subject as a mere economic operator "responsive" to factors which can themselves be calculated, registered, and assessed in economic terms. In this way, any kind of behavior can be translated as economic behavior through the analysis and modulation of environmental controls. Thus, environmental governmentality works like a cybernetic system: taking all possible socio-technical inputs, translating them into economic variables in relation to the paradigm of competition, and feeding the results back for the optimization of the system, rather than acting on the subject itself.[16] The subject is therefore not controlled directly, but rather the environment itself presupposes a particular behavior for the subject:

> From the point of view of a [liberal] theory of government, *homo oeconomicus* is the person who must be let alone. With regard to *homo oeconomicus*, one must *laisser-faire*; he is the subject or object of *laissez-faire*. And now, [the neoliberal] *homo oeconomicus*, that is to say, the person who accepts reality or who responds systematically to modifications in the variables of the environment, appears precisely as someone manageable, someone who responds systematically to systematic modifications artificially introduced into the environment. *Homo oeconomicus* is someone who is eminently governable. From being the intangible partner of *laissez-faire*, *homo economicus* now becomes the correlate of a governmentality which will act on the environment and systematically modify its variables.[17]

Neoliberal environmental economization thus provides a frame by which governmentality (power) may hide itself in plain view; it is hard to see because it is everywhere at once. Through this particular kind of *econo-subjectivization,* integrally bound to competition and productivity as social paradigms, neoliberal subjects are performatively *made* by acting in their environment, with no apparent need to meddle with the subject's internal dimensions (its particular body, psychology, social context, or history). This makes for a purely formal subject; a subject without subjectivity as far as power is concerned, yet "eminently governable."[18] Rather than normative, economic, or ideological regulations, cultural techniques become the method by which neoliberalism designs social reality in the form of a socio-technical "game"; like a chess board or a computer interface, an artificial "environment" brings together a set of protocols and a material plane.[19] Environmental power literally actualizes and materializes the ideological paradigm of a society based on market economics. It allows for an epistemology, a rationality, and a valuation system to become operative in society, and thus to affect socio-political reality *ergonomically*, rather than "from above."[20]

Architecture and creativity under environmental governmentality

As demonstrated by the lectures included in *The Birth of Biopolitics*, Foucault was deeply aware of how contemporary scientific discourses, particularly behavioral economics, were at the heart of the neoliberal reprogramming of society. He was also, however, certainly aware of the extent to which the term "environment" had become the crucial ground for the intersection of these same sciences with architecture and design in the 1960s and 1970s.[21] Many of the neo-avant-gardes' work from this period already clearly presented architecture as a socio-technical means for registering and channeling "behavior" in all its manifestations, placing its emphasis on the operationalization of programmatic rationalities ("languages," "scripts," and "codes") rather than on discrete forms or aesthetics.[22]

Today, these tools and strategies have become absolutely hegemonic projects. Advances in computer science and engineering, behavioral economics, and the various "sciences" of the service economy (marketing, advertising, branding, public relations, etcetera) have led to the deployment of quasi-universal neoliberal programs of *economo-subjectivization*. After the tentative, speculative projects of the 1960s and 1970s, today there are plenty of offices, studios, and campuses (such as those in Silicon Valley or other global "creative city" hubs) planned and designed according to the paradigm of *gamification*.[23]

Architecture in this context plays much more than a passive, testimonial, or merely symbolic role. As mentioned earlier, one of the main ways neoliberal environmental power takes hold is through the category of "creativity." The rhetoric of creativity certainly has its effects at the level of ideology, but some of the specific cultural techniques associated with architectural creativity constitute, in themselves, processes of *economo-subjectivization*. This means that when we are being most "creative" in certain architectural environments, we are also working at greater rates toward the actualization and dissemination of neoliberal space and logics.

The relationship between architectural creativity and neoliberal environmental power appears through two interrelated planes: on one hand, the material-formal configurations of neoliberal space itself, which has transformed *all* spaces into workspaces—this is one of its typological achievements, architecturally speaking; and on the other, the modes of living and working that these neoliberal spaces presuppose and engender. These are two sides of the same coin that come together in the physical tools the contemporary designer employs (surfaces, typically) that collapse the distinctions between work-space, work-mode, and work-purpose altogether and which make up the techno-cultural substrate of contemporary architecture: computer screens, parametric software and visualization tools, open-plan-and-play production spaces, Google researchology and infotainment, etcetera.

We tend to think creativity is what animates these surfaces. In fact, it is precisely the opposite: creativity is an effect of these tools and technologies. Creativity is the animation these environments and interfaces produce in ourselves.[24] This is not a metaphoric reflection, but a material condition, and can be found as much in the products and spaces of the giant technological corporations as in the most "creative" global architecture studios.

The creativity of environmental power is animated by way of at least three main channels: (1) through managerial logics and products; (2) through the use of particular parametric tools of governmentality; and (3) through the proliferation of media and project-driven modes of labor. Each of these interconnected channels is large and complex, and related to many others; their main qualities can only be introduced here but they point to a modulation of "creativity" in the neoliberal workspace.

The anti-politics of the techno-managerial workplace

The contemporary workplace of large design and engineering firms has long abandoned the old "command-and-control" model of earlier times.[25] Taylorist and Fordist models gave way in the post-World War II period to corporate structures in which managers had the safest and most important roles within the company. The general model was one of "producers competing for consumers," led by managers, who thus wielded tremendous power as well as becoming increasingly constrained by the political demands and pressures of these various groups.

Such a model was in place due to the particular socio-economic and political conditions of the period, with capital regulated to encourage a steady degree of re-investment within the economy. But it was also sustained technologically by the semi-open-plan office and the various levels of coordination and control such an architectural apparatus could provide: a separate but always alert community of managers that could oversee the companies' workers and operations. The spatial and social distinctions were somewhat clear, making the office or shop floor a highly political—clearly territorial—environment, where plans concerning the entire constituency of the company as well as the State (via unions, consumers, and regulators) could be discussed and disputed.

With the advent of neoliberal policies of deregulation from the 1970s onwards, the market becomes an end in itself: the State begins to govern for the market. Thus, at the level of the company, the model turns from one of "producers competing for consumers" to one of "producers competing for investors," as capital owners penalized managers for their balancing acts between consumers and workers—demanding a more flexible workspace to induce higher levels of productivity and thus higher returns on capital investment.[26] This transfer of power from labor to capital occurs through a shift in the function of the law: from a political instrument (for instituting and contesting substantive principles, i.e. rights), to a formal instrument (for adjudicating disputes based on the technical and "objective" law of competition). The law thus becomes the opposite of a social fundament for politics and planning. It facilitates the economic game but does not contain or regulate it. Law defers to the self-regulated rule of those in power.

The neoliberal model thus implied an intensification of the post-World War II shift from vertical modes of management to "horizontal" ones. In this new model, workers are not so much governed from the outside or from above, but rather through environmental regulation. Discipline turns into *environmentality*, giving more responsibility to the now-autonomous worker but without the benefits of old. Management thus shifts from external control and internalized self-policing (discipline) to encouraging competitive self-expression ("creativity"): the principle of environmental *economo-subjectivization*. Government regulation becomes corporate "governance"—from the site of social disputes, workspaces become environments that have tacitly coded within them a whole set of procedures and operations, including "disruptive" ways of acting, seeing, and being; places where power circulates most effectively because it circulates without any apparent management, directly through *us*.[27]

The rhetoric of "governance" in management theory and practice shifts the earlier top-down, command-control rule of the semi-open-plan office, to fully-open-plan, networked, and self-organized teams and spaces. Governance implies a topological system of organization (no inside, no outside) where procedures rule themselves without there being any apparent rules. Sovereignty dissolves into processes we ourselves set in motion. This political anomie is mirrored at the level of the individual worker: individuals (or semi-autonomous teams) become responsible for themselves while remaining vulnerable to structural conditions and fluctuations.

The language of governance, in identifying itself with the whole environment and rarely acknowledging any missing parts (physical or social), tends to deny the existence of deep struggles. No substantive conflict is possible (it is literally not recognized); rather there is always a strong emphasis on consensus. Disagreements are merely technical aspects of problems that can only have a technical solution.[28] Technocracy is validated by its presumed quantitative efficacy, not by its record in upholding qualitative ways of doing things. Knowledge is validated by incentives and personal experience, rather than a serious engagement with history. The appearance of jovial neutrality, through physical design and personal demeanor, provides a veneer of legitimacy and authority that is structurally—socially and legally—safe from serious contention, despite the repeated references to creativity or disruption.

From all these perspectives, the corporate post-Fordist workplace is a thoroughly anti-political one, if by "the political" we understand the logic of disagreement.[29] Governance is the correlate of a "post-political" management of social productivity—the thesis that capitalism is "the end of history." In its aim to supersede antagonism, neoliberals mobilize the language of "stakeholders" to replace interest groups or classes. These substitutions deny a political vocabulary: they configure a social space ruled by a depoliticized epistemology. For neoliberal governance, any democratic political interruption signifies the stark opposition of irrationalism versus expertise: politics stands for provincialism versus the "open doors" of the universal free market. The reason for managerialism's air of moral superiority has nothing to do with a historical-political position. Rather, it is a function of the way environmental governmentality channels and registers interferences. Environmental power involves the absorption of what are public, political, and moral concerns into market logics, and hence these kinds of interferences can only be "dealt with" if they are homologated to the systems' own means and ends. Any other format remains exogenous to the model, as economists like to say. Thus, any initiative that vies for recognition or hegemony is necessarily funneled and translated into a market-oriented episteme, an episteme that structurally elides the political dimensions and norms it tacitly runs on—the miracle of pure performance with no "ghost in the machine."[30]

This technocratic context—the cultural and political poverty of which is only obscured by its enormous power—reduces questions of principle to the management of disputes contained within the dogmas of economic competition and other ideologically enshrined parameters of productivity. Thus, despite all the cartoonish spatial and symbolic references to playfulness, disruption, or even "hacking the system" present in the corporate-creative industries, these environments all require and promote the same kind of defanged "creativity."[31] In material terms, creativity is the measure by which workers will cannibalize themselves for the sake of the company—extreme work hours, no parallel commitments (love, friendship, community, etcetera), and no separation between the private, the public, or the social. This kind of creativity rewards competition-induced nervous breakdowns and narcissistic pathologies. In most architecture offices, creativity is defined by the necessary over-production of senseless images and models for the feeding of the offices' media spectacle machines. This goes hand in hand with the depletion of valuable resources for other spheres of architectural practice and imagination that are in sore need of creative input, such as the articulation of a different, richer epistemology and cultural techniques to be able to engage the complexity of urban development beyond the tired aesthetic and discursive clichés disseminated by neoliberal governance.

The parametric governmentality of neoliberal interfaces

One of the reasons architecture is immune and impotent toward the politics of the city is that it does not have adequate instruments—technical, epistemic—to engage and transform this arena. In such an impoverished condition, architectural creativity is doomed to reproduce the effects and the metrics that neoliberal environmental interfaces set for it. This kind of creativity is therefore an effect—a reproduction—of the animations generated by neoliberal managerial tools, rather than a challenge to it.

In architecture, the logics of managerial governance are increasingly embedded in a set of tools for design that have transformed the discipline entirely. Digital design platforms such as parametric scripting packages or Building Information Modeling (BIM) have dramatically shifted the means of representation and working for architects. The old modern paradigm of scaled representation and mechanically-drafted drawing has given way to the possibility of representing objects at any scale, at any point in their development, and in any possible state in relation to any other parameter that can be quantitatively defined: energy consumption, rate of return on investment, structural efficiency, and so on. Virtual models synched to physical products, assembly and construction logistics, market fluctuations, and data on territories, climate, and users in real time will increasingly replace the static physical drawing. These virtual interfaces usually run on computers through proprietary computer aided design (CAD) software packages, but also take the form of interactive reports, online services, and databases, making it possible to register and operationalize data in an architectural project. Thus, such interfaces have a curious capacity for turning parameters—data that responds to narrowly-defined conditions, usually in market terms—into unquestionable, essential facts. As Foucault theorized, the market discloses "truth" as the performative result of discrete market representations. Neoliberalism enacts an intensification of this elliptical market truth-logic, extending it to the whole environment—cultural, personal, and physical—and further upturning the political logic of rights (legality) for the sake of unquestionable "performance."[32]

The problem with such market-driven devices is that they do not disclose, as is often presumed, "reality itself," but they merely reproduce and satisfy the epistemic conditions that generated them. Thus, when one uses parametric software to identify the most cost-effective shape for a tower's floor plan, certain "costs" are structurally excluded from the computation (i.e. labor costs). In other words, why should real estate-defined metrics drive housing design exercises? These are political questions that cannot be reduced to market-oriented, technical, problem-solving exercises.

As these tools are still in the early stages of development (at least with regards to the promise of their full potential in terms of systemization of integrated project delivery, quality control, risk assessment, enhanced collaboration in design and construction, etcetera), architects tend to utilize them superficially—predominantly for formal experiments. This is also an ideological determination, of course, as the market constantly demands sensationalist architecture while keeping delivery systems and existing power relations as intact as possible. Aesthetic experimentation (including technological and material fetishism) is certainly the remit of the architect, but if we want to be truly creative and have any kind of impact on the politics of buildings and cities, we will have to transform these tools to go beyond formalism and environmental management as usual.

Media and project-driven modes of labor

Despite the common utopian rhetoric around the proliferation of media and project-driven modes of labor—positively and negatively referred to in contemporary discourse by many different names, such as post-Fordism, cognitive capitalism, the sharing economy, affective labor, communicative capitalism, etcetera[33]—these modes of labor must be seen in the wider context of increasing labor precarity and social inequality. The innovations in technology described above (particularly network communications) and the new media forms they have spawned—post-internet culture, the possibility of global collaborations, online cultural events, the closer interweaving of producers across the world, and other positive practices of freedom enabled by these tools—have to be placed in perspective. These practices are not just the result of genial technological advances, but are also the outlet through which cultural producers manage the pressures of neoliberal power, sometimes just barely.

In this mode of labor we can locate the (youngish) sole practitioner, usually involved in more than one project and discipline (often courting art production, curation, academia, publishing, journalism, and architecture all at once), although more and more the fully-employed architectural worker is subjected to the same logics as a strategy of survival. The state of permanent migration that cultural producers, including architects, are supposed to endure—working and living out of a suitcase from one city, residency, project, or teaching position to the next—is aided and abetted by neoliberal institutional policies and the lifestyles of these migrants themselves. The generalization and intensification of student debt—a centerpiece of neoliberal governmentality—is largely responsible for this permanent state of exception. Constant flux disables any kind of serious engagement with place (and thus, serious political commitment), as well as personal development. Family and future become part of an ever-receding mirage in the real-time dictatorship of screens and transfers. In return for the circulation of bodies and ideas, the internet and its various physical outlets (magazines, galleries, seminar rooms, biennials) bloat with more content than can ever be viewed, managed, or edited. The result is an overproduction of content and media delivery channels—media itself usually framed as the most valuable kind of content, as it gives the presentation of work the veneer of a *gesamstkunstwerk's* magisterial authority. Cultural production thus ironically attempts to emulate and somehow pierce through the overarching environmental systems that constrain it.

The greater ease of online collaboration and communication, however, does not compensate for the general downgrading of the necessary physical infrastructures that support cultural production: less funding for education, theaters, art spaces, studios, housing, etcetera. With a permanently migrant workforce adept at instant transplantation and adaptation, and focused on the sole purpose of achieving individual survival in the form of securing the next oversubscribed and short-term job, grant, residency, or project, contemporary architectural workers are a very easily managed and docile group.[34] The systemic pressures—as well as the ideological drive to compete—make this kind of labor difficult to recognize *as* labor. Neoliberal policy does not want to label it as such, nor does the architecture industry, as it would sunder current institutional arrangements, from the academy to the starchitect system that now runs the show. Architectural workers themselves are either too caught up in survival or playing the neoliberal script to take collective action.

This inertia begins right at architecture school, where the media and project-driven mode of labor is presented as a necessary state of affairs to the young architecture student. Projects tend to be short, encompassing two or three months at most and, at the same time, diffused, distinguishing dubiously between "skills," "history & theory," and "practice." Lightning site visits and engagements with complex socio-economic conditions teach the student to effectively misread context while learning to deliver blurb-precision discourse. Individualistic competition is encouraged and prized above collective work or experiments in collaboration—a sensibility that is fire-etched on students' consciousness through the ineffective and petty cruelties of the jury system of evaluation. "Star" architects, more interested in spinning their own careers than in pedagogical questions, unashamedly model education to their own image. The student is caught up in a paradoxical relation, as she is both client and service provider for the university or firm, acquiring intangible knowledge at the firm (often unpaid or underpaid), or "branding" the university through the ceaseless publication of her projects and activities—a paradoxical and paralyzing condition in which actual self-development or real political positioning is almost impossible. Here again, the focus on narrowly-defined categories at school replicates market epistemologies.

Far from engaging "creativity" in and of itself, media and project-driven modes of labor flatten the anthropological content of sites and subjects, as they demand a speed and a concrete type of result that prevents other temporalities, other values, or more resistant logics (such as that of the family, of political commitment, or of deep ecology) to affect it. When such an allegedly "global" model actually involves problematic global sites—such as through international field trips—the impulsive overlaying of the media and project-driven format automatically leads to a one-dimensional and self-satisfying reading of context. Serious issues like racialization, social inequality, urban or infrastructural dispossession, and environmental fallout are treated, if at all, as token factors to be checked-off in the project's "deliverables." The old imperialistic logic of development or "aid" flaccidly animates the projects' true focus: the production and dissemination of more and more images and posts for debased circulation, obscuring the tame engagement with the actual place, its history, and its complexity.

Conclusion

From these three points on how neoliberal environmentality dominates contemporary "creativity" in architecture, at least three interconnected consequences can be extracted.

First, the system of managerial technocracy, market-driven parametric interfaces, and structural precarity, work, in architecture as in other fields, to elide "externalities" while claiming to be seriously engaging the whole of the environment. This issue reflects how the rhetoric of "performance"—as an apparently objective and technical mode of reason, but in effect utterly saturated with ideology—operates at the level of the State and at the level of industry. The State (the law; regulatory bodies) guarantees competition for the market (itself a highly *unfree* and asymmetrical arena, despite neoliberals' continuous pronouncements to the contrary[35]), but does not adequately respond to the "externalities" such market competition entails.

Within the architecture industry, the lack of comprehensive planning, adequate political representation, or accountability can be observed in the schizophrenic approaches to "sustainability" and around the inability of the industry to address its problematic modes of labor. Both sustainability and labor are mediated via neoliberal interfaces and are thus subject to market-oriented homologization—they are not allowed to be addressed as political issues stemming from the privatization of resources, including the architectural "general intellect."[36] This inability to deal with the damaging and dangerous externalities of the system may, by itself, bring down the whole apparatus of environmental governmentality through the sheer force of its own weight.

The second consequence is that we may not yet have an adequate representation of the subjects of environmental power.[37] Beyond old and worn categories such as the modern master-architect or the post-modern pluralist, the neoliberal subject is politically and socially complex, and contradictory. She often has a collectivist disposition, but is far from being anarchic or anti-capitalist. The civil rights and liberties associated with liberal subjectivity (privacy, property, dignity) are thoroughly transformed by *environmentality*: workers uneasily submit to all manner of digital surveillance practices in exchange for mere access to the industry. Attachments of any kind must be dispensed with. These environments demand a specific brand of hyper-flexible, defanged non-conformism that enhances rather than destroys capital—a paradoxical condition that only works when the workers themselves are aware of the contradictions they are in, as it requires a lucid awareness of the power diagram in which they operate. Transgression has to be carefully managed as a valuable asset—neither totally avoided nor totally accepted.[38] Thus, the neoliberal subject faces complex questions of selfhood and power involving values and culture that the architecture industry does not usually recognize. Yet these are important, substantive issues that have to be addressed if we are to succeed in politicizing a collective body of architectural workers.[39]

Third, an epistemic re-wiring of the discipline is necessary to enable the possibility of thought at any level of structural or infrastructural significance, not just to address issues of rights, but to be able to change the politics of the city itself.[40] The establishment of neoliberal models of urban governance has generated a paradox for architects' political capacities: the more we seek to participate in urban policy, the more we become entangled in its messy and questionable politics—but the gamble of troubling compromise for positive influence rarely seems to pay off. Despite architects' best efforts, the neoliberal city's managerial class (real estate developers, financial brokers, public relations agencies, and the whole massive industry of business management consultants) contains and lubricates planning processes within strict neoliberal parameters. This sphere of urban administration, masquerading as objective professionalism, has utterly replaced the politics of the city at the expense of democracy—and arguably, of architects' expertise for figuring out what the forms of democracy could be.[41]

In this sense, environmental governmentality's technological foundations in behavioral economics, cybernetics, and computer science make the naturalization of market-logics and market-truth claims ever more difficult to identify and disentangle, as political assumptions are so thoroughly bonded to techno-scientific models. Their anti-political dimension is due not only to the elision between market-oriented epistemology and epistemology in general. Neoliberal interfaces deny intellectual speculation (particularly anthropological, political, and historical thinking) also by virtue of their obsession with the contemporary, the dictatorship of and addiction to "real-time."[42] This injunction—to always stick to the present, to the surface, to the already-existing—prevents any conceptualization or even lived physical experience that would allow a different reality to emerge from a given situation.[43] Crudely put, these managerial interfaces deny the possibility of political thought. With its fierce and totalizing focus on behavior as an economic function, neoliberalism challenges us on a number of fronts: to conceive of ways in which to organize life as a public (that is, political) thing, to conceive of wealth as worldliness instead of privatized capital, and to democratize creativity without simultaneously anaesthetizing it.

It is important to note that when we challenge the neoliberal definition of creativity it is not to suggest there is an underlying, essential human nature beneath it—a "real" creativity that is being suppressed by spectacle. It is to assert that there are multiple types of creativity—and forms of life—that do not have to follow the neoliberal capitalist script. We are not necessarily "entrepreneurial" by nature, nor should we be coerced into this mode of being by environmental power. Creativity in architecture today should have less to do with gaming or hacking the received tenets for the management of capital in its various guises (the old business as usual of non-conformity made productive), and more to do with a search for decolonized environments—a quest for understanding and enjoying worldliness beyond capitalist imperatives.[44]

Architecture ought to have a lot to say on these matters, as both planning and creativity are familiar grounds for its practitioners. Other design interfaces must be constructed out of different epistemic configurations.[45] To finish with Foucault's own words of advice against seeing texts as scriptures, the task still lies before us:

> There is no governmental rationality of socialism. … [W]e ask what rules it adopts for itself, how it offsets compensating mechanisms, how it calculates the mechanisms of measurement it has installed within its governmentality. … [T]o define for itself its way of doing things and its way of governing. … What governmentality is possible as a strictly, intrinsically, and autonomously socialist governmentality? In any case, we know only that if there is a really socialist governmentality, then it is not hidden within socialism and its texts. It cannot be deduced from them. It must be invented.[46]

Notes

Acknowledgments: The author would like to thank Professor Wendy Brown for her seminar on "Marx & Neoliberalism" at Columbia University during the spring of 2014, which inspired many of the theoretical reflections in this chapter. Thanks also to the editors, Peggy Deamer and Dariel Cobb, for their helpful and incisive comments on the chapter's early versions.

1. Here I am referring to Timothy Mitchell's analysis of "the economy" as a constructed category that only emerged as such in the first half of the twentieth century. This chapter is an attempt to combine Mitchell's methods (working within a comparative, postcolonial, Science and Technology Studies (STS) framework) with Foucault's theory of subjectivization. Unlike Mitchell, this chapter will only describe the West European and North American context. A richer comparative analysis including the relations between so-called developed and developing nations is beyond the scope of this chapter, but it would present a fundamental aspect of neoliberal economization and subjectivization: the problematic distinction between "material" and "immaterial" labor is absolutely geopolitically determined. See: Timothy Mitchell, *Rule of Experts: Egypt, Techno-Politics, Modernity* (Berkeley: University of California Press, 2002), especially Chapter 3: "The Character of Calculability." See also: Koray Çaliskan and Michel Callon, "Economization, Part 1: Shifting Attention from the Economy Towards Processes of Economization," *Economy and Society* 38.3 (2009): 369–98. Çaliskan and Callon denote economization as

the processes that constitute the behaviours, organizations, institutions and, more generally, the objects in a particular society which are tentatively and often controversially qualified, by scholars and/or lay people, as "economic". The construction of action(-ization) into the word implies that the economy is an achievement rather than a starting point or a pre-existing reality that can simply be revealed and acted upon. (370)

2. Michel Foucault, *The Birth of Biopolitics: Lectures at the Collège de France, 1978–79* (Basingstoke: Palgrave Macmillan, 2008). I use the term "neoliberalism" in the sense used by Foucault during his lectures: as a diffuse but relatively coherent intellectual project born around the 1930s and developed throughout the twentieth century, aimed at re-invigorating, renewing, and transforming the economic principles of classical liberalism, thus generating a new theorization and normative project for society and politics. There is a wealth of volumes on the many geographical and actually-implemented variants of "neoliberalism." For a brief overview, see: Jamie Peck, *Constructions of Neoliberal Reason* (Oxford: Oxford University Press, 2010).

3. Foucault theorized a large paradigmatic shift in the history of government: the transformation of power, evolving since the Middle Ages, from "sovereignty"—an external, transcendental, and self-serving rule of law chiefly dedicated to maintaining territorial power—to "governmentality"; a form of power emerging roughly around the middle of the eighteenth century which is integrally bound with the population, governed and governing by and for itself through not only laws, but also "tactics" that are at once internal and external to the State:

> By this word "governmentality" I mean three things. First, by "governmentality" I understand the ensemble formed by institutions, procedures, analyses and reflections, calculations, and tactics that allow the exercise of this very specific, albeit very complex, power that has the population as its target, political economy as its major form of knowledge, and apparatuses of security as its essential technical instrument. Second, by "governmentality" I understand the tendency, the line of force, that for a long time, and throughout the West, has constantly led towards the pre-eminence over all other types of power—sovereignty, discipline, and so on—of the type of power that we can call "government" and which has led to the development of a series of specific governmental apparatuses (*appareils*) on the one hand, and, on the other to the development of a series of knowledges (*savoirs*). Finally, by "governmentality" I think we should understand the process, or rather, the result of the process by which the state of justice of the Middle Ages became the administrative state in the fifteenth and sixteenth centuries and was gradually "governmentalized."

(Michel Foucault, *"Security, Territory, Population": Lectures at the Collège de France, 1977–78* (New York: Picador, 2007), 108.) See also: Michel Foucault, *"Society Must Be Defended": Lectures at the Collège de France, 1975–76* (New York: Picador, 2003).

4. Foucault, *The Birth of Biopolitics*, 61.
5. F. A. Hayek, *The Road to Serfdom: Texts and Documents—The Definitive Edition*, ed. Bruce Caldwell (Chicago: University of Chicago Press, 2007 [1944]); Joseph A. Schumpeter, *Capitalism, Democracy, Socialism*. (New York: Harper Perennial, 1962).
6. Foucault, *The Birth of Biopolitics*, 121. My emphasis.
7. Foucault, *The Birth of Biopolitics*, 119:

    This is where the ordoliberals break with the tradition of eighteenth and nineteenth century liberalism. They say: Laissez-faire cannot and must not be the conclusion drawn from the principle of competition as the organizing form of the market. Why not? Because, they say, when you deduce the principle of laissez-faire from the market economy, basically you are still in the grip of what could be called a "naive naturalism," ... For what in fact is competition? It is absolutely not a given of nature. The game, mechanisms, and effects of competition which we identify and enhance are not at all natural phenomena; competition is not the result of a natural interplay of appetites, instincts, behavior, and so on. ... Competition is an essence. Competition is an *eidos*. Competition is a principle of formalization. Competition has an internal logic; it has its own structure. Its effects are only produced if this logic is respected. It is, as it were, a formal game between inequalities; it is not a natural game between individuals and behaviors. ... competition as an essential economic logic will only appear and produce its effects under certain conditions which have to be carefully and artificially constructed.

8. This formalist mode of governmental reason is illustrated by Foucault with an example of agricultural policy proposed by one of the fathers of ordoliberalism in 1952, Walter Eucken, where he outlines what must be done to create a competitive agricultural market. Eucken's approach is to act exclusively on socio-technical variables, such as the "population, technology, training and education, the legal system, the availability of land, the climate." Foucault continues:

    The idea was not, given the state of things, how can we find the economic system that will be able to take account of the basic facts peculiar to European agriculture? It was, given that economic-political regulation can only take place through the market, how can we modify these material, cultural, technical, and legal bases that are given in Europe? How can we modify these facts, this framework so that the market economy can come into play? You can see here ... that to the same extent that governmental intervention must be light at the level of economic processes themselves, so must it be heavy when it is a matter of this set of technical, scientific, legal, geographic, let's say, broadly, social factors which now increasingly become the object of governmental intervention.

    (*The Birth of Biopolitics*, 141)

9. Foucault, *The Birth of Biopolitics*, 146. The "social" dimension is normative also in the sense that, according to Foucault, ordoliberalism included a compensatory social

policy to what they called the "coldness" of pure economic competition. American neoliberal theorists shrugged off such niceties.

10. Foucault, *The Birth of Biopolitics,* 260–61. This crucial shift from a disciplinary society to a society of environmental control is the result of a reflection on the efficacy of the relation between law, political economy, and technologies of "enforcement" in liberalism; liberal governmentality based on the law appears weak or deficient to neoliberal thinkers: "It is necessary," Foucault writes, "to change the conception of law, or at least elucidate its function. In other words, not confuse its form (which is always to prohibit and constrain) and its function, which must be that of rule of the game. The law is that which must favor the game" of economic competition, "i.e. the … enterprises, initiatives, changes, and by enabling everybody to be a rational subject, i.e. to maximize the functions of utility." The law, as governing principle, is thus deemed too monolithic, rigid, and removed—not *ergonomic* enough—for the control of a population understood entirely through market principles and for the sake of competitive differentiation:

> [I]f you do not want to get out of the law and you do not want to divert its true function as rule of the game, the technology to be employed is not discipline-normalization, but action on the environment. Modifying the terms of the game, not the players' mentality. … An environmental technology whose main aspects are: the definition of a framework around the individual which is loose enough for him to be able to play; the possibility for the individual of regulation of the effects of the definition of his own framework; the regulation of environmental effects; … the autonomy of these environmental spaces. … Not a standardizing, identificatory, hierarchical individualization, but an *environmentality* open to unknowns and transversal phenomena.

(*The Birth of Biopolitics,* 261) My italics: "environmentalité" (environmentality) in the original French edition was mistranslated as "environmentalism" in the English edition. It is worth noting the similarities between Foucault's various notes and allusions to this shift from disciplinary to environmental power in *The Birth of Biopolitics* and Gilles Deleuze's own speculations on the future of Foucault's model of power, which Deleuze termed "Control Society"; see: Gilles Deleuze, "Postscript on the Societies of Control," *October* 59 (1992): 3–7.

11. Foucault, *The Birth of Biopolitics,* 147–8:

> [W]hat is sought is not a society subject to the commodity effect, but a society subject to the dynamic of competition. Not a supermarket society, but an enterprise society. The *homo oeconomicus* sought after is not the man of exchange or man the consumer; he is the man of enterprise and production. … I think this multiplication of the "enterprise" form within the social body is what is at stake in neo-liberal policy. It is a matter of making the market, competition, and so the enterprise, into what could be called the formative power of society.

12. Foucault, *The Birth of Biopolitics,* 221:

    [I]t is precisely because classical economics was not able to take on this analysis of labor in its concrete specification and qualitative modulations, it is because it left this blank page, gap or vacuum in its theory, that a whole philosophy, anthropology, and politics, of which Marx is precisely the representative, rushed in. Consequently, we should not continue with this, in a way, realist criticism made by Marx, accusing real capitalism of having made real labor abstract; we should undertake a theoretical criticism of the way in which labor itself became abstract in economic discourse.

13. Foucault, *The Birth of Biopolitics,* 226.
14. Foucault, *The Birth of Biopolitics,* 223: "Economics is not therefore the analysis of processes; it is the analysis of an activity. So it is no longer the analysis of the historical logic of processes; it is the analysis of the internal rationality, the strategic programming of individuals' activity."
15. See, for instance: Gary S. Becker, "Irrational Behavior and Economic Theory," *The Journal of Political Economy,* 70.1 (February 1962): 1–13. "Even irrational decision units must accept reality and could not, for example, maintain a choice that was no longer within their opportunity set. And these sets are not fixed or dominated by erratic variations, but are systematically changed by different economic variables." (12)
16. Foucault, *The Birth of Biopolitics,* 253:

    We only move over to the side of the subject himself inasmuch as ... we can approach it through the angle, the aspect, the kind of network of intelligibility of his behavior as economic behavior. The subject is considered only as *homo oeconomicus*, which does not mean that the whole subject is considered as *homo oeconomicus*. In other words, considering the subject as *homo oeconomicus* does not imply an anthropological identification of any behavior whatsoever with economic behavior. It simply means that economic behavior is the grid of intelligibility one will adopt on the behavior of a new individual. It also means that the individual becomes governmentalizable, that power gets a hold on him to the extent, and only to the extent, that he is a *homo oeconomicus*.

17. Foucault, *The Birth of Biopolitics,* 270.
18. Here we find a weakness in Foucault's analysis, as he appears to underplay the internal dimensions of the subject of neoliberalism: we are "eminently governable" because we have a stake in the game, not because we are an empty signal in its circuits, as Foucault sometimes seems to suggest. Which is not to disagree with Foucault's description of "environmentality," but to point at neoliberalism's successful "environmentalization" of our motivations and desires. Critical discourses of desire in the symbolic economy (sometimes labeled "semiocapitalism") are crucial here, as well as the various critiques of bourgeois subjectivization: consumer society, interiority and domesticity, metropolitanism and empire, practices of sexuality, hygiene, and

so on. See, for instance: Franco "Bifo" Berardi, *The Soul at Work: From Alienation to Autonomy* (Cambridge, MA: The MIT Press, 2009).
19. See: "Special Issue: Cultural Techniques edited by Geoffrey Winthrop-Young, Ilinca Iurascu, and Jussi Parikka," *Theory, Culture, & Society* (November, 2013) 30 (6).
20. On "ergonomics," see: John Harwood, "The Interface," in *Governing by Design: Architecture, Economy, and Politics in the Twentieth Century*, ed. Aggregate (Architectural History Collaborative) (Pittsburgh, PA: University of Pittsburgh Press, 2012), 73:

> A neologism—coined at a British military research laboratory in 1949 from the Greek ergon ("organ" or "work") and nomos ("natural law")—ergonomics is a normative, synthetic discipline, seeking to apply the findings of psychiatry, psychology, physiology and anthropometrics, cybernetics and information theory, engineering, medicine, business management, and all branches of design to "the scientific study of the relationship between man and his working environment." As such, ergonomics constituted a new configuration and instrumentalization of human sciences. Earlier sciences of work, such as the system of "scientific management" championed by Frederick Winslow Taylor, had deployed anthropometric data and efficiency studies to "fit the worker to the job." ... Instead of fitting the worker to the job, a new applied science [ergonomics] would do just the opposite: "fit the job to the worker."

21. Felicity D. Scott, *Architecture or Techno-Utopia: Politics After Modernism* (Cambridge, MA: The MIT Press, 2007), 97. Foucault had been invited to a conference at the Museum of Modern Art in 1971, eventually called: "Institutions for a Post-Technological Society: The Universitas Project," and earlier subtitled "The Future of the Man-Made Environment." Foucault did not attend, but he did correspond with the curator Emilio Ambasz about the proposal.
22. Manfredo Tafuri was also very attuned to this development. See: "Architecture and Its Double: Semiology and Formalism" in *Architecture and Utopia: Design and Capitalist Development* (Cambridge, MA: The MIT Press, 1979). See also Arindam Dutta, ed., *A Second Modernism: MIT, Architecture, and the 'Techno-Social' Moment* (Cambridge, MA: The MIT Press, 2013).
23. Ian Bogost, "Gamasutra – Persuasive Games: Exploitationware," *Gamasutra Blog*, 3 May, 2011, http://www.gamasutra.com/view/feature/134735/persuasive_games_exploitationware.php (accessed 15 August, 2014):

> In the modern marketing business, the best solutions are generic ones, ideas that can be repeated without much thought from brand to brand, billed by consultants and agencies at a clear markup. Gamification offers this exactly. No thinking is required, just simple, absentminded iteration and the promise of empty metrics to prove its value. Like having a website or a social media strategy, "gamification" allows organizations to tick the games box without fuss. Just add badges! Just add leaderboards!

> ... gamification proposes to replace real incentives with fictional ones. Real incentives come at a cost but provide value for both parties based on a relationship of trust. By contrast, pretend incentives reduce or eliminate costs, but in so doing they strip away both value and trust. ... Gamification replaces these real, functional, two-way relationships with dysfunctional perversions of relationships. Organizations ask for loyalty, but they reciprocate that loyalty with shams, counterfeit incentives that neither provide value nor require investment. When seen in this light, "gamification" is a misnomer. A better name for this practice is *exploitationware*. ... Google and Facebook's seemingly free services also could be called exploitationware of a different kind, since they use the carrot of free services (their purported product) to extract information that forms the real basis for their revenues (their real product).

24. Alexander R. Galloway, *The Interface Effect* (London: Polity, 2012).
25. As already noted, the remarks in this and other sections refer mainly to the Euro-American context. See: L. Boltanski and È. Chiapello, *The New Spirit of Capitalism* (London: Verso, 2005). In Sebastian Budgen's concise account:

    > How has a new and virulent form of capitalism—they label it a 'connectionist' or 'network' variant—with an even more disastrous impact on the fabric of a common life than its predecessors, managed to install itself so smoothly and inconspicuously in France, without attracting either due critical attention or any organized resistance from forces of opposition, vigorous a generation ago, now reduced to irrelevancy or cheerleading? ... Ready to take advantage of even the most inhospitable conditions, firms began to reorganize the production process and wage contracts. Flexible labour systems, sub-contracting, team-working, multi-tasking and multi-skilling, 'flat' management—all the features of a so-called "lean capitalism" or "post-Fordism"—were the result.

    (S. Budgen, "A New 'Spirit of Capitalism,'" *New Left Review* (2000): 149–56)
26. I owe this general account to a seminar with Wendy Brown on "Marx & Neoliberalism" (including a guest presentation by Michel Feher). Columbia University, Spring 2014.
27. Maurizio Lazzarato, "Immaterial Labour" in *Radical Thought in Italy: A Potential Politics*, eds. Paolo Virno and Michael Hardt (Minneapolis: University of Minnesota Press, 1996). Regarding the nexus between creativity, autonomy, and productivity, Lazzarato claims: "Participative management is a technology of power, a technology for creating and controlling the 'subjective processes.' ... First and foremost, we have here a discourse that is authoritarian: one *has to* express oneself, one *has to* speak, communicate, cooperate, and so forth." (135)
28. Evgeny Morozov, *To Save Everything, Click Here: The Folly of Technological Solutionism* (New York: PublicAffairs, 2014).
29. Jacques Rancière, *Disagreement* (Minneapolis: University of Minnesota Press, 1999).
30. Arjun Appadurai, "The Ghost in the Financial Machine," in *The Future as Cultural Fact: Essays on the Global Condition* (Brooklyn, NY: Verso, 2013).

31. See, for instance: Quentin Hardy, "The Monuments of Tech," *New York Times*, 1 March, 2014, http://nyti.ms/1d7QKBf (accessed 28 April, 2014).
32. Despite the resonance of "performance" with the idea of modulation, neoliberal apologists still tend to see their system as a monolithic form: one is either completely for or against it, there can be no critical discussion of its relative merits or problems. This totalization makes it impossible to distinguish between means and ends, as they are always framed as pre-given—all that can be discussed is the management of the situation. There is no possibility of challenging the principles underlying the system. Hannah Arendt already warned of the danger in such thinking associated with liberalism. See: Hannah Arendt, "What Is Freedom?," in *Between Past and Future; Eight Exercises in Political Thought* (New York: Viking Press, 1968).
33. See: Jodi Dean, "Communicative Capitalism: Circulation and the Foreclosure of Politics," in *Digital Media and Democracy: Tactics in Hard Times* (Cambridge, MA: The MIT Press, 2008).
34. As artist Andrea Fraser has reckoned, with an almost cringing lucidity:

    Artists, like other arts professionals, are often highly entrepreneurial. I would go even further and say that we are the very model for labour in the new economy, a fact that's not an odd irony or quirk of fate, but deeply rooted in our "habitus"— as Pierre Bourdieu calls the habits, dispositions and preferences generated within a given field. We're highly educated, highly motivated "self-starters" who believe that learning is a continuous process. We're always ready for change and adapt to it quickly. We prefer freedom and flexibility to security. We don't want to punch a clock and tend to resist quantifying the value of our labour time. We don't know the meaning of "overtime." We're convinced that we work for ourselves and our own satisfaction even when we work for others. We tend to value non-material over material rewards, which we are willing to defer, even to posterity. While we may identify with social causes, we tend to come from backgrounds which discourage us from seeing ourselves as "labour." Finally, we're fiercely individualistic, which makes us difficult to organize and easy to exploit. … If artists have long served as ideological figures for 'independent professionals' as well as entrepreneurs, the answer should be obvious: the promise and privilege of recognising ourselves and being recognised in the products of what is supposed to be uniquely unalienated and autonomous labour.

    (Andrea Fraser, "A Museum is not a Business. It is Run in a Businesslike Fashion," in *Art and Its Institutions: Current Conflicts, Critique and Collaborations*, ed. Nina Möntmann (London: Black Dog Publishing, 2006), 94)
35. On this point, the work of Ferdinand Braudel, an economic and social historian, is of great help to clarify the terms and assumptions propounded by liberal economists, in contrast to the actual unfolding of history. See, for instance: *The Wheels of Commerce*, trans. Siân Reynold (Berkeley, CA: The University of California Press, 1992).

36. Italian philosopher Paolo Virno borrows this notion from Marx's *Grundrisse* to critique the "post-Fordist" commodification of common intellectual potential, as in

   > formal and informal knowledge, imagination, ethical tendencies, mentalities and "language games". Thoughts and discourses function in themselves as productive "machines" in contemporary labour and do not need to take on a mechanical body or an electronic soul. ... General intellect needs to be understood literally as intellect in general: the faculty and power to think, rather than the works produced by thought – a book, an algebra formula etc.

   ("On General Intellect" in A. Zanini, U. Fadini, and C. Herold, eds, *Lessico postfordista: dizionario di idee della mutazione* (Milan: Feltrinelli, 2001) Available in English online at: http://libcom.org/library/on-general-intellect-paulo-virno. See also: Berardi, *The Soul at Work*.

37. On this point, also see note 18.
38. Rem Koolhaas is the contemporary "master" of this cynical game. On this kind of constant self-modulation for the sake of cultural capital, see: Brian Holmes, "The Flexible Personality: For a New Cultural Critique," *EIPCP Blog*, January 2002, http://eipcp.net/transversal/1106/holmes/en/base_edit (accessed 1 August, 2014).
39. Some interesting work trying to bridge the divide between the technological dimensions of economic systems and the anthropological questions on modes of valuation (including and exceeding capitalist modes) can be found with the STS. For instance:

   > At the theoretical level, the sociology of economy prefers to focus on sociology's favourite objects—networks and social relations, institutions, rules, conventions, norms and power struggles. Yet the empirical research that it has generated increasingly points to the decisive role played by techniques, sciences, standards, calculating instruments, metrology and, more generally, material infrastructure in market formation.

   (384, Çaliskan and Callon, "Economization, Part 1: Shifting Attention from the Economy Towards Processes of Economization," *Economy and Society* 38.3 (2009): 369–98) See also: Donald McKenzie, *An Engine, Not a Camera: How Financial Models Shape Markets* (Cambridge, MA: The MIT Press, 2006), and Ian Hacking, *The Taming of Chance* (Cambridge: Cambridge University Press, 1990).

40. This appears to be a broad sentiment shared by critical architectural and spatial practitioners today, one that manifests itself in a renewed interest in the anonymous histories and workings of "infrastructure"—that which persists, that which connects—rather than singular architectural objects and subjects. The new critical literature on infrastructure tries to understand the places where the system reproduces itself—the inertial drudgeries of administration (what Jacques Rancière erroneously dismisses as "the police" as opposed to "politics" proper)—rather than the moments of exception (the self-congratulatory self-assertion of self-appointed avant-gardes). Examples could include Keller Easterling's work on Free Economic Zones (in *Extrastatecraft: The*

Power of Infrastructure Space (London: Verso, 2014)), or the focus on infrastructure by contemporary anthropologists and historians. See, for instance: Timothy Mitchell, *Carbon Democracy: Political Power in the Age of Oil* (London: Verso, 2013), and Brian Larkin, "The Politics and Poetics of Infrastructure," *Annual Review of Anthropology* 42 (2013): 327–43.

41. For an example of this problem, see the UK's extremely conformist "Farrell Review" 2014, http://www.farrellreview.co.uk/ (accessed 1 August, 2014).
42. John May develops this point with reference to "electronic-statistical surfaces." John May, "Logic of the Managerial Surface," *Praxis: Journal of Writing + Building* 13 (2011): 116–24.
43. Mark Fisher, *Capitalist Realism: Is There No Alternative?* (London: Zero Books, 2009).
44. On this point, see the author's article "Fundamentals of Architectural Work," *Fulcrum* 95 (2014).
45. This assertion might lead to the paradoxical hypothesis—from a critical perspective—that we are, in some ways, just not neoliberal *enough*, as part of a critical project toward neoliberalism also involves sorting what aspects of its governmentality ought to be salvaged, repurposed, or simply understood and celebrated. For instance, one connected but in certain ways parallel development to the political project of neoliberalism has indeed been the integration of communications technology and finance. This techno-social development has no doubt generated a deluge of horrifying landscapes of debt and death, the causes of which are both technical as well as political. But understanding financialization beyond indignant scandal or ironic cynicism also opens the door to a potentially huge development: the democratization and multiplication of "credit"—the potential for greater numbers of people to speculate on the future and to collectively plan ahead. Financialization is no panacea, of course, but it should be cause for serious investigation and experimentation, not just lamentation.
46. Foucault, *The Birth of Biopolitics*, 91–4.

Part V

The profession

Chapter 13

Three strategies for new value propositions of design practice

Phillip G. Bernstein

America's first professional architect, Benjamin Latrobe, arrived from England in 1796 after a gentleman's education and apprenticeship in England. Before immigrating, Latrobe was a member of the Architect's Club, an early professional association founded in 1791 that included John Soane as well as other architects and engineers of the gentleman's class. Historian Mary Woods, citing Soane's *Plans, Elevations and Sections of Buildings*, summarized the gentlemanly stance on architecture:

> The architect … occupied a position of "great trust" between the client and the mechanic; he protected the former's interests but also defended the latter's rights. The architect was a gentleman, like a clergyman, physician, and barrister, who must be above crass commercial interests. If the architect worked as a builder, Soane continued, he jeopardized his honor and authority as the wise paternal figure mediating between client and mechanic.[1]

More than two hundred years later, the roots of today's profound challenges of practice are entirely legible in Soane's formulation of the architect's role. While we may aspire to be above the "crass commercial interests" of the market, salaries, benefits, and working conditions for architects are hardly commensurate with our equally educated colleagues in medicine and law.[2] Relations with builders and other technicians in the construction process range from ambivalent to hostile. As indicated by their poor pay and small numbers, architects today are hardly seen as "wise and paternal figures" operating in the balance of interests between the participants in the building industry.

In reality, architectural labor serves the enterprise of building at a difficult intersection of professionalism and commodification. While no building can be created without the services of an architect—who is empowered by the state to take responsibility for the public's health and safety—his or her work is often characterized and paid for as if it were any other lowest-cost commodity in the construction supply chain. Architects often "bid" against one another for work, allow the resulting fees to deteriorate accordingly, and convert efforts into compensation that does not represent the unique value that they provide. Given that architects are extensively educated, meticulously certified through licensure, relatively rare compared to other similarly trained professionals like doctors or lawyers, and provide a necessary service to building, why is the value proposition of architecture so poorly converted and why are profit margins so narrow? In an era of radical changes in technology and project delivery business structures, what can architecture learn from other professional and creative business models to convert opportunity into value?

The business model of the typical architectural practice is a relatively simple mechanism that can be understood through the diagram in Figure 13.1. The inputs of the model are simple: clients pay architects (fees) and the firm hires intellectual resources in the form of staff, which provides labor hours. Each is

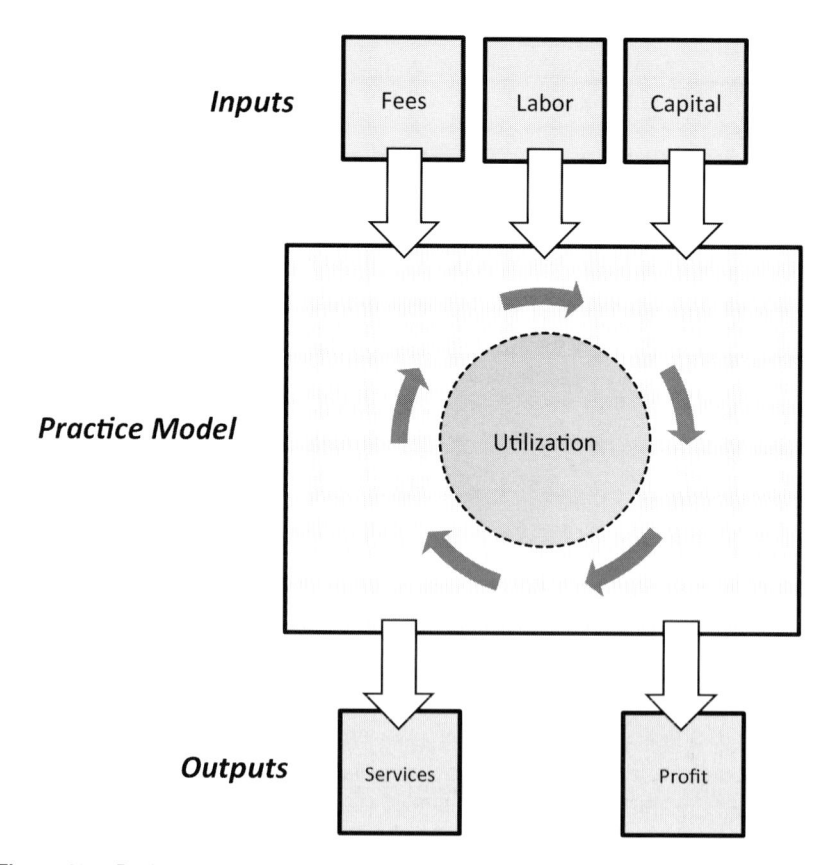

Figure 13.1 Basic practice business model.

fed into a services conversion machine (the firm practice model), which, based on its strategy and efficiency of doing work, translates revenue and labor inputs into services, and, if there are funds remaining after the conversion, profit. The "utilization engine" of the practice is dependent on many factors including talent, experience, procedural effectiveness, and ability to manage externalities that might disturb the work process like unruly clients or unforeseen economic conditions. This business model poses two basic challenges to the architect: business risk (Can I do the work and still make money?) and professional liability risk (Am I going to make an error that will cause me to lose money from a claim?). Working efficiently mitigates both risks, in that an effective practice does good work and is less likely to be sued, and makes enough money to buffer unanticipated difficulties like a lawsuit or non-paying client.

The canonical structure of architectural services, as defined by the American Instiute of Architects (AIA) standard contracts or the Royal Institute of British Architects (RIBA) Plan of Work, follows the contours of the associated business model. Organized in successive phases of work during which design is elaborated and client decisions memorialized (while creating a template for sending invoices), the phasing plan defines what an architect is expected to do within the fixed fee. In the United States, the sequence of schematic design, design development, construction documents, procurement, and then construction contract administration comprise the architect's "basic services" or the work that is to be performed in exchange for the fixed fee. The concept of basic services comprises a bilateral agreement between client and architect that attempts to define for the client what the architect is supposed to do for the fee while protecting the architect from extramural work imposed by forces outside her control—like that same client. At its core it is a risk management maneuver created to make sure the business risk (of spending or losing too much money) is reasonably well understood by the parties, and the contracts that define basic services are lengthy explanations of these services (tasks, deliverables) and the punishments to be inflicted should they not be performed adequately (dispute resolution and penalties). Basic services seem like a simple deal: "do this stuff well and you will be paid this fixed amount of money … unless …" Of course, the definition of basic services explains what tasks the architect is expected to perform but is largely silent on what this work is intended to accomplish.

A parallel concept of "additional services" also appears in typical owner-architect contracts, comprising a lengthy list of all the things that the architect is not going to do as a part of basic services and the procedure for claiming same should the occasion rise. Alleging additional services protects the architect's resources while simultaneously provoking the client to wonder just exactly where all that fixed fee money is going. And like change orders on a hard bid construction job, the tougher the fixed fee negotiation, the more likely the architect is to fight for—and need—additional services in order to not lose her shirt.

Contractual services definitions are weak attempts at value conversion for architects. They attempt to codify a process by which difficult and ineffable design tasks are remunerated and fail to address several correlated questions, to wit: How long does it take to have a good idea that the client will like? How long does it take a client to make a decision? What is the underlying value of a good building and how is it measured? What comprises adequate instructions to the builder? The answers to these questions lie just beneath the surface of every architectural business deal, but that deal is just one of a chain of many commoditized exchanges that in concert comprise the contractual network to create a typical building and, at the same time, shortchange the architect's value proposition.

Architects have pushed the limits of this model to the edge of reason, or at least comfort. Commoditized fees are depressed by intense competition where many architects are, intentionally or otherwise, creating a value proposition based only on price. Commodity pricing occurs in markets where other differentiators—like quality—are absent and the only difference between two providers is lowest cost. Salaries—the cost of labor hours—are low relative to comparable professions, and in the case of unpaid interns, zero. Improvements to the value proposition would result in increased fee inputs, higher wages in return for labor hours, and more residual profits after conversion of hours to services. Short of radically revising the fundamental processes for providing those services that would change utilization, there are no other obvious approaches available given the model itself.

To address this, inspiration can be found in three non-normative places: other learned professions, other practices that produce designed results, and innovative architects operating far outside today's traditional models.

Architects are similar to doctors and lawyers in that they have, by dint of education, experience and certification, a special status as service providers. As professionals created by society in a particular class of individuals who can provide specialized advice in exchange for a payment and no expectation of other financial gain, doctors and lawyers are like architects,[3] except that they are compensated far better than architects.[4] Attorney compensation has traditionally been based on the concept of the billable hour, where time spent on a legal matter was converted, by high hourly multipliers, to fees charged to the client. The related value proposition is predicated on two assumptions: that the lawyer's time is very valuable and that it is impossible to predict how much of that time is necessary to resolve a client's case. Lawyers handling larger cases involving greater risk or money charge hourly rates accordingly, but even young associates who work with these high-priced barristers bill high numbers in the reflected glory of their prowess. Deals closed, divorces resolved, and cases won are the measure of success. The value proposition is clear: a perception of return on investment sufficiently high that the financial risk (in everything but contingency cases) is shifted entirely to the client.

Physicians have deployed several different strategies to leverage their particularly privileged perch on the social ladder toward high compensation. Hyper-specialization has created sub-classes of providers with very particular skills who are part of a self-referential network that is also self-reinforcing, assuring a constant flow of paying patients. Those same specialists often have a financial interest in the infrastructure of health delivery. Radiologists own their imaging centers, obstetricians their birthing facilities, and each take a cut of the various payments that flow through as a part of health care delivery. Soane would be horrified, of course, but the apparent conflict of professional interest has not adjusted the value proposition: deliver services at a price and increase "sales" by monetizing part of the delivery apparatus.

Other enterprises that create products in the intersection of design and technics are based on business models far different than architecture. Fashion designers leverage reputation to monetize design by either scarcity (a unique couture dress) or abundance (replication of a popular item). Product designers create both the production strategy and the artifact to solve a specific problem and license that idea to the supply chain for manufacturing and distribution. Film producers leverage the box office attractiveness of a star to raise capital to produce a movie that will make money in distribution on local, foreign, or mobile screens. Advertising firms produce design strategies in the hopes of winning business that is monetized as a percentage of media buys based on their ideas. Each of these models translates perceived value of the created asset (be it clothes, products, stories, or ads) into revenue without specific regard to fixed resources or an exchange of effort for compensation. In this sense they highlight the disparity in value perception between their work and that of architects.

Architects themselves have experimented with approaches that break the tyranny of commoditized fees. Star firms leverage reputations to garner higher fees by differentiating their services from the norm. Firms like Gluck + in New York deliver integrated design and construction services, convinced that being both the architect and builder is the only way to garner trust from the client that Soane desired. Taking that model even further, Brooklyn-based Alloy

Development LLC, not unlike John Portman several decades prior, develops, designs, builds, and sells residential property in a self-contained supply chain that needs no clients—just customers. Mega-practices like AECOM can provide every possible building-related service across their pantheon of capabilities. Young firms across the United States leverage their new-found digital fabrication skills to bridge design and artifact with computer controlled manufacturing; New York's Sharples Holden Pasquarelli (ShOP) has gone so far as to serve as curtainwall manufacturer on one of their projects. LMN Architects of Seattle leverages their team LMN Technical Services to create and sell digital information across the design-construction divide to fabricators and builders to smooth building.

The business models described above are different from those of traditional architectural design in two interesting and potentially exploitable ways (with the exception of the billings rate model). First, Soane's radical distinction between design and mechanics is largely abandoned in each as design ideation is closely tied to the characteristics and performance of the result. The designer's relationship to the broader expanse of the delivery chain is greater, from project inception through completion and operation. Second, as is the case in most markets, assumption of risk generates both unique positioning in the market (a willingness to assume risk makes you more attractive than the competition) and a resulting return. And since architects largely avoid risk on the assumption that they can't properly manage it, the opportunity to use it to value advantage is lost.

It would seem that each of these approaches, both within and without architecture, do a better job of value conversion than traditional practice which characterizes the vast majority of work. But the profession's responses, at least as embodied by efforts by the AIA, are typically ineffective. In the aftermath of the devastation wrought by the 2008 crash, the AIA embarked upon a project called "Repositioning the Institute" that concluded, in a systematic restatement of the obvious, that its members wished that the value of architects and architecture were better understood. The resulting PR campaign of advertisements and radio commercials,[5] not unlike those of previous years, extolled the virtues of architects, architecture, and good design—as if this would solve the problem.

It won't. Efforts to revamp the professional reputation of architects in the hopes that billing rates rise to those of our attorneys is doomed to fail in the heavily commoditized supply chain where architectural services are delivered. A radical shift in the value proposition will go much further in the name of value conversion than marketing and hope.

Thus new methods are suggested here that break from commoditized models of basic services. Each generates value through unique positioning as firms willing to try them will stand out from their commoditized competition in what is known in the business world as a "blue ocean" strategy.[6]

The first is to provide new services adjacent to or in support of traditional work. Along the continuum of services that begins with schematic design and ends with construction contract administration, architects could consider expanding their work along the time horizon of a project, starting with project inception. Applying design sensibilities to the early conceptualization of a project (including financing, siting, programming, feasibility analysis, and financial performance), or the operational phase after completion (helping optimize, manage, or maintain a building) positions the architect as a more full-service provider of building services while building credibility—and value—with clients. Interstitial work within the rubric of basic service might include continuous modeling and analysis of project finances, greater control of construction cost and strategy, systems, or material procurement, or building commission and operational mobilization. This strategy was anticipated by Paolo Tombesi in a concept called "flexible specialization" that advocates for a broader understanding of the constellation of services necessary to complete a building and willingness to apply the architect's sensibilities and professionalism to their delivery.[7]

Of course, providing the sorts of services that extend the architect's responsibilities beyond the bounds of typical practice brings, by definition, additional risk on two fronts, a realization that brings us to the second strategy for value conversion: assuming controllable risks that are of clear value. For this, conceptual shifts need to be in place. A client willing to trust the architect with additional responsibilities presumes the architect's competence, but architects have been conditioned over the years to only assume those risks that can be reasonably controlled and managed. If you are going to provide financial modeling for your client's project, make sure you understand how to do so—and have done it before. But more difficult is the hurdle created by the negligence standard that applies to all professional services, to wit the "standard of care."[8] This principle is the mechanism that defines competence for professional behavior and is by definition backward-facing in that the skill and care suggested can only be "measured" by comparing it with the past behavior of other allegedly competent architects. Practitioners venturing into the blue ocean of services have no such definitional protection and must proceed with great care. Failing to do so, however, leaves architects back in the commoditized, bloodied red ocean.

Neither of these strategies—expanding services and/or taking greater responsibility—is meaningful for value conversion unless they are freed from commoditized pricing, bringing us to the third method for value conversion: the exchange of commodity pricing with outcome-based profit based on measured results. Providing more services for similarly low prices, or worse—providing more services without compensation by allowing them to be considered basic—raises salary and improves working conditions not at all. A new method of value calibration must be overlaid on new ways of working that allow provable, not merely asserted, results. Lawyers and physicians "prove" their value by providing services with demonstrable outcomes that are well understood by society at large as officers of the court or keepers of the Hippocratic Oath. Cases are won and people made healthy, largely unambiguous results that don't rely on subjective judgment of taste, cultural value, or artistic merit. It is not that these qualities are unimportant but in the parlance of this analysis they do not convert well to value for architects.

The third leg of the strategic "stool" proposed here, then, is the most important: freeing the architect from the tyranny of the fixed fee by defining, measuring, and achieving specific outcomes related to projects, irrespective of how or when the services related to those outcomes are delivered. If players in the industry supply chain, and particularly clients, believe that architects can predict, measure, and then deliver specific results related to their projects then value conversion becomes strictly a function of a job well-done—and proven to be so. Outcome-based methods, a significant break from service provided in exchange for set fees, require the architect to take the risk of a result (rather than the risk of running out of money under basic services) and then take the necessary measures to achieve it. Two specific mechanisms evolving in current building practice today open the door for such an approach.

Innovation in project delivery models—the organizational and informational approaches by which owners, designers, and builders configure themselves to create a building—include compensation strategies based in part on project outcomes. Known collectively as "integrated project delivery," these methods encourage deep collaboration between project participants (to the would-be horror of Soane and Latrobe, no doubt) based on complete, transparent sharing of information and collective responsibility (and reward) for measurable project outcomes. Early integrated project delivery (IPD) projects have been based on simple and controllable items like construction schedule, construction cost, and sustainable certification, but as building industry professionals gain experience and confidence in the approach, it is inevitable that juicy, performance-related measures will define value creation and conversion.

As has been argued in detail elsewhere,[9] digital technology has begun to provide the analytical and simulative tools that offer increased confidence in such predictions. Digital models combined with powerful, cloud-based algorithmic simulations allow architects to generate, refine, and validate more alternatives and understand the implications of design choices at greater resolution than ever. Today's ability to predict more prosaic characteristics of a design like materiality, cost, or energy consumption will give way soon to agent-based behavioral modeling, or sociological evaluation of a building's impact on the neighborhood and city. Considerations of the ineffable aesthetic quality of design will never be computerized, but the architect's digital assistants will provide more time, insight, and financial resource to improve design on that front as well.

The most important of these potential improvements—and perhaps the architect's greatest opportunity to improve our lot—is at the intersection of design and construction or the boundary line between the architect and the mechanic. The importance of the accurate, clear, and useful transfer of information between design intent and construction execution cannot be understated, as it lies at the heart of many of the ineffective approaches in modern building. Blurring that boundary means architects must understand, control, and take responsibility for construction outcomes in ways that we spent much of the latter part of the twentieth century avoiding. Leveraging the information and insight generated from the design process to predict built results and taking responsibility for outcomes while managing the attendant risks addresses the client's greatest concern in the building enterprise: the quality and efficacy of the finished product. This combination of expanded service, managed risk assumption, and commitment to measured and compensable outcomes is the architect's best bet for creating and converting value. Perhaps architects can no longer be defined in the tradition of the gentleman but we once again serve our clients with the honor and dignity we both deserve.

Notes

1. Mary N. Woods, *From Craft to Profession: The Practice of Architecture in Nineteenth-Century America* (Berkeley, CA: University of California Press, 1999), 265.
2. Phillip G. Bernstein, "Money, Value, Architects, Building," *Perspecta 47: Money* (2014): 14–20.
3. This tradition derives directly from the notion of the gentleman's profession espoused by Latrobe, Soane, and their contemporaries, who largely found commercial considerations beneath their station but often had other sources of income on which to live.
4. It should be noted, however, that with the advent of outsourced legal services and managed medical care, doctors and attorneys are beginning to experience the pressures of commoditized payment. But some healthcare providers are considering

outcome-based compensation that pays doctors and hospitals on patient wellness rather than time spent or number of procedures performed. "Health Insurers Are Trying New Payment Models, Study Shows" 9 July, 2014, http://www.nytimes.com/2014/07/10/business/health-insurers-are-trying-new-payment-models-study-shows.html?emc=eta1 (accessed 11 July, 2014).
5. See: "Telling Our Stories" at http://progress.aia.org/public-outreach (accessed 11 July, 2014).
6. "Blue ocean" strategy, as formulated by W. Chan Kim and Renée Mauborgne, professors at INSEAD, posits that firms can profit greatly by avoiding intensely competitive markets (red ocean where the sharks are fighting for the chum) and instead operate in a blue ocean where new products and services are provided. See http://en.wikipedia.org/wiki/Blue_Ocean_Strategy (accessed 10 July, 2014).
7. Paolo Tombesi, "On the Cultural Separation of Design Labor," in *Building (In) The Future: Recasting Labor in Architecture*, eds. Peggy Deamer and Phillip G. Bernstein (New York: Princeton Architectural Press, 2010), 117–36.
8. The standard of care is defined in AIA Owner-Architect Agreement Form B103/2007 Edition in Section 2.2 as:

   The Architect shall perform its services consistent with the professional skill and care ordinarily provided by architects practicing in the same or similar locality under the same or similar circumstances. The Architect shall perform its services as expeditiously as is consistent with such professional skill and care and the orderly progress of the Project."

9. Phillip G. Bernstein and Matt Jezyk, "Models and Measurement: Changing Design Value with Simulation, Measurement and Outcomes," in *Building Information Modeling: BIM in Current and Future Practice*, eds Karen Kensek and Douglas Noble (Hoboken, NJ: John Wiley & Sons, 2014), 79–84.

Chapter 14

Labor and talent in architecture
Thomas Fisher

Roger Martin, the former Dean of the Rotman School of Management at the University of Toronto, argued in the *New York Times* that the global economy now has three main players: *capital*, "the owners and investors who provide the means of production;" *labor*, "the workers who turn invested capital into profits;" and *talent*, employees who are "highly skilled and portable."[1] Martin wrote about the lockout of referees by the National Football League (NFL) to make his point. The NFL owners viewed the referees as replaceable labor, but it turns out, after some controversial calls by their replacements, that referees are more like players, with irreplaceable talent in demand by fans and teams alike.

Martin's insightful distinction goes far beyond football. It defines an important dividing line in the global economy between labor, which capital views as an easily replaceable commodity, and talent, which has become prized by capital for the value it creates and yet resented because of its portability, which capital cannot control. This leads to the question that every employee needs to ask: How can I become irreplaceable talent rather than expendable labor?

The discipline of architecture provides a particularly useful lens through which to look at this question. On one hand, because of our creative skills, architects seem to stand clearly in the talent camp, but on the other hand, capital views most—but not all—of the design community as replaceable labor. Low fees, job insecurity, and depressed wages all stem from the latter view. As a result, the architectural field reveals some important nuances in the distinctions that Martin makes that can help illuminate how to move from the labor to the talent side of the ledger.

Star talent

To understand those nuances, let's imagine some different types of architects at the front line of the struggle between capital on one hand, and labor and talent on the other. Star designers clearly stand at the talent end of the spectrum:

highly skilled and highly in demand, they have greater leverage than most architects to command higher fees. That does not mean that they pay their staff higher wages, since many star architects seem to have highly inefficient operations. Such operations reveal how the owners of architecture firms can act like capitalists, seeking the lowest-cost labor from those who work for them.

Talent has a limited shelf life, and if architectural stars do not continually innovate in ways meaningful to capital, they disappear from public view. That cycling of talent also reflects the fact that the value of something in a capitalist economy often depends upon its scarcity, suggesting that only relatively few architects can have star status at any one time. As Martin puts it, capital is "not amused" by having to pay a premium price for talent, and so it will do all it can to keep the number of such people to a minimum. The media aids and abets this process by continually seeking out new stars and ignoring talent considered past its prime, which plays right into the hands of capital.

The more talent can boost the profits of capital, the more leverage talented people have in terms of compensation. In the design fields, those whose work leads to replicable results—graphic design, interactive design, product design—seem to have more leverage in terms of fees than those who do one-off projects, like architects or landscape architects, who even when famous, have to compete mightily for commissions. On the other hand, architectural talent seems more in demand among one-of-a-kind institutional clients, such as museums and universities, whose value also lies in the scarcity of what they have to offer.

Still, some star architects, like Frank Gehry, Rem Koolhaas, and Zaha Hadid, have expanded their portfolio into product and furniture design, whose replicable results offer capital more potential profit. Indeed, the more star designers become defined as brands rather than as members of a particular discipline, the greater ability they have to diversify their offerings, and the more leverage they have with owners and investors. Ironically, the more radical or daring the work of these designers, the more distinct their brand, and the longer they can hold on to the slippery slopes at the top of the talent pinnacle.

Labor becoming talent

Too many young designers make the mistake of imitating the work of one of these stars, rather than understanding the nature of talent and seeking their own way. Becoming prized talent mainly involves innovating in a way that creates new demand, meets an unaddressed need, attracts positive media attention, and increases the profits, or at least the public profile, of capital. You might think that capital would welcome such efforts, but it doesn't make it easy. As Martin writes, "Capital is outraged because it is being beaten up by talent ... and it takes out its anger on the easiest target: labor."[2]

We have to earn the talent moniker in the face of capital that wants to treat us as much as possible like labor. Let's see what this means on the ground. Consider late-career architects, with higher wages and fewer computer skills, who have found themselves permanently out of a job; or recent architecture-school graduates, unable to find a job with benefits and depending on a combination of freelance work and non-design employment to pay the bills; or adjunct faculty members, cobbling together low-paid and often last-minute teaching assignments along with work in a firm, or running a small practice on the side.

All of them have talent, but all of them find themselves treated, even by their professional peers, like low-wage, expendable labor, with little leverage in the market and a great deal of job insecurity as a result. This raises other nuances within Martin's capital/labor/talent distinction. Architectural firms will compete with each other for talented staff, even while treating other staff in their office like replaceable labor, and so there are talent-labor struggles within offices having to do with the type of expertise or the nature of the talent in question. The more staff members can distinguish themselves in some way critical to the firm's success, the more they will be able to compete as talent rather than as labor.

Architecture firms, of course, also compete with each other for commissions, and here, too, the talent-labor struggle emerges. Some commodity-oriented clients may not care about an architect's creativity or innovation and may make their decision based solely on price, viewing their consultants as interchangeable labor. Too many practitioners accept such situations and lower their fees, sometimes to the point of unprofitability. Yet there always remains the potential to move even these clients toward an appreciation of talent. As in an office, so in an interview; talent can get a client to think about a problem in a new way and to see possible profits where others have not.

How, though, can unemployed or under-employed architects move from expendable labor to valuable talent? As the former Secretary of Labor Robert Reich wrote in the *New York Times* about this phenomenon, "It's important to distinguish between entrepreneurial zeal and self-employed desperation," to distinguish, in other words, between the increasingly portable nature of talent, able to move to where it has the greatest value, and the increasingly dire situation of labor, unable to control the conditions of its employment.[3]

To the unwillingly unemployed, proving their talent in a tough labor market can seem daunting, and impossible to do alone. Reich has proposed some policy ideas such as "earnings insurance," paid for by the payroll tax, to help buffer the income decline of laid-off employees, or tax credits to match 401(k)s or IRAs to help prevent unemployed workers from depleting their savings. While those policy proposals might help older workers with long-held, permanent jobs, such ideas do little to aid the recent graduate who has yet to get a job, or the adjunct faculty member who may have a job one semester and not the next.

Talent outsmarting capital

The tension between capital and talent that Martin identifies arises, in part, from the latter's ability to create value where none existed before, and to imagine new products or services never considered before. While that ability can bring enormous profits, which capital likes, it also means that capital cannot control talent—and should not want to control it—in the way it tries to control labor. Talent, in other words, can continually outsmart capital. This offers the best way—and maybe the only certain way—for talented people to ensure they are paid well and not treated as easily replaceable labor.

The architectural profession, and the design fields generally, should excel at this. A design education provides some of the best training available in imagining new paradigms, envisioning better alternatives, and conceiving of that which does not yet exist. Architects engage in these value-creating activities every time we design a new building, develop a new strategy, or devise a new solution to a seemingly irresolvable problem.

Many architects, however, do a terrible job demonstrating or even talking about the value we create. I have been in too many interviews with architectural firms in which they show their completed work as if its value were self-evident, with little or nothing tangible offered in terms of how their projects, for example, improved the productivity, profitability, or performance of their clients' organizations, or innovated in a way that created new demand or satisfied an unmet need. As a result, both architects and their work tend to look alike, leading selection committees to base their decision on equally shortsighted criteria, such as which architect had the lowest fees or the best presentation. No wonder, then, that so many clients view architects as interchangeable entities and treat us like overworked and underpaid labor.

The misunderstanding of design's value on the part of designers themselves starts in school. Most architectural programs focus on developing students' design intentions and evaluate students' work based on how well their final project meets those original goals. Rarely do schools examine the consequences of design decisions over time, with students documenting, analyzing, and assessing the performance of a completed project and the value it has created for its client and its community. This represents a huge missed opportunity for both the architectural profession and the schools. While low project fees often do not allow firms to return to their projects to assess the value they have generated over time, architectural schools could—and should—include that work as an integral part of the curriculum, sensitizing students to the need for such evaluative information, and thereby making it available to the profession.

Talent stuck in the past

This hasn't happened as much as it should, in part, because too many architectural firms and schools seem stuck in the past when it comes to demonstrating value. The profession and its first schools emerged in the nineteenth century in response to the need for new kinds of buildings and new types of programs, which emerged as a result of the first industrial revolution. Talented architects thrived by providing unprecedented structures—steel-framed skyscrapers, concrete factories, balloon-framed houses—for new kinds of human activities—white-collar office work, machine-based fabrication, affordable worker housing. In that context, the value of these new types of buildings may have seemed self-evident, with architects simply having to show their work in order to get more of it. And with the rapid growth of the economy and the relatively small number of architects, capital paid for the talent of those able to conceive of such innovations.

This also drove architectural education in those early years. Schools focused on developing students' skills in rapidly developing a building's layout and massing and on organizing design studios around particular building types, echoing the increasing pace of repetitive, machine-based production in the nineteenth-century economy as a whole. While that made sense in the context of the first industrial revolution, it remains telling that the curriculum in most architecture schools still follows this format. Most studios, for example, still focus on a particular building type and have the same basic pedagogical structure and even the same Monday/Wednesday/Friday-afternoon meeting times as those in the nineteenth century.

The demand for talent began to change with the rise of the second industrial revolution in the twentieth century. Characterized by assembly-line mass production and the need to boost consumption of an ever-increasing supply of goods, that economy really took off after World War II. Architects responded with the development of modern facilities for mass production and consumption, such as large-scale and often indistinguishable office buildings, factories, and malls. With the standardization of their products, though, architectural firms started down the road of becoming indistinguishable labor, with capital increasingly using competitions and fee-based selection processes to decide which firm to commission. At the same time, other design disciplines—graphic design, product design, and apparel design—began to receive more of the talent pay as they fueled consumer desire in ways that buildings rarely could.

Post-modern marginalization

Post-modernism emerged in the late twentieth century as an implicit acknowledgment of architects' growing economic marginalization. The recognition by Robert Venturi and Denise Scott Brown, for example, that many commercial buildings had become little more than backdrops to billboards or neutral enclosures for media-driven experiences highlighted the problem of architecture having become a commodity and its practitioners an interchangeable labor pool.[4] The architectural profession tended to focus on the aesthetic and theoretical aspects of Venturi and Scott Brown's perception, while paying relatively little attention to its implications for practice or pedagogy. If buildings had become commodities, for example, then did architectural talent need to look elsewhere for more fertile areas of innovation?

That question has become even more pressing in the twenty-first century, as we enter what the economist Jeremy Rifkin has called "the third industrial revolution."[5] This revolution has moved us away from a mass-production and mass-consumption economy to one characterized by mass customization, in which new digital technologies allow consumers to personalize the information they receive, the services they seek, and even the goods they buy or produce themselves. Just as the first industrial revolution saw the rise of innovative building programs and structures, and the second, the rise of innovative spatial experiences, the third has seen the miniaturization and integration of digital technology into almost all aspects of our lives and with it, a disruption of almost every industry that has depended on the making of physical stuff, whether it be compact discs or printed newspapers or, in the case of architecture, retail malls now competing with e-commerce or corporate office buildings now competing with telecommuting.

People still need shelter and places to gather and buildings remain even more in demand with a rapidly growing human population. But the role of architecture has dramatically changed. The third industrial revolution has raised the possibility of people downloading design files and fabricating parts—or even the whole—of buildings themselves using digitally controlled equipment. In such an economy, the value of architects lies in how well we customize a design not only for fee-paying clients, who will constitute an ever-shrinking amount of work for architects, but also for the masses of people who previously had no access to design services. Rather than a scarcity economy, the third industrial revolution also recognizes that humanity needs to move to an economy of abundance, using renewable resources, making information freely available, and leveraging the vast, untapped potential of people's social, cultural, and intellectual capital.

At first glance, this economy of abundance, with much that's free, may look like the final triumph of capital over talent and a fatalistic acceptance of architecture as a commodity produced by the lowest-cost labor. But that will happen only if the architectural community lets it. Viewed from another perspective, the third industrial revolution represents the ultimate revenge of talent and its liberation from the repressive hold that capital has had on us for so long. How so? Because a digitally enabled, mass-customization economy puts the means of production in the hands of the workers, as Marx might have said. The technologies fueling this economy—3D printing, CNC fabrication, virtual reality, e-commerce—all have relatively low purchase and operational costs, allowing ordinary people to kick-start companies and launch products and services without the high capital costs and organizational structures that the previous two revolutions required.

This has profound implications for a field like architecture, which has suffered over the last century from capital's success in treating most architects as expendable labor and in keeping the number of high-paid talent to a minimum. With such low capital requirements, the new economy gives everyone with access to these technologies an opportunity to demonstrate their talent and to succeed according to how well they meet the needs of the greatest number of users. Capital no longer guards the gate by doling out funds in ways that keep most people in perpetual labor with little reward. As we have seen in this socially mediated environment, innovative ideas have gone viral, companies have kick-started themselves to prosperity, and talented individuals have come seemingly out of nowhere to achieve amazing success.

Many of these success stories have also had a design undercurrent, be it President Obama, who once aspired to become an architect before taking up a political career, or Steve Jobs, who mentioned graphic design and typography as his favorite course in college, or Brad Pitt, who also wanted to pursue architecture but chose acting instead. On one hand, such stories may indicate how much architecture, in its current underpaid and often-underappreciated state has lost some of its appeal to talented people. But these stories also show how people with an architectural orientation have taken that design way of thinking into new areas and accomplished great things. Talent combined with a design sensibility can outsmart capital by envisioning what others thought unimaginable (an African American president), by creating something people didn't know they needed (Apple's products), and by doing something no one else dared (Make It Right Foundation).

Reimagining ourselves

In other words, we escape the trap of low-paid labor to become higher-paid talent not by complaining about our plight, or claiming that we deserve it, or even by collaborating to join or form a union. As Martin observes, capital has so successfully "worked to diminish the power of unions," that "labor (has) been forced to capitulate entirely."[6] In the new economy, talent arises out of meaningful innovation. That has probably always been the case, but it seems particularly true today, in a world very much in need of new and innovative ways of living, working, and making if we hope to sustain ourselves on this planet with over seven billion mouths to feed in the midst of a changing climate and diminishing resources.

Design offers one of the best educations in innovation. It teaches us how to develop creative solutions to extremely difficult problems and to conceive of compelling ideas for things or processes that have not existed in exactly the same form before. But the design community needs to apply its methods to itself. By not doing so, by adhering to professional practices and educational methods that date back to the nineteenth century, too many architects find themselves treated as replaceable labor even as they continually come up with innovative designs for their clients. It may seem as if architects simply need to do a better job explaining and demonstrating their talent and they will get recognized for it and compensated accordingly. But that will not resolve the paradox that many architects face. Architects will cross the line from underpaid labor to higher-paid talent when we finally recognize that buildings represent just one of many ways—and maybe not the best way—to address many clients' needs.

In the new economy of abundance, innovation comes from figuring out how to accomplish the most with the least: the least cost, the least disruption, the least impact on the planet. People will still need buildings, but buildings as we have traditionally conceived of them represent not only huge costs, but also a great deal of disruption and resource consumption. Capital will increasingly pay for talent that figures out how to provide the shelter and gathering spaces that humans still need, with as minimal a cost and impact as possible. This will, in turn, demand the architectural profession to redefine itself as populated by strategic thinkers rather than the designers of buildings. In the future, the most highly paid architects will be those who figure out how to meet people's spatial needs by building as little and as lightly as possible, and by maybe not building something new at all.

This prediction may sound odd to a field that has for so long associated itself with buildings and been paid according to how large and lavish they are. Yet, as in the past, the new industrial revolution arising all around us promises to overturn much of what we took for granted following the old one. In that change lies the key to architects being treated as well-compensated talent rather than under-paid labor. The latter does what we already know how to do and what has already become a commodity service. Talent surprises us, creating that which we have never imagined before and didn't know we needed until we saw what it can do for us. The new economy has made the potential of becoming talent available to everyone, and those who don't take this opportunity—those who remain laboring in the ways of the past—have nothing to complain about.

Notes

1. Roger Martin, "Talent Shows," *New York Times*, 28 September, 2012, A23.
2. Ibid.
3. Robert Reich, "Entrepreneur or Unemployed?" *New York Times*, 1 June, 2010, A27.
4. Robert Venturi, Denise Scott Brown, and Steven Izenour, *Learning from Las Vegas* (Cambridge, MA: The MIT Press, 1972).
5. Jeremy Rifkin, *The Third Industrial Revolution, How Lateral Power is Transforming Energy, the Economy, and the World* (New York: Palgrave Macmillan, 2011).
6. Martin, "Talent Shows."

Chapter 15

The (ac)credit(ation) card
Neil Leach

Introduction

Let me start with a simple comparison:

1 Many countries in the world require architects to be accredited by national associations in order to call themselves "architects."
2 Only around five percent of all buildings constructed in the world are designed by registered architects.[1]

There appears, in short, to be a mismatch between the influence that national associations exert on architectural education, and the influence that they exert on the general marketplace. The question therefore arises that if national associations are not protecting the profession of architecture (thus allowing its diminished footprint in the market) why are they given such authority in terms of the accreditation of architectural students within the educational marketplace?

The definition of the architect

Who, then, is an architect? Leon Battista Alberti was one of the first to offer a definition of the architect:

> Him I consider the architect, who by sure and wonderful reason and method, knows both how to devise through his own mind and energy, and to realize by construction, whatever can be most beautifully fitted out for the noble needs of man, by the movement of weights and the joining and massing of bodies. To do this he must have an understanding and knowledge of all the highest and most noble disciplines. This then is the architect.[2]

Alberti is well known as a great *uomo universale* of the Renaissance. Not only was he the designer of a number of highly significant buildings in fifteenth-century

Italy, but he was also the author of the first published treatise on architecture, *De re aedificatoria* (1452). He was also an artist, sculptor, mathematician, sociologist, and writer. In short he had a profound impact in a variety of fields, and his designs and books form part of the foundation of any history course in any accredited program. But could we call him an "architect?"

According to the logic of accreditation, only those who have graduated from accredited programs, and who have fulfilled other necessary conditions, are entitled to call themselves architects. As such, we might ask which of our iconic "designers" featured in history of architecture courses in accredited programs should actually be called "architects." Renzo Piano is reportedly not registered as an architect, and the Architects Registration Board (ARB) of the United Kingdom has requested that he should not be described as an architect, but rather as a "building designer."[3] Likewise Daniel Libeskind was not accredited in the United States until after he won the competition for the World Trade Center tower.[4] If we apply the same logic to the past, we might surmise that—contrary to what one might glean from consulting most textbooks on architectural history used in accredited architecture programs—no architects existed before the introduction of accreditation.

Attitudes towards accreditation vary across the world. In Japan, architectural education itself is not governed by accreditation, but architectural graduates are required to take an examination following a statutory period working in an architectural office before calling themselves architects. In the UK, Australia, Turkey, New Zealand, and the Netherlands anyone may undertake the work of an architect, but only those who are accredited may call themselves "architects."[5] Meanwhile in Denmark, Finland, Ireland, Norway, and Sweden anyone can design a building. The key constraint is whether or not it conforms to building regulations.[6] In the United States the title is more closely controlled, and only those who are registered may do the job of an architect, although in California anyone can design a small-scale residential building.[7] In Austria, meanwhile, only those who both have a degree from an Austrian university and who are also Austrian nationals may practice there.[8]

All this is set in perspective by the fact that the globalization of the marketplace has broken down regional barriers to the extent that architecture is now truly a global profession. Not only do many architects practice in different countries, but many offices contain architects trained in other countries, to the point that standard emails from the office of Zaha Hadid Architects are forced to contain the following disclaimer: "Where used, the term 'architect' may include architects qualified in other countries apart from the UK."[9] In short, the regulations are many and various, and for a profession that is becoming increasingly global, the entitlement to call oneself an architect is grounded in decidedly local accreditation procedures.

The global marketplace

One of the remarkable features of recent developments in architectural education worldwide has been the growth of non-accredited, post-professional masters programs, including a number of postgraduate programs in Europe and Masters of Architecture II post-professional degrees in the United States. Most of these programs do not offer any substantial financial aid, and unless students have independent funding they have to expose themselves to financial hardship in a profession where it might be difficult—if not impossible—to recoup the investment in their education. It is therefore worth reflecting on this development and asking why students opt for these non-accredited programs. While the reasons behind such a choice in postgraduate education must be many and varied—and let us not overlook the simple issue of educational tourism that has developed in recent years—one primary factor must surely be that students are eager to acquire knowledge that they have not gained in their previous accredited architectural programs. In other words, the primary motivation would seem to be not the logic of the National Architectural Accrediting Board (NAAB) or any other accreditation body, but the logic of self-improvement. An obvious outcome of this is the notion that in focusing on a set of standards to define the architect, accreditation bodies have failed to grasp what actually motivates the student marketplace. Nor is it that these educational initiatives are unrelated to the practice of architecture. Indeed they are often tied to professional opportunities. For example, part of the attractiveness of the highly popular Architectural Association (AA) Design Research Lab (DRL) has been the opportunity for many graduates of working subsequently for Zaha Hadid Architects, a practice that employs several DRL graduates. Likewise, part of the attractiveness for companies such as Zaha Hadid Architects has been the fact that the DRL program effectively prepares graduates for employment in their office by skilling them up with various tools.

One is left to surmise that accreditation is failing to ensure that students are taught appropriate skills in their education. Either this or they are catering simply to the basic, lowest common denominator in architectural education, and are assuming that these post-professional programs will cater to whatever it is that professionally-accredited courses do not provide. Either way, it is clear that standard accreditation programs have been deemed insufficient by a significant number of students within the educational marketplace.

It is, however, the very notion of the "basic, lowest common denominator" that also gives cause for concern. A further issue is the background impact that accreditation processes are having on standard architectural education in terms of creativity. Within the prevailing architectural climate—where almost all schools still subscribe to a logic of accreditation—maintaining one's accreditation status remains vital, since the loss of it would have an inflated impact on attracting potential students and as a result on the financial wellbeing of a given school. From my own empirical observations from teaching in several architectural schools on both sides of the Atlantic for over twenty years, I have witnessed only too often the tendency among schools to stifle creativity and dumb down architectural education in order to maintain a school's accreditation status.[10]

At the same time we need to recognize the globalized arena in which these programs operate. Indeed many students in post-professional programs around the world come from countries other than their school's. China has emerged as the dominant market in this regard. In other words, the very fact of a nation-based accreditation logic fails to cater to the international market of students that are the customers in architectural education. Clearly what architectural education needs is a model of reciprocity and exchange within a global marketplace that sees a certain commensurability in architectural education between different countries, and that has the flexibility to develop a model such as the Bologna Process in Europe that allows for viable forms of educational exchange. NAAB comes across as perhaps the most parochial of all accreditation systems with its insistence that architectural graduates are only qualified to practice in one particular state. The logic of the parochial NAAB model also fails when we consider that many architects will end up designing buildings for foreign markets, such as China. Clearly the model adopted by architectural accreditation bodies is too parochial and does not offer the skill sets that many architectural graduates are looking for.

The situation is exacerbated when we take into account the highly mobile marketplace for architectural education. Given the opportunities afforded by international travel today, it is very common not only for students to go on study abroad or exchange programs to explore the architecture of other countries, but also for professors to teach in many different schools at one time. One only needs to look at a school like the Angewandte School of Applied Arts in Vienna to notice that almost all professors teaching there are largely itinerant, often teaching in other schools at the same time. Clearly architectural education operates in a highly mobile, globalized marketplace, and yet this does not seem to be acknowledged by NAAB and other national- (or state-) based accreditation bodies.

At the same time a note of caution needs to be voiced here. Over the past few years at the University of Southern California (USC) we have been somewhat bemused by the number of Chinese applicants who have applied for our standard NAAB accredited Masters of Architecture program instead of our post-professional Masters of Advanced Architecture program, when they had already completed accredited programs in their native country. For sure, these students would have found it difficult—in the then-dominant economic climate—to obtain a visa to stay on long enough in the United States to become accredited architects. Nor did many of them opt to stay in the States as there were far more job opportunities in China. So why were they registering for the NAAB accredited course and not for the more experimental and ambitious post-professional program? Eventually, it became obvious to us that they were applying for the program not to become licensed in the United States, but rather to make themselves more marketable back in China. To some extent, then, we need to recognize an additional way in which a NAAB degree might appeal to the global marketplace, not in order to license students to work in the United States, but rather to improve their employability elsewhere. This, however, only feeds into the general critique of NAAB. If it can be used to authorize graduates in other countries, does it not need to be more global in its orientation?

The sustainability of the profession

Sustainability has become something of a buzzword in the architectural profession of late, as companies vie with one another to establish which is the most environmentally sustainable in their construction techniques and energy consumption. LEED certified buildings have become the vogue, whether or not they subscribe to genuinely high standards of environmental sustainability. But what about the sustainability of the profession itself?

With increasing challenges to the Western capitalist model mounted by alternative economic models offered outside the United States by countries such as China, the very foundations of what was once regarded in the West as the only viable economic structure are being called into question. China subscribes not to the standard, Western, libertarian model of capitalism *per se*, but rather to state-controlled capitalism. Whether or not this Chinese model would seem to offer a viable alternative to the standard Western model, it is clear that its construction industry has remained buoyant while that in the West has not. What has also become abundantly clear, however, is that a profession tied so closely to a Western, libertarian model premised on economic growth will suffer when there is no such growth. Moreover, periods of sustained downturn may well have long-term consequences for the profession.

A recent survey of student applicants for university places to study architecture-related disciplines in the United Kingdom found that there had been a decline of 16.3 percent in applications nationwide.[11] This trend might be a temporary one, engendered by the recent slump in construction activity, but if not, it is a worrying sign that the profession is no longer attracting the same caliber of students, and is losing its cultural capital.[12] In such a situation, it is pointless to posit a simple return to a condition that was once dominant, as though history itself could simply be rewound, without understanding the precise cause of this development.[13] A more productive strategy might be to consider other ways of expanding the potential scope of the remit of the architect.

Given that the architect has not been in the strongest financial position in the building industry, it might be worth exploring how the profession of architecture might mutate so as to give architects more economic control of the construction process. It is well known that far greater financial gains—while also incurring greater risk—can be made by developers and others involved in the financing of buildings, and yet there are still relatively few schools of architecture that offer courses in real estate or development. Moreover, as Rem Koolhaas once observed, the primary problem with architects' salaries is that ordinarily their fees are based on a percentage of construction costs, and no account is taken of the quality of the work itself.[14] Thus one of the world's leading architects might find him- or herself being paid on the same scale as one of the world's least respected architects. The same situation would not happen in the art market where, for example, the price of a work of art is based on consumer demand, rather than on the cost of its fabrication, and where there is no absolute scale of remuneration.

Another option—given that building design, the ground occupied traditionally by architects, is being colonized increasingly by other professionals in the construction industry—is to expand the remit of the architect and explore other creative outlets for the architectural imagination. Here we might cite the example of Koolhaas's AMO, which demonstrates the capacity for architects to branch out into other areas loosely defined as "spatial consultancy" or "design consultancy," areas which are far better remunerated than the design of buildings.[15]

The potential to expand the remit of the architect's operations is also facilitated by the digital revolution. If Leon Battista Alberti, Filippo Brunelleschi, and others were instrumental in heralding the Renaissance itself, introducing a new set of tools such as the invention of perspective that changed our fundamental understanding of architecture, are we not witnessing a similar moment now with the introduction of computation? Indeed, Douglas Rushkoff has even described our contemporary digital era as being a "renaissance moment" in that all our values are now being shaken up and reconfigured in an age where the advent of the digital has challenged many of our previous assumptions:

> Renaissance moments happen when we experience a shift in perspective so that the stories, models, and languages that we have been using to understand our reality are suddenly up for grabs. But these renaissance moments are transitory, because almost as soon as our perspectives are shifted, we settle into new conventions.[16]

Back in 2002, Mark Burry questioned whether the use of the computer had served to bring architects and engineers closer together in that engineers—traditionally weak at sketching—could improve their draughting skills by using the computer, while architects—traditionally weak at structural analysis—could improve their understanding of structural performance by using new structural software programs.[17] But this issue can be taken further given the developments in terms of computational design techniques and fabrication technologies since then. It is clear that advances in technology have broken down the differences between architecture and other disciplines. What we see emerging in this present "renaissance moment" is a new breed, a form of *uomo universale* or *donna universale* of the digital renaissance—without the gender assumptions of the Renaissance itself. Architects, such as Zaha Hadid, are designing anything from jewelry, clothes, and shoes to interactive installations to entire urban districts and even cities.[18]

Another arena of potential development, then, is that with the introduction of new technologies that effectively efface the difference between architecture and other disciplines, architectural graduates are proving very attractive to other disciplines. By way of anecdote, a recent graduate from the post-professional masters program at the USC School of Architecture took up a place to study in the Interdivisional Media Arts and Practice Ph.D. program at the USC School of Cinematic Arts. The attraction for the School of Cinematic Arts is that it gained a student with a skill set far more varied than most film school graduates.[19] For example, this student was able not only to use certain software programs—such as Grasshopper, Maya, 3D Max—that were not commonly grasped by film school graduates, but also had a far more advanced skill set than most film school graduates in her capacity to deal with design, material behaviors, and 3D awareness. Another student whom I taught at the Southern California Institute of Architecture (SCI-Arc) is currently working for Disney Imagineering in their research and development section. He finds that not only is the workload more consistent than architectural work, but the remuneration is considerably higher. One is left to surmise that the discipline of architecture endows graduates with a highly marketable set of skills that could be deployed in many other disciplines, and yet its primary objective—as defined by accreditation boards—is to channel graduates into a poorly marketed profession within the construction industry where they receive meager financial compensation for a relatively long and expensive education.[20]

For a profession supposedly valued for its capacity to design and think ahead, architects have been notoriously bad at designing their own profession. The present model, it would appear, is rapidly becoming unsustainable. What is clearly required is a rethinking of the basic economic model on which the architectural profession is based.

Towards a new educational model

How then might we rethink architectural education in our contemporary age? Somewhat paradoxically I wish to suggest that the Bauhaus—an historical model from the past—might provide a way forward for the future. The Bauhaus offered one of the most influential educational models from the twentieth century. What is remarkable about the Bauhaus is that it was actually operational for only a few years (from 1919 to 1933), and yet its influence has been profound. Not only did the Bauhaus provide the original model for the recently developed international market for progressive, skill-based programs, such as the AA DRL, but it also engaged with emerging technologies in a highly prescient way. Moreover, it was extremely marketable in an international arena, as is evident from the reception of many of its former professors, such as Walter Gropius or Mies van der Rohe, in leading schools of architecture in the United States. Indeed, what the Bauhaus managed to produce above all was a successful brand name—so much so that the College of Architecture and Civil Engineering in Weimar decided to rebrand itself in 1996 by renaming itself "Bauhaus University Weimar." Yet if we look back at the Bauhaus itself we might recognize that it operated as an open, interdisciplinary platform, with architectural students studying alongside industrial designers, artists, sculptors, photographers, textile designers, and so on. As such, it represented the kind of working environment that is required again today, as technological developments within the digital field have effaced the differences between architecture and other disciplines. Furthermore, despite its success and influence within the global marketplace, it remained unfettered by the constraints imposed by accreditation.[21]

If, then, we think through the dominant logic of today's consumer society—a society in which branding has proved the most successful form of promoting a product—we can see that the Bauhaus offers us a tantalizing glimpse of a thoroughly international approach that frees architecture from its narrow definition of the recent past, and yet which remains outside of the logic of accreditation. Might we therefore not look towards a "New Bauhaus," as a more sustainable model for architectural education that is more flexible and adaptive to ways of operating within an ever-changing global marketplace, where the very definition of the profession of architecture is being renegotiated?

Nonetheless, the question remains as to who would be willing to risk student applications by abandoning the accreditation system and introducing unaccredited degrees. However, in a more recent development within the United States we might point towards the increasing popularity of Architectural Studies programs in schools such as Massachusetts Institute of Technology (MIT), as evidence of changes that are already appearing in the educational marketplace. The main attraction of these programs would seem to be their capacity to leave students time to decide on the path of their future careers, by allowing them to take a range of courses across campus which would otherwise have been precluded by the limited and prescribed nature of an NAAB accredited degree.[22] Moreover, in terms of nomenclature as least, we might observe that the more open "design based" model of the Bauhaus has already been accepted. Given that the Harvard Graduate School of Design—regarded by many as one of the market leaders in the field of architectural education—does not refer to itself as a "Graduate School of Architecture," we might even surmise that the educational marketplace might tolerate a shift not only towards an "architectural studies" model, but also towards a broader "design studies" one, such as operates in other leading schools, like the Rhode Island School of Design, that include architecture alongside other design-based disciplines.

To conclude, then, there seems to be little sense in using accreditation to protect the name of the architect in a professional context where the position of the architect seems to have become increasingly marginal within the building industry. Certainly, accreditation will do little to help reverse global trends for the future, given that it has done so little in the past. Moreover, internal fighting on the part of local accreditation boards as to who gets to call him- or herself "an architect" seems utterly irrelevant, especially in the context of an architectural profession that has become global. At the same time some kind of legal protection for the consumer/client remains desirable, and this protection should have the capacity to extend to other design disciplines where architects are becoming increasingly engaged. It is abundantly clear that consumer society as a whole is looking increasingly towards the logic of certification, insurance, quality control, and risk management. It is therefore worth considering different alternatives of consumer protection within the present scenario while acknowledging the new opportunities opening up to architectural graduates.

One obvious way to address these issues is to decouple architectural education from the architectural profession, and defer accreditation until after university education is complete. This is the model followed by the architectural profession in Japan, as noted above. It is also the model followed in other disciplines. Law, for example, is viewed as an academic discipline in universities within the UK, and is decoupled from professional constraints. Students may first study Law at university purely as an academic discipline, and then attend a postgraduate law school to obtain their professional qualifications. The advantage of this model is that it allows for a degree of flexibility in the marketplace whereby students might branch off into related disciplines. Architecture, in this context, would be treated as a generic background discipline that might offer a platform for a variety of other professional pathways in related disciplines, such as real estate, property development, landscape architecture, urban planning, urban design, industrial design, and other forums for design and spatial consultancies—not forgetting architectural practice itself.

Another way to address these issues is to rely on alternative mechanisms to protect the client/customer within the building industry. For example, in Ireland and Scandinavia, as has been noted above, a building is deemed acceptable if it conforms to building regulations, and there is no need to regulate who designs it. Alternatively, in many countries the term "architect" is already protected by legislation. As George Oldham points out, there is no need for the Architects Registration Board (ARB) to protect the name of the architect, since within the UK the title "architect" is already protected by the Fraud Act of 2006.[23] Indeed within the UK, there is a sizeable group of distinguished architects—including Norman Foster and Richard Rogers—who have voiced their support to the ARB Reform Group that has attempted to limit the remit of the ARB.[24] In other words, umbrella legal concepts could be foregrounded to provide global protection for the client and so too the architect/designer.

Whatever option is taken, it would seem to make sense to offer a flexible model of education more in tune with a globalized marketplace, where architects are not only operating in a range of different countries, but are also branching out into related design-oriented professions. But the issues are far reaching. It is not simply a question of challenging prevailing attitudes towards accreditation. Not only does the definition of the architect need to be overhauled, but our whole understanding of what constitutes architectural education also needs to be rethought in a profound way.

Notes

1. There appears to be no accurate survey to support this figure, although it has been cited in many instances (see, for example: http://archinect.com/forum/thread/82605/how-much-of-the-built-environment-is-designed-by-architects). Even in the developed world it is not always easy to ascertain the extent of an architect's involvement in a project when the project falls outside the standard relationship between architect, client, and construction company.
2. Leon Battista Alberti, *On the Art of Building in Ten Books*, trans. Joseph Rykwert, Neil Leach, and Robert Tavernor (Cambridge, MA: The MIT Press, 1988), 3. Alberti's motive behind this was in part conditioned by the development of the cult of the individual in the Renaissance itself. We know little about the designers during the Middle Ages largely because of the prevailing culture where the client was seen as more significant than the architect. Indeed few records exist from that period of the actual designers of buildings. Alberti's approach was also an attempt to set standards in an age living in the shadows of the glory that had been the Roman Empire. Indeed a common phrase in medieval Italy, surrounded by the great monuments of antiquity falling into disrepair but fraught by internecine disputes, was: "If you want to see how great Rome was, just look around you." But importantly also Alberti knew his audience. His treatise was addressed not to architects, but to patrons. Alberti operated within the papal *curia*, and the first edition of his published work was dedicated to Federigo da Montefeltro, one of the great patrons of the arts of the time. For further discussion of Alberti's definition of the architect see: James Ackerman, "Architectural Practice in the Italian Renaissance," *Journal of the Society of Architectural Historians* 13 (1954): 3–11.
3. Stephen Hopkins and Daniel Kent, "Daniel Libeskind is No Architect," *Fast Company Innovation by Design Blog*, 1 November, 2013, http://www.fastcodesign.com/3021001/innovation-by-design/daniel-libeskind-is-no-architect (accessed 30 July, 2014); Andrea Klettner, "Arb Says BD Cannot Call Piano an 'Architect,'" *BD Online*, 5 October, 2012, http://www.bdonline.co.uk/arb-says-bd-cannot-call-piano-an-?architect?/5043677.article; for the ARB definition of "an architect" see: http://www.legislation.gov.uk/ukpga/1997/22/section/20 (accessed 30 July, 2014).
4. "The Name of the Architect," Architectural Blatherations, http://www.archsoc.com/kcas/Namearchitect.html (accessed 9 September, 2014).
5. "On Regulating Architects," Architectural Blatherations, http://www.archsoc.com/kcas/RegulatingArchitects.html (accessed 9 September, 2014).
6. Ibid.
7. "National Council of Architectural Registration Boards," NCARB, http://www.ncarb.org
8. Ibid.
9. Disclaimer taken from standard email from office of Zaha Hadid Architects.
10. I have been struck by the lack of general educational awareness among those on accreditation boards. At a recent NAAB accreditation visit none of the visiting inspectors had heard of the French architect François Roche, an architectural

educator who has taught in many of the leading schools of architecture in the world. I am tempted to suggest that accreditation boards themselves should be subject to more rigorous quality controls.

11. David Rogers, "Architecture Student Numbers Drops by 12%," *BD Online*, 12 July, 2012, http://www.bdonline.co.uk/architecture-student-numbers-drops-by-12/5039556.article (accessed 29 July, 2014).
12. Cultural capital is a concept associated with Pierre Bourdieu: "Cultural capital acts as a social relation within a system of exchange that includes accumulated cultural knowledge that confers power and status." Chris Baker, *The Sage Dictionary of Cultural Studies* (London: Sage, 2004), 37.
13. At a meeting of the RIBA Building Futures "think tank" group in 2003, I was surprised to hear a colleague advocating a "return to the values of the past," where the architect was accorded more respect. Such conditions cannot be simply reactivated without a thorough understanding of what caused their demise in the first place.
14. Rem Koolhaas, lecture at the Architectural Association, 2007.
15. It is perhaps no coincidence that Koolhaas himself developed AMO as an alternative branch to OMA, and that AMO was instrumental in saving OMA during a period of acute financial difficulties, and has remained financially buoyant with regular commissions from clients such as Prada.
16. Douglas Rushkoff, "The Digital Renaissance," in *Designing for a Digital World*, ed. Neil Leach (London: Wiley, 2002), 24.
17. Mark Burry, "The Aesthetics of Calculus" (Roundtable Discussion), in *Digital Tectonics*, eds. Neil Leach, David Turnbull, and Chris Williams (London: Wiley, 2004), 145.
18. Indeed, the present moment also resembles a digital renaissance in that instead of the bankers and popes of the Renaissance, a new generation of patrons—often hi-tech companies, such as Amazon, Autodesk, eBay, Google, YouTube, and so on—have become significant sponsors of the arts.
19. The attraction for the student, meanwhile, is that this program is relatively well funded—compared to most architecture programs—and even pays a basic stipendium for Ph.D. students that is greater than the salaries offered in many architectural offices.
20. As an academic who has taught architectural graduates in the city of Los Angeles for many years, I can report that several of my former students have moved into other industries, such as the movie industry, space industry, or to other local employers such as Disney Imagineering, where salaries are not only higher than those offered in the architectural profession, but also more stable.
21. One is left wondering how the existing professional bodies in Germany at the time viewed the Bauhaus. Would it have achieved the equivalent of accreditation today? And what would be the status of architects trained in Germany, such as Walter Gropius and Mies van der Rohe, within the narrow NAAB accreditation logic of today?
22. I am grateful to Xavier Costa for this observation.
23. Laura Mark, "Last Chance to Fill Out the Survey: Should the Title of Architect be Protected?" *Architects' Journal*, 8 April, 2014, http://www.architectsjournal.co.uk/news/

last-chance-to-fill-out-the-survey-should-the-title-of-architect-be-protected/8659752. article (accessed 4 August, 2014).

24. According to the manifesto of the ARB Reform Group, the ARB has been pursuing unnecessary and restrictive policies:

> The Group argues that the ARB was set up in 1997 as an architects' registration body—hence its name. It points out that Hansard confirms that Parliament intended that it would be a minimalist body, but that the Board has instead progressively sought to involve itself in regulation of the profession, in indemnity insurance, education, accreditation of architectural courses, CPD and regular revalidation of those on the register. Members of the group believe the Board's expansionist policies cannot be justified by reference to the Architects Act, and are unnecessary and restrictive; they believe that evidence shows that the profession has no need for oppressive regulation, and feel that the Board damages the reputation of the profession by acting as though the public interest requires it. ARB has succumbed to the maxim that an organization tends, once created, to work to increase its own position and existence whether or not that is in the public's best interest.

"ARB Reform Group 2009 Manifesto," ARB Reform Group, http://www.aaruk.info/ARG/ARG%20manifesto.htm (accessed 9 September 2014).

Afterword
Michael Sorkin

A ubiquitous German big box is *Bauhaus*. On first seeing one, I was buoyed by the thought of a repressed's return, modernism's Jerusalem diffused on the landscape of the Jerry everyday. That this turned out to be the Teutonic equivalent of *Home Depot* didn't exactly sink my reverie. The stores, crammed with pressure-treated plywood, plumbing fittings, and hand drills, represented an idea of empowerment, the means by which the priesthood of architecture might be circumvented by citizens with *access to tools.* Bauhaus is no less than a festival marketplace for the consumption of the means of production.

Pier Vittorio Aureli describes the factory as the materialized degree-zero of the Marxian conception of labor, the outcome of a particular historical moment in the development of capitalism. Marx was our primal modernist and—in thrall—architects of the Bauhaus and matching stripes who rejected the effete perquisites of *haute bourgeois* practice, had deep labor—rather *laborer*—envy. As an outgrowth of an egalitarian, mainly socialist tradition that revered the worker as ideal, that architecture found both form and purpose in response to the imagined requirements of this model subject. Industrial building systems, the domino frame, the minimalized (i.e. equalized) housing unit, the celebration of the sites of production—from the Dnieper Dam to the Rouge Factory to the grain elevators of Buffalo—were where modernism sought to site its project and where its aesthetic of aesthetic denial took shape. There's a reason that the Bauhaus in Dessau took the form of a factory, why, in standard histories, its photo invariably follows Fagus.

But there's a divide in design's conception of labor—with Marx's proletarian on one side and William Morris's yeoman on the other—that forecasts our own ongoing split in systems of meaning in architecture, a hoary craft vs. factory fork between historicism and "new" urbanism and the divergent modernisms now incarnate especially in the anxiety and prospect of both parametric ("automated" and ecological ("save the earth") design. This serial bifurcation tends to fix the location of architecture's own work either on the side of symbolization or remediation and thereby founds its complex politics. Thus, any analysis of the nature of *human* architectural labor (and related questions of compensation, working conditions, etcetera) must take into account the differing conceptual and ethical impetus behind it, the ongoing imbrication of the cultural meanings of handicraft (with its imputations of individuality, self-fulfillment, and communal service) and the production line (with its attendant alienation, exploitation, and stoking of the mass-consumption engine). The expectation that architectural activity on behalf of squatters or typhoon survivors will be part of the same ethico-fiscal calculus as that of building condos on 57th Street only points up that there is a morally-valenced class system within architecture that cannot easily be collapsed, much as the doctors at Médecins Sans Frontières cannot be *simply* identified with the Park Avenue plastic surgeon doing nose jobs. These are category confusions that underpin ideas both of redress and entitlement and greatly influence how and who we organize: I don't think of David Childs as a brother in struggle but many of SOM's employees sure are. That some of us think of our "practice" as more closely allied to art or politics or social work than to computer science or real estate development clearly begs the issue of one profession, two systems. *Many* systems.

This ethically grounded doubling is represented in a variety of "professional" circumstances. A tiny subset of those posh surgeons—all signatories to the Hippocratic Oath—spend time in Africa fixing cleft palates for the poor. Even Rand Paul periodically goes to Nicaragua to do cataract surgery for those without other access to care. Lawyers take cases *pro bono* as part of their understanding of the civic nature of their calling and the state sanction that allows them to pursue it. Architects sign on to a code of professional conduct rich with encouragement to be of service. Much of this depends on what might be called the economics of the tithe—charity—as its enabling (if voluntary) authority. In this broader context of inequality—the fact that an underpaid junior architect in New York is immeasurably better off than a rag-picker in Cairo (if with a similar discrepancy with her boss)—there is a certain parochialism to the fight for a (better) living wage. This is not an argument against the struggle but a call to recognize the unevenness both within and without the discipline and to deal with it.

But there's a further confusion, induced by the artistic character of architectural practice. How to parse this? There's a liminal blur generated by the "relative autonomy" of the artistic side of architecture, which does radically distinguish it from the professions with which it is grouped and distorts any attempt to claim it completely for one side or the other. For architecture, questions of politics are partially distributive and partially representational. This is not the dualism of C. P. Snow's two cultures of humanism and technology but the site of an inborn contradiction that animates the *nature* of architecture and suggests that it's a mistake to see the "architect" as a unitary subject. Given that the most fundamental predicate for any politics is *organization*, what can be done about an activity that is susceptible to so many different modes of both self-production and the production of its outcome in something like building? It's urgent to establish a set of useful differences between the work and the workplace.

In the latter case, a struggle comparable to our current battles for fair pay and treatment was the fight of medical interns and residents to curtail their insane hours. Their success was in part due to their union affiliation and, in part, to several high profile cases (the death of Libby Zion, whose father was a writer for the *New York Times* most prominently) in which patients died as a clear outcome of mistakes by over-tired and over-taxed doctors in training. Many in the academic medical profession were appalled that there would be objections to this boot camp crucible, the incredibly stressful demands held integral to the formation of the medical personality and to the development of the reflexes under pressure that would, in theory, stand doctors in good stead in future crises. The adversity of an architect's professional apprenticeship shares this same idea of ennobling degradation but begs a question of the reasons (and the rhetoric) for enduring it. There seems very little cause to suggest that laboring under squalid and exploitative conditions in an architectural office has any positive impact, save on the employer's bottom line and in creating the expectation in the young architect that she will one day be in a position to pass it on.

What employers often exploit, ironically, are two characteristics of architectural education that seem, on the whole, to be worthwhile. The first is the charrette and its hyper-focus, which both tests individual capacity for performance and discipline and prepares for the natural difficulties of scheduling and production—not to mention boom and bust—that are endemic to architectural practice. Whether better management could smooth the output curves is neither here nor there if the circumstances of compensation are fair (take a week off, earn overtime, aid the poor, etcetera) and the inborn enthusiasm for the job on the part of participants is present and motivating. The other piece of the educational experience, also native to the charrette, is the tradition of mutual aid, the second year who helps the third year in the final hours of thesis preparation. This too is precious but may also conduce a form of false consciousness.

The measure of exploitation is inequality. While I am as shocked, shocked, as the next *sans-culottes* by the thought of the engorged Norman Foster piloting his own jet to the job site in some despotic Shangri-La while lesser staff are relegated to the middle seat in coach, this version of the architectural Gini Coefficient is typical of the widening gap between CEO salaries and those of average employees in the corporate world more generally. And, as with other corporate employees, architects are challenged not simply by an endemic culture of greed but by the same off-shoring that has decimated so many American industries, which increasingly ship both physical and "immaterial" production to sites of low-wage expertise, to computer coders in India, or to architectural renderers in China. These big offices and these strategies are logical sites for insurgency but cannot simply be collapsed into a single architectural field, denying the many social and economic models that comprise its complex ecology.

Not to go all Trotsky, but we can only solve the challenges of our own privileged predicament through contemplation of our increasingly globalized economy, by making common cause with brothers and sisters who underpin our own efforts. Just as the media focused on the dreadful conditions in the electronics factories of Shenzhen, with their toxicities, cruel schedules, and suicides, so there's been a sudden interest in the condition of exploited labor constructing starchitect projects in the Gulf. One of the problems with an exclusively professional organization is that it can perpetuate the very ideas of stratification and exclusion it seeks to overturn and further reify an undercurrent of privilege. Which suggests that the prospects of revolution in one profession, while appealingly efficient, also amount to a betrayal of those non-professionals lower down the chain of implementation. Or of the non-professionals who are responsible for constructing 98 percent of the built environment. The point is not to de-professionalize in the sense of surrendering expertise but to practice in a conscious way, one that acknowledges that we do not build alone. One big union?

A paradox of architectural practice is, in fact, the social compression that has become typical of American offices. Where once the output of drawings was largely the work of draftsmen—who learned their skills in trade schools or apprenticeships—now every bathroom tile is drawn by an Ivy League architectural graduate with aspirations to be a star. This narrowed cadre of producers models the big office on the small (witness also the way in which many megafirms are organized in individual studios, each with its own "master"). As a practical matter, how are we to distinguish this camouflaged corporatism from more authentic, less hierarchical, forms of organization? One approach is to look at thresholds of relative expense, of earnings, of the size and density of the "production unit," and at the level of empowerment, intimacy, control, and authority down the ranks. There are many sites where old-fashioned forms of trade unionism are called for.

For this, we happily have a history to look to: during the period from the end of World War I to the end of World War II, there were a number of successful attempts to unionize architectural workers in the United States. The first serious effort was the International Federation of Draftmen's Unions. This originated as the Society of Marine Draftsmen in 1913—a company union—at the Norfolk Naval Shipyard but an insurgency established its independence and, in 1918, the AFL (until 1937, the only national labor federation) granted it a charter. Far more important, though, was a successor, the Federation of Architects, Engineers, Chemists, and Technicians (FAECT) born of the Great Depression.[1] According to Robert Heifetz, "By 1932, architects had one-seventh of the work they had had in 1928, and six of every seven draftsmen, specification writers, and construction superintendents had lost their jobs." In 1929, a militant wing of the earlier union had emerged in New York—the Union of Technical Men— which was soon expelled from the AFL for "excessive radicalism." FAECT began in 1933, following publication—by the AIA—of suggested minimum wage standards for draftsman (fifty cents an hour!) to be promulgated as part of the National Industrial Recovery Act. This was not simply pathetically low but the rates were devised without consultation with membership and the push-back was immediate. By 1934, FAECT had over 6,500 members in 15 locals and declared itself "the progressive vanguard of the technical professions." In 1937, it became part of the CIO, formed that year under the leadership of the immortal John L. Lewis.

During World War II, FAECT strongly advocated for an increased role for labor in industrial decision-making and made it clear that it expected such a cooperative model would also be central to peacetime production. Management thought otherwise and the union was viciously red-baited: the revolting Rep. Martin Dies—of HUAC fame—described the union as "under the complete control of the Communist Party." It didn't help that FAECT members were involved in atomic research, including Robert Oppenheimer (and his brother) and Julius Rosenberg, and, in 1943, the War Department called for FAECT to be banned from the Berkeley (now Lawrence) Radiation Lab. Heifetz quotes no less a figure than General Leslie Groves, head of the Manhattan Project, who wrote in a memo, "activities of the FAECT Local No. 25 have already seriously compromised the security of the Berkeley work … It is essential that action be taken to remove the influence of FAECT from the Radiation Laboratory."

In the post-war red scare, FAECT continued to be tarred as a tool of the Kremlin and, to stay alive, it merged, in 1946, with the leftish Union of Office and Professional Workers of America, which was itself purged from the CIO— then drifting protectively right—in 1948. During its brief heyday such important architectural figures as Simon Breines, Percival Goodman, James Marston Fitch, Vito Battista (representing the union's own right wing), Morris Zeitlin, and Tom Creighton, the editor of *Progressive Architecture*, were members of FAECT which also ran its own school to help members prepare for licensing exams and to top up their knowledge of current technology. The school conducted two design studios, one along beaux-arts lines, the other modernist, and, at its height, enrolled 600 students. In the end, what was most consequential about FAECT was its consistently progressive orientation, its structural efforts to build bridges between professional and technical workers of all stripes (its membership was never more than 15 percent architects), its efforts in culture and education, and its allegiance to the idea of a broad labor movement, empowered by wide solidarity and the fight for social justice.

FAECT offers an object lesson in both forgetfulness and possibility. Recalling this struggle—and it is not the only instance of architects organizing outside institutional professional structures—is critical to our possibilities today, especially in the context of the increasing dominance of corporate offices. We must disabuse ourselves of the notion that, as "professionals," we stand outside the fundamentals of the contest of labor in general, while at the same time recognizing our own heterogeneity. Because so many who theorize this question are also involved in academic "practice," our approach is greatly informed by struggles in our beleaguered universities where we see the rapid emergence of a new mode of production: the pressures to be "entrepreneurial" in seeking funding for design studios, the appalling salaries and lack of benefits offered to piece-working adjuncts, the speed-up in workload, and the general decline in importance of full-time faculty—the creation of a two-tiered class system. These workers are our natural allies: the professoriate offers a far closer parallel to the situation—and pay scales—of architectural labor than do most lawyers or doctors.

Our academic pickle is underwritten by a special historic conceit in professional education: the idea of teaching is a supplementary responsibility of practitioners, a remnant of the earlier system of apprenticeship, the white man's *noblesse oblige*. This has morphed into a rhetoric of involuntary altruism that is deployed as an unspoken pressure to sacrifice, disguised as civic duty and a route to initiation into our priesthood, an *opportunity*. Indeed, rates of compensation for visiting professors are sometimes inversely proportional to the "prestige" of the institution and the job represented as either résumé-building fodder or a chance for insider trading in the recruitment of talented students. However, the majority of practicing architects (as opposed to the majority of publishing architects), while not part of this academic-architectural complex, still suffer from (or exploit) the expectations and habits it creates. The press of students and recent graduates seeking internships in high gloss offices is enormous, creating a buyer's market of such magnitude that it has produced a class of willing slaves, ready to work for nothing for their own CV-burnishing brush with celebrity. Again, this is not exclusive to our profession and perhaps even greater numbers queue up for a chance to lick Anna Wintour's Louboutins than do chez Zaha. The cult of celebrity is an incitement to *not* organize and that's why its critique is so important.

Speaking of Hadid, her inopportune remarks about working conditions in Qatar beg questions not simply of responsibility, liability, and the vertical organization of the building process but of the architect's role in the *design* of the process of construction, often very difficult to influence. We are, at the moment, seeing a resurgence of interest in modular building and in factory fabrication of various components (including very large ones) that were previously put together on site. While this has a fine old modernist flavor and certain attractions—especially when it's foregrounded as a solution to housing cost or scarcity—it's also an obvious ploy to dodge higher-cost union labor by exploiting lower wages typical of factory work, even when unionized. A current case in point is the construction of the Atlantic Yards project in Brooklyn, touted for the bargain costs of its production line modules but now arrested by quarrels between builder and developer over questions of the quality of its components. Is it for architects to have an opinion about the comparative merits of producing housing for less and paying workers more? You bet it is. One argument for a big tent organization—for unionization in league with others—is precisely to foreground such issues of solidarity and cause.

Questions of our relationship to labor—material or im—define who we are, just as the nature of patronage or the content of a program requires us to make hard choices. These decisions must have results that are more than ornamental. In my day, the fashionably attired MIT architecture student expressed solidarity and defiance by wearing bib-overalls and carrying a big measuring tape and a claw hammer, the better to instantly reconstruct our congenial slum of a studio—we too were squatters! Not that such cultural manifestations of resistance were useless: we also wore our costumes and long hair in the streets and were well aware of corruption of our aspirations by racist urban renewal and the burning villages in Vietnam. Many of us refused to work for what we understood to be "the man" which surely bolstered our self-regard as subjects and had legible effects on the ground. But refusing architecture was a dead end and too often resulted in ineffectual abstention rather than real resistance. The beast just rumbled on.

Time to turn this around and the model of the union (interestingly, FAECT, recognizing problems with traditional union organization for architects, always identified itself as a "federation," "an economic organization functioning in much the same manner as a labor union") is both bracing and material. Unions have always, at their best, had a double agenda. The first is the workplace, the assurance of fair wages and rules, of a safe and humane environment, and of access to jobs by all who are qualified. Second, though, is a broader objective, the idea that these conditions should characterize society as a whole and this impetus has led to the labor movement's role in the vanguard of struggles for peace, civil and human rights, and an ethical internationalism. Our own organization should likewise embrace both. A focus on the immaterial qualities of intellectual labor—or on our vaunted professionalism—is to miss the point. It's the solidarity that we need and the forms of subjugation—the Taylorism and the terror, the power of the one percent, the grotesque environmental injustices—that remain our constant foe.

Our fight is to assure equity and justice both in architecture's effects and in the means of its production. Let's organize together!

Note

1. I owe virtually everything I know about FAECT to Anthony Schuman's article, "Professionalization and the Social Goals of Architects, 1930–1980: The History of the Federation of Architects, Engineers, Chemists, and Technicians (FAECT)," in *The Design Professions and the Built Environment,* ed. Paul L. Nox (Croom Helm, 1988) and to "The Role of Professional and Technical Workers in Progressive Transformation," by Robert Heifetz (*Monthly Review*, December 2000), which draws heavily on the work of Schuman. My summary borrows shamelessly from both and they have my gratitude.

Index

abstraction xxxiii; in architecture 103–7, 113; of labor in general 109–10
abundance, economy of 225–6
accreditation of architects 228–32, 235–7
Actors Equity 74
"additional services" provided by architects 211–12
Adorno, Theodor 65
advertising films 213
AECOM (architectural practice) 214
Alberti, Leon Battista 109, 228–9, 233
alienation 6
Allot, Tony 136–8
Alloy Development LLC 213–14
American Express 14, 66
American Institute of Architects (AIA) 211, 214, 245
Amhoff, Tilo xvi, xxxiii; *co-author of Chapter 8*
Amnesty International 151–2
Amsterdammer cities 165
Angewandte School of Applied Arts 231
Appadurai, Arjun 154
architect, definition of 228–30
architect-as-worker xxv
architect-entrepreneurs 51–2
architects: and control over construction 233; in the 18th Century 209; group characteristics of 192; remuneration of 73–4, 88, 212, 226–7, 233, 246–7; role of 233; status as workers 61; using their skills in other disciplines 235–7
Architect's Club 209
Architects Registration Board (ARB) 229; Reform Group 237
Architectural Association (AA) 230
architectural education 222–3, 230–1, 243; decline in number of candidates for 233
"architectural studies" programs 236
architectural work 72, 82–97, 242; efficiency of 90–1, 94; present-day 209–10; seen as "abstract labor" 83; and value-creating activities 222–3
architecture: change in role of 224–5; definitions of 11
Arendt, Hannah xxxi, 83, 113
art history and theory xxx
Artist Placement Group (APG) 65–6
assembly-line production 110
Atlantic Yards, Brooklyn 247
Aurell, Pier Vittorio xv–xvi, xxxiii, 241; *author of Chapter 7*
Australia 88, 93
Austria 229
automation 5

Ball, Michael 123
Bartholomew, Alfred 122, 129
"basic services" provided by architects 211, 216
Battista, Vito 246
Bauhaus, the 148, 235–6
Bauhaus factory, Dessau 241
Bauhaus University Weimar 235
Baxi, Kadambari xvii, xxiv, xxxiv; *co-author of Chapter 9*
Beaton, Lauren 163
Beck, Ulrich 22, 27
behavioral economics 184, 186
Bellamy, Edward 68
Benedict, Saint 107
Benjamin, Walter 65–6, 104–5
Berardi, Franco xiii, xxxii; *author of Chapter 1*
Bernstein, Phillip G. xviii, xxviii, xxxv; *author of Chapter 13*
Biernacki, Richard xiv, xxxii; *author of Chapter 3*
Bierut, Michael 26
"Bilbao effect" 145
Bloch, Marc 162–3
book fairs 32
Bosworth, William W. 111

Bourriaud, Nicholas 65–6
Brecht, Bertolt 65
Breines, Simon 246
Bröcking, Ulrich 51
Brooklyn 163, 247
Brunelleschi, Filippo 233
Buckley, Craig 54–5
budgets 90, 95
building information modeling (BIM) xxviii, 73, 98, 152, 154, 190
Burry, Mark 234
business models for architectural practices 210–17

Caffentzis, George xxii
capitalism xxi–xxii, xxiv, xxx, xxxiv, 3, 11, 64, 148, 172–3, 184, 232
Carla's List (documentary) 20
Carrió, Alicia xvii, xxxiv; *author of Chapter 11*
Carver, Jordan xvi, xxxiv; *co-author of Chapter 9*
"La Casa Invisible" 175–8
Childs, David 242
China xxiii, 231–2
Christianity 61
cities, cultural cores of 21
city-states 164–5
Clarke, Linda 140–1
Cobb, Dariel (assistant editor) xx
Coco Chanel bag 20–1
coherence in design 20
Collins, Suzanne 171
commodification of architecture 224–5
communism 68
The Communist Manifesto 25, 28
computers, use of 234
Congrès International d'Architecture Moderne (CIAM) 148
Connor, Maureen 62, 71
constructivism 64–6
consumer protection 237
consumer society 236–7
"contracting in gross" 125–9, 134, 140
"contractual services" provided by architects 212
cost-reduction strategies 94, 99
"creatives" 30, 40
creativity 181, 186–96; architectural 61, 186, 190–6, 231; of environmental power 187; modern concept of 30–2, 37–40; multiple types of 195; in the neoliberal workspace 187–8
Creighton, Tom 246
critical theory xxx
Crystal Palace xxiii
custom house clearing 91
customization 224–5
cybernetic logic 47

Dance, George the younger 126–7
Davis, Howard 124, 132
"daylight factory" concept 111
Deamer, Peggy xv, xxxiii; *author of Introduction, author of Chapter 5 and editor*
Debray, Régis 23, 28
Deleuze, Gilles 107
Del Ponte, Carla 20–1
deregulation 188
design and designers 72, 213–14, 223–6, 236
"design drawings" 139
Design Research Lab (DRL) 230
Dewey, John 70
Dies, Martin 245
digital technology xxxi, 97, 234
division of labor 63–4, 148, 154
doctors compared with architects 212–13, 216, 242–3
Doha 144–5
Donaldson, Thomas 129–30
Draxler, Helmut 53–4
Drucker, Peter 70–1

Easterling, Keller xxxi
École Polytechnique Fédérale de Lausanne (EPFL) 112
The Economic Lexicon (1753) 36
economics and economists 9–11, 40; *see also* behavioral economics
"economization" 181
economo-subjectivization 186, 188
Eisenman, Peter xxx
Engels, Friedrich 25
engineers 9–11, 234
environmental governmentality 184–7, 189, 193–5

Index

Evans, Robin xxxi
exchange value 18
exploitation of labor xxii, xxiv, 7, 113, 244

factory architecture 109–13
fake versions of products 20
fashion designers 213
Fédération Internationale de Football Association (FIFA) 144
Federation of Architects, Engineers, Chemists and Technicians (FAECT) 245–6, 248
fee scales 86–90, 97; as labor boundaries 88–90
feudalisms 162–7
film producers 213
financialization 8
First Things First (FTF) Manifesto (2000) 25–6
Fisher, Thomas xviii, xxxv; *author of Chapter 14*
Fitch, James Marston 246
"flexible specialization" (Tombesi) 215
Flitcroft, Henry 125–6
Florida, Richard 40
football facilities 144
football referees, lockout of 219
Ford, Edward xxviii
Fordism 44, 47
Ford Plant, Highland Park, Michigan 110
formalism in architecture xxx
Foster, Norman 237, 244
Foucault, Michael xxxiv, 107, 181–4, 186, 190–1, 196
Fourier, Charles xxiv, 68
Frampton, Ken xxxi
Frankfurt School 64–5
Franzen, Jonathan 32
Fraser, Andrea 65–6
Freelance Workers Union 74
Free Speech Movement 4, 7
Freire, Paulo 179
Freud, Sigmund 6, 68

Galloway, Alexander 69–70
Gehry, Frank xxiii–xxiv, 155, 220
Giddens, Anthony 22, 27
Gille, Bertrand 134
globalization 149, 229, 231, 237, 244

Gluck + (architectural firm) 213
The GNU Manifesto 28
Goethe, Johann Wolfgang von 33, 35–6, 38
Goodman, Percival 246
Gropius, Walter 148, 235
Groves, Leslie 245
Guangzhou xxiii
Guattari, Félix 107
Guggenheim Museum, Abu Dhabi xxiv, xxx, 74, 155
Guggenheim Museum, Bilbao xxiii, 19
Guggenheim Museum, Dubai xxx
Guggenheim Museum, US 66

Hadid, Zaha xxiv, 146–7, 155, 220, 234; *see also* Zaha Hadid Architects
Halley, Peter 103
Hannoverisches Magazin 34
Hanseatic League 165
Hanson, Brian 134
Hardt, Michael xxii–xxiii, 26–7, 69
Hardwick, Thomas 133
Hartmann, Florence 20–1
Harvard Graduate School of Design 236
Hays, K. Michael xxx–xxxi
Heathcote, Sir William, house of 122, 125–6
Heidegger, Martin 179
Heifetz, Robert 245
Herder, Johann Gottfried 37
Hill, Christine 63, 65
Hollein, Hans xxxii–xxxiii, 44, 48–56
Holmes, Brian 174
home pages 16
Hong Kong 166
Horton, Scott 155
Howard, Ebenezer 68
Huizinga, Johann 163
human capital 181, 184
Human Rights Watch xxiv, 74–5
The Hunger Games (film) 171–2
Huyghe, Pierre 66

"ideal forms", buildings represented as 141
Illich, Ivan 173
"immaterial labor" xxi, xxiv–xxv, xxxii, xxxv, 27, 47, 52
An Incomplete Manifesto for Growth (2000) 24–5

industrial revolution: *first*, *second* and *third* 224–5, 227
integrated project delivery (IPD) xxviii, 72–3, 191, 216
International Federation of Draftsmen's Unions 245
internships 154
Ireland 237
Ivain, Gilles 179

Jameson, Fredric 22
Janssen, Jörn 140–1
Japan 229, 237
Jefferson, Thomas 35
Jobs, Steve 225

Kahn, Albert 110
Kant, Immanuel 31, 38–9
Kinross, Robin 26–7
Klein, Norman M. xvii, xxxiv; *author of Chapter 10*
knowledge production 112
Koolhaas, Rem 220, 233
Krantz Engineering 151–2, 154
Kruk, Vinka xxxii
Kuhn, Thomas 9–10

labor: *abstract* and *concrete* 83–4, 88, 90, 94–5, 106; architectural work as 83–4; art as 64–7; concept of 63; as distinct from work 82–3; *see also* division of labor
"labor power" (Marx) 106
Lash, Scott 22
Latrobe, Benjamin 209
lawyers compared with architects 212–13, 216, 237, 242
Lazzarato, Maurizio 27–8, 47, 52, 69
Leach, Neil xviii–xix, xxxv; *author of Chapter 15*
Le Corbusier 68, 104, 108
Lefebvre, Henri 111–12
leisure society 47–8
Lessing, Gotthold Ephraim 33
Lewis, John L. 245
liberalism 182
Libeskind, Daniel 229
Lloyd Thomas, Katie xvi, xxxiii; *co-author of Chapter 8*

LMN Architects 214
London County Council 134–6
Louis Vuitton bag 20–1
Luther, Martin 39

Macchiavelli, Niccolò 23, 25
McGregor, Colin 136
Maclaurin Buildings at MIT 111
McLuhan, Marshall 23–4
Madl, Franz 49
Maison Dom-ino model for housing 104
Málaga 175–6
Malinovsky, Alexander 64
manifestos 22–8
Marcuse, Herbert 5–6, 65–6, 68–9
Marinetti, Filippo 24–5
market processes 182–3, 188, 191, 194–5
Martin, Reinhold xxxi
Martin, Roger 219–22, 226
Marullo, Francesco 110
Marx, Karl xxi–xxii, xxiv, 4, 10, 17, 25, 62–4, 67–8, 72–3, 83, 99–100, 106, 109, 125, 184, 241
Marxism xxx, xxxi
Massachusetts Institute of Technology (MIT) 111, 236
masters programmes, non-accredited 230, 232
Mau, Bruce 24–5
Mayakovsky, Vladimir 64
Médecins Sans Frontières 242
mercantilism 165–6
Merck, Johann 32
meritocracy 7
Metahaven xiv, xxxii; *author of Chapter 2*
Mies van der Rohe, Ludwig 148, 235
migrant workers xxiv, 151
Mobile Office (installation) 44–56
mobile phones 15
Modernism 148
modular buildings 247
monasteries 107–8, 113
Moritz, Karl Philipp 37–9
Morris, William xxix, 68, 241

Nanterre University 111–12
National Architectural Accrediting Board (NAAB) 230–2, 236

Index 253

National Building Specification (NBS) 124, 136–8, 141
Negri, Antonio xxii–xxiii, 26–7, 69
Neill, Thomas 122
neoliberalism xxxiv, 4, 7, 181–96
Newgate Gaol 122, 126–7, 132
New York City 163, 165–6

Obama, Barack 225–6
Ockman, Joan xiii; *author of Foreword*
Oldham, George 237
Oppenheimer, Robert 245
outcome-based profit 216
Owen, Robert xxiv, 68

paradigm shifts 9–10
parametric software 190–1
Parreno, Phillipe 66
Paul, Jean 33, 36–7
Paul, Rand 242
peripheries 14
Peterson, Lowell 74
Peter the Great 165
phenomenology xxvii
Piano, Renzo 229
Picasso, Pablo 31
piece-work 72–3
Pitt, Brad 224
Pittsburgh xxiii
play, role of 67–8
pleasure principle 68–9
poetry, requirements of 64
Popova, Liubov xxiii
Portman, John 213–14
post-criticality xxxi
post-Fordism 44, 47, 189, 191
post-modernism 22, 224
product designers 213
professions and professionalism 172–4, 212–13, 232–5, 248
protection for professional titles 237
Pugin, August Welby 134

Qatar 144–7, 151–2, 247

Rancière, Jacques 66
Ras Laffan Emergency and Safety College (RLESC) 151–4
Ray-Jones, Allen 136

Rebentisch, Juliane 56
Rebmann, Georg Friedrich 32
Reich, Robert 40, 221–2
Relational Aesthetics (Bourriaud) 65–6, 74
Rhode Island School of Design 236
Rifkin, Jeremy 224
risk management 214–17
"risk society" (Beck) 22
Rock, Michael 26
Rodchenko, Alexander xxiii
Rogers, Richard 237
Rolex Learning Center 112–13
Rosenberg, Julius 245
Ross, Gary 171
Royal Institute of British Architects (RIBA) 121–2, 124, 136, 211
Rumpfhuber, Andreas xiv, xxxii–xxxiii; *author of Chapter 4*
Rumsfeld, Donald 69–70
Rushkoff, Douglas 234
Ruskin, John 97, 134

Saint Gallen library 107
La Sarraz Declaration (1928) 148
Savio, Mario 3–4
Schapiro, Mark xxiii
Schiller, Friedrich 31–3, 67–9
Schön, Donald 70
Schumann Smith (consultants) 138–9, 141
Schwartzberg, Manuel xxxiv
science, definition of 9–10
Scott, Felicity xxxi
Scott Brown, Denise 104, 224
Screen Actors Guild 74
Seifart, Ina 18–19
Semper, Gottfried 67
Sennett, Richard xxxi
Serlio, Sebastiano 108–9
Shanghai 166
Sharples Holden Pasquarelli 214
Shenzhen 244
Shorto, Russell 166
Shvartzberg, Manuel xvii–xviii; *author of Chapter 12*
Snow, C. P. 243
Soane, John 121–3, 127, 130, 136, 209, 213–14
social housing 179
socialism xxx, 68

social networking sites 16
software 16–17
Sohn-Rethel, Alfred 105
Sorkin, Michael xix; *author of Afterword*
Spain 174
Specification (journal) 130–2
specifications, architectural xxxiii–xxxiv, 93, 121–41; "open" and "closed" 138; trades-based 130–5, 140
Spencer, Herbert 172
Stallman, Richard 28
standardization of architectural products 223–4
"standard of care" principle 215
"star" architects 192–3, 213, 219–20, 244
Steinmetz, John 123–4
Stepanova, Varvara xxiii
student architects 192–3
subcontracting by architecture firms 154
Summerson, John 132
sustainability of the architectural profession 232–5
Swiss Army Knife 18
Switzerland 87–8

Taft-Hartley Act (US, 1947) 161
Tafuri, Manfredo xxx–xxxi, xxxv
talent xxxv, 219–27; specifically architectural 220
Taylorism 248
Tendring Hall 123, 127–8, 130
Tetra Tech 152
"Third Way" politics 21–2, 27
Timeless Bracelet 18–19
Tiravanija, Rirkrit 66
Tocqueville, Alexis de 163
Tombesi, Paolo xv, xxxi, xxxiii, 154–5, 215; *author of Chapter 6*
totalitarianism, high-tech 6

Tromlitz, Friedrich Jakob 34–5
Tronti, Mario 47, 113

UNICLASS (UN Classification for the Construction Industry) 137–9
Union of Technical Men 245
unions 74, 161, 226, 243–5, 247–8; for architectural workers 244–5, 248
United Nations 137–8, 152
United States Supreme Court 166–7
universities 7–8, 111–13, 172, 246
University of Southern California (USC) 233; School of Cinematic Arts 234
urban politics 195
Urry, John 22
user-generated content 15–16, 27
use value 18

van der Velden, Daniel xiv, xxxii
Venice 165
Venturi, Robert 104, 224
Virno, Paolo 52–3
Vitruvius 105
Vogt, Adolf Max 104
"voids" 164–7

Walker, Rob 18
Weber, Max 68
Wilkerson, Isabel 163
Wilson, Mabel O. xvi, xxiv, xxxiv; *co-author of Chapter 9*
Woods, Mary 209
work as distinct from labor 82–3
World Cup football 144, 147
Wright, Frank Lloyd 68

Zaha Hadid Architects 229–30
Zeitlin, Morris 246
Zion, Libby 243